Storming Toward
Armageddon

Essays in Apocalypse

A Storming Toward Armageddon

Essays in Apocalypse

Texe Marrs • Tim LaHaye
David Breese • David A. Lewis
Robert Lindsted • Ray Brubaker
Joseph Carr • Joseph R. Chambers
with William T. James

New Leaf Press

First printing: December 1992
Second printing: February 1993
Third printing: August 1993
Fourth printing: April 1994
Fifth printing: September 1994

Library of Congress Catalog Number: 92-64450
ISBN: 0-89221-228-4

Cover photo: Barry Blackman Studio, Inc., New York, NY 10010

To the Saviour,
our Lord Jesus Christ

Strange winds whisper sounds of storm;
judgment may fall soon.
Awake, brother, sister, awake!
I see a harvest moon.

— Arbra Carman

Acknowledgments

First and foremost, to the Lord of Heaven, whose Holy Spirit sparked the thought to begin the work and provided all that was necessary to sustain and complete it, belongs all thankfulness, honor, and glory.

To my dad, Bill James, and my mother, Kathleen James, who by raising me in His ways and admonitions proved Him absolutely true to His promises, my love and appreciation.

To Margaret and our sons, Terry, Jr. and Nathan, whose patience, while my attention sank ever deeper into the project, proved *almost* infinite and whose love boosted morale beyond measure — just knowing they were there, my love.

To my Christian brothers and friends, Dave Breese, Ray Brubaker, Joseph Chambers, Tim LaHaye, David Allen Lewis, Rob Linsted, Joe Carr, and Texe Marrs — all spiritual giants in my view — whose gifted insights and immense talents, kindnesses, and generosities contributed more than my ability to express — my deepest gratitude and admiration. Especially to Dave Breese and Texe Marrs for their wonderful counsel, and to Wanda Marrs for taking time to pass along notes of encouragement, my thanks.

To Kathy Brown, without whose hours of dedication spent over the computer keyboard and in manuscript preparation, such as proofreading and suggestions in the editing process, this book would have been greatly delayed in coming to publication, and to her husband, Randy, and children, Renee and Geoff, for allowing her the time, my special thanks.

My gratitude goes to Carolyn Bradshaw, Joanne Kalassen, Sandra Shappert, Tanya Turner, Mary Beth Williams, and to all others who so graciously helped in the coordination of shuffling correspondence, messages, and materials between the various ministries they serve and my office.

My special thanks and appreciation to Rev. Robert and Nancy McDaniel for the word processor which — after the pain of struggle in learning to use it proficiently — made the work faster, easier, and even more enjoyable.

Finally, to Cliff Dudley, my friend and brother in Christ who has since gone home to be with the Lord in Heaven, my deepest, heartfelt gratitude for having seen merit in the work. And to my friend and Christian brother, Tim Dudley, for so expertly guiding the book through the publishing process, as well as to his associates at New Leaf Press for their expertise and work on the book's behalf — my fullest appreciation.

Contents

INTRODUCTION

WHAT THE FUTURE HOLDS

by William T. James

Desert Storm broke with fury in a surge of violence that instantly riveted the attention of every man, woman, and child who had access to media coverage of the event. Worried, fascinated eyes and ears focused on the area of planet earth where human life began, and where, prophets foretold, human history as it is now known will — in one catastrophic day — culminate at a killing field called Armageddon.

Official pronouncements at first indicated that Desert Storm had given way to Desert Rainbow. Rather than ending a problem by liberating Kuwait, however, the bold and courageous actions of American-led coalition forces seemed to energize movement toward a cataclysm beyond the ability of military might or diplomatic process to control.

Turmoil of eternal, cosmic significance was brewing. Earlier, its stirrings had become startlingly evident when even hardened geopolitical observers confessed shock over unfolding events in the Soviet Union. A Western-style Kremlin leader swiftly emerged to dramatically turn the world-domination-bent "evil empire" into a seemingly benign, live-and-let-live neighbor.

Communism suddenly appeared to be a docile and subsiding ripple on the ideological seas of the past. Soviet leaders had obviously seen the light and were anxious to adopt and adapt to the ways of the formerly despised, mistrusted, capitalistic imperialists.

Mischief Makers

The cold war thawed; the Soviet Union released its grip on its economy-draining Eastern Bloc sphere of influence; the Berlin Wall crumbled; Germany became one again, in a fashion, and with rapidity that dazzled. More global pyrotechnics burst forth.

The previously impotent United Nations organization suddenly grew teeth as former antagonists in the Security Council's permanent voting block coalesced to implement the use of military force against a would-be conqueror of the whole Middle East and exterminator of Israel. In lightning-like fashion, and with technological precision never before witnessed in warfare, the newly formed United Nation police force crushed the vaunted million-man war machine of the self-styled Saladin/ Nebuchadnezzar.

Victory for the United Nation forces was not without flaw and uncertainty, however. Despite the surface cohesiveness and supposed spirit of cooperation, an undercurrent of double-dealing flowed just beneath the euphoria of the one-sided Desert Storm campaign. The Soviets seemed to be — as global strategist Dr. Henry Kissinger conjectured in an interview during the Gulf War period — engaged in "mischief making" of some sort in proposing last minute cease-fire negotiations with Iraq.

All the while the United Nation coalition's declared position was clearly full implementation of all United Nation adopted resolutions. Also at this time, Iraq's archenemy — Iran — seemed to join the duplicitous collusion to become part of the process of shuttling the ground war — forestalling "initiatives" between Baghdad and Moscow.

George Bush, the best prepared, most astute man in international and world affairs ever to hold the office of president of the United States, deftly, yet gently, stiff-armed Mikhail

Gorbachev's "mischief making." That allowed General Norman Schwarzkopf to loose his forces and those of the coalition partners, thereby decimating remnants of the Iraqi military. These remnants included top of the line, Soviet-made weaponry, which their former client, Saddam Hussein, purchased with Iraq's oil billions at the expense of his hapless people.

A New World Order

According to George Bush, a New World order marched forth out of that Persian Gulf conflict, having taken its first breaths and steps between August 2, 1990, and early March, 1991.

During the president's appointment of Robert Strauss to be ambassador to the Soviet Union, George Bush jokingly remarked, "What is it about August?" Nervous laughter from the journalists and others gathered in the White House Rose Garden erupted at this reference to the invasion of Kuwait by Saddam Hussein's barbaric horde the previous August.

An even more dramatic crisis gripped the world in August 1991, as President Bush spoke. Kremlin hard-liners were in the process of staging a coup d'etat, apparently having sequestered Premier Gorbachev and his family while they vacationed somewhere in the Crimea.

Moscow was in turmoil with tanks rolling ominously toward what western journalists quickly dubbed the "White House" — the Russian Parliament Building in which Russian President Boris Yeltsin courageously vowed to resist. Thousands of Soviet citizens backed him, facing down Soviet soldiers and KGB thugs.

The coup, poorly organized the world was told, crumbled, and Gorbachev returned to what should have been — according to analysts — sympathy and a rousing welcome. Instead, the head Communist was greeted by some very hard questions put to him by Soviet and other journalists who, for the first time, were allowed to freely question in-depth a Soviet leader.

Gorbachev sternly warned against "witch hunting" for Communists who were involved in the coup attempt, and he stated flatly that he would not disavow Marxist-Leninism but would set about to reform the Party, seeking to merge its principles with democratic methods. Yeltsin and the people, disillusioned by seventy-four years of Communist tyranny, convinced Gorbachev otherwise. He expediently quit the Party and made all Communist Party activity illegal. The total dissolution of the Soviet Union quickly followed; Gorbachev resigned as leader.

But is communism dead? Has the final chapter been written in the blood-stained history that sprang from Karl Marx's *Communist Manifesto?* Can we now welcome with open arms the new leadership, with absolute certainty that we no longer need fear the former Soviet Union, which, after all, is now in the struggling stages of trying to become a responsible world citizen?

Can we now, without much pause for reflection on the Soviet Union's record of oppression, go confidently forward into George Bush's New World order? Can we count on the Russian bear, and whatever republics ultimately remain within its sphere, to labor cooperatively at our side while Utopia is built?

God's Word has much to say about the subject of end-time Russia and also about a world governing system that will have at its heart ideology and aspirations very similar to what some leaders are proposing today. Essays within this book address these matters, always considering them in the light of God's prophetic Word.

Signposts to the Future

Desert Shield, Desert Storm, Desert Rainbow; Russia becoming a distinct entity again with the splitting-up of the Soviet Union; a New World order — these are not insignificant matters in the light of biblical prophecy.

Some signposts warn those who are spiritually attuned to the truth of God's Word concerning prophecy of terrifying times just ahead. Some of these spiritual markers are the following: the link between Persia (Iran/Iraq) and a destabilized, almost chaotic, former Soviet Union; the birth of a global order; and the near-future unification of a once considered irreparably fragmented Europe in 1993.

Purveyors of information in electronic and print media alike report an upsurge of interest among their viewers, listeners, and readers concerning what the future might hold for their troubled world. Many people, claiming to be prophets, fortune tellers, futurists, gurus, psychics, and other types of soothsayers, eagerly promise to satisfy public hunger to know what comes next.

From the predictions of sixteenth century seer, Nostradamus, to the incantations and gobbledygook of whomever is the latest astrological rage, the deluded rush from one Babylonian type feast to the next. The only appetite that is satiated, however, is the greed of the charlatans who feed these hungry ones the occult-rooted, false prophecies they crave.

Will Desert Rainbow and the Kremlin's new-found benevolence produce a New World order through which mankind will achieve lasting world peace? Would such peace bring about the fulfillment of all the utopian wonders aspired to by the dreamers of the Human Potential movement? Or will a different rainbow, the rainbow of New Age promises, bedazzle a gullible world populace anxious to build a one-world heaven on earth? Will they find at the end of that rainbow the proverbial pot of gold or a cauldron bubbling with unprecedented terror?

The Promise of Enlightenment

Facts and figures attest that we live in a world system built on deception. That being so, can we ever hope to understand what the future holds with certainty that truth rests at the heart of prophecy? Is there a benchmark by which one can determine that what is prophesied will absolutely come to pass in every detail?

The answer is a resounding yes! You can know what the future ultimately holds for you; the benchmark by which to measure the integrity of prophecy is the Word of God — the Bible. If the prophecy is recorded in God's inspired Word, it is 100 percent truth. God cannot lie.

The Word of God is in reality a person — One who was and is at the same time fully man and fully God — the Word made flesh, Jesus Christ. The Holy Scriptures tell us He knows the end from the beginning because, "In the beginning was the Word and the Word was with God, and the Word was God." He alone can know all future matters. Any and all so-called prophets, psychics, astrologers, spiritists, or whatever they might call themselves, are deceivers.

The living God alone knows the details of things to come in the unfolding of world history and of your own life. Still, there are large portions of prophetic truth within God's written Word for the very purpose of being understood. The secret to understanding is really no secret at all. Anyone who is a true child of God has the promise of enlightenment in all aspects of God's recorded Word. If he or she diligently studies and seeks to understand with the prayerful desire that God's will and purpose be accomplished in his or her life, the truth will be revealed.

Some are especially gifted in understanding and disseminating God's truths. *STORMING TOWARD ARMAGEDDON: Essays In Apocalypse* brings together a number of God's most dedicated students of the prophetic Word — accomplished scholars and writers in the fields of prophecy and eschatology.

Having sifted these matters through the filter of God's prophetic Word, each of these renowned authors analyzes and gives insights into the most relevant national and global issues and events of recent and current times. They are in agreement that the world is on a collision course as apocalyptic events and Armageddon are coming into view. In that light, they have concluded that the once sealed book of Daniel 12:4 has now been opened for this generation to see, hear, and understand.

The Blessed Hope

Although this volume covers a broad range of issues believed to be definite signals of future end-time events, one sign in particular stands out most starkly from the pages of God's Word and from the pages of history. This sign concerns the nation of Israel.

Headline reports involving the nation Israel leap at the true student of prophecy from major newspapers and television screens on a daily, even an hourly, basis. As was predictable even before the first Scud missile slammed into Tel Aviv and now following Desert Storm, the world community is demanding that this tiny nation submit to a diplomatic process through which a lasting peace in the Middle East can be achieved. The Palestinian homeland issue/problem, secure borders for Israel, and the elimination of strategic weapons in the region (i.e., Israel's nuclear defensive capability) are terms and phrases destined to loom larger and larger in the media and within the circle of powers that be.

The first rider of the Four Horsemen of the Apocalypse will soon gallop across the world stage apparently carrying — the masses will believe — the answer to the Arab/Israeli problem and solutions to all other dilemmas confronting mankind. A Middle East peace process and then a treaty with the nation of Israel at its core; a worldwide cry for peace and safety; the greatest, most charismatic leader and negotiator the planet has ever produced — these are keys that fling open the gates to Apocalypse.

But, there is hope. The Blessed Hope is the only pathway of escape from a world soon to rush headlong into the Valley of Jezreel at Meggido — the place called Armageddon.

The writers of these essays do much more than warn of future judgment. They point to God's supreme love sacrifice, the only safe haven from the unimaginable devastation that is surely coming. His name is Jesus Christ. He is the Son of God, the Saviour, the Prince of Peace!

Section One

A World
Gone Mad!

1

Characteristics of End-Time Man

by William T. James

There was a time, early in this century, when reports of children being sold to makers of pornographic movies and magazines would have been met with disbelief by the reader or hearer of such allegations. News of gang rape, mass killings, of genocide on an unfathomable scale would have — among civilized people at least — been considered as acts of barbarism predating the Renaissance, or as happening only in earth's most primitive cultures. Almost certainly, such acts in early twentieth century life would have been catalogued as aberrations or isolated incidents of insanity.

World War I brought news of chemical warfare — of mustard gas searing the lungs of men at war.

The 1920s and 1930s were ablaze with gangland killings. Capone, Pretty Boy Floyd, Bonnie and Clyde, John Dillinger — all are names infamous for their bloody trails of violence across the face of naive America. Naive because many people, enamored with Hollywood and all the glitter emanating from the silver screens, viewed these brutal murderers as modern day Robin Hoods getting even on behalf of middle Americans.

These criminals were seen as outwitting the banking tyrants, the law, and lawmen with clever maneuvering. For many the outlaws were, for the most part, merely misunderstood rather than truly evil men and women. They were people forced into their nefarious molds by sour, vindictive injustice.

Globally, the strategists in geopolitical affairs tried to hammer out a League of Nations, but the world, despite coming together in war, would not come together in peace. The league failed, other than to lay groundwork for a uniting of a bloc of nations that would come at a later, more amenable date.

In the United States crime and violence — the ugly side of life — while festering within the nation, remained isolated from the mainstream of society for the most part. The nation forged ahead, producing labor-saving machinery and creating a more leisurely way of life for the middle class.

But clouds of war were boiling in Europe. Anger over terms forced on Germany at Versailles at the end of World War I inflamed passions and the political thought processes of those who would have their revenge. Adolph Hitler wrote and dictated to Rudolph Hess from his jail cell where he had been gingerly exiled for rabble-rousing. The genocidal blueprint for avenging Germany's humiliation, by the world he would one day come close to conquering, emerged from his twisted mind. The resultant holocaust and aftermath, with six million Jews mass-murdered, forever wiped away the naivete and head-in-the-sand innocence of America and the world.

From that shocking moment in history when the corpses of the Jewish holocaust victims were filmed and shown to a gasping world, man brutalizing man has taken on new dimensions, and humanity now seems desensitized to the point of being almost shockproof.

Worse and Worse

In 2 Timothy 3:13 the apostle Paul, under inspiration of the Holy Spirit, prophesied: "But evil men and seducers shall wax worse and worse . . . ."

From the daily news accounts, the accuracy of this prophecy cannot be denied. The front pages of our newspapers do not provide adequate space to contain the number of stories flowing from the news services across America and the world.

Reports of man's degenerate acts spill over into and fill other pages from front to back. The rare exception in today's world is the story of people doing something beneficial to others; the norm is bad news.

Throughout the centuries there have been the Jack-the-Rippers, the Bluebeards, the Attilas, the Rue Morgue-type horror stories. Never, however, have these grisly accounts come in such profusion as now. We are bombarded hourly by accounts that bear witness to the fact that despite our professed civility, we are in a period as barbarous and perverse as any in human history.

It can truly be said that we live in a world in the process — perhaps in the final stages — of going mad. Jesus himself told us in the Scriptures that there would come a time at the end of the age when, if God did not physically intervene, no flesh would be saved. Man would, collectively, commit suicide.

Since that sunlit mid-day of November 22, 1963, in Dallas, Texas, when Americans watched the murder of the president of the United States, the floodgates of evil seem to have opened wide, and it appears that no one and nothing can stem the flow of violence.

The Scriptures tell us that the end will come like a flood. All the signs given by God's prophetic Word will be gushing through the generation that is alive at the time Jesus Christ returns to put an end to man's insanity. While the Apocalypse looms and Armageddon sucks all of fallen mankind into its vortex, the time will resemble the days of Noah and the days of Lot.

God's holy righteousness demanded that the generation alive in Noah's time be destroyed. The contamination that sin wrought had finally so corrupted mankind physically, mentally, and spiritually that the earth had to be cleansed. Noah and his family were the only people perfect in their generation. They were not sinless because God's grace saved them just as it saves all who believe in Him. Noah and his family were saved from the flood because they chose to remain free of the genetic and spiritual contamination that ran rampant over all the earth of that pre-flood era.

Sodom and Gomorrah, of Lot's day, were similarly affected and infected. The thoughts of the people, according to

God's Word, were only on evil continually. Homosexual activity was not an alternate lifestyle, it was the predominate lifestyle. Society festered as well with all other manner of reprobate human interaction. Man had reached the point of incorrigibility that demanded a just and righteous God destroy them in order for cleansing to take place.

Jesus said in Luke 17:26: "And as it was in the days of Noah, so shall it be also in the days of the Son of man." In verse 28, Jesus said it will be "as it was in the days of Lot" when He returns to set right this wayward planet.

The Final Diagnosis

Exactly how, then, will things be in the period just before Christ returns? According to God's Word, how will man be conducting human affairs at the time of the end?

Let us attempt to find answers to this question by examining the only truth there is — God's truth, His holy, inerrant Word.

The apostle Paul delineated the precise societal symptoms of man's last gasp of living death. God, who loves man and wants to give him the life and freedom that is in His Son Jesus Christ, must in the final analysis give God-rejecting man up to his vile affections. The symptoms are clear, unmistakable in their presentation, as the Apostle minces no words in outlining them. We will look at these one at a time to see if any or all fit the generation in which we live.

Jesus said in Luke 21:28: "And when these things begin to come to pass, then look up, and lift up your heads; for your redemption draweth nigh."

Jesus was speaking to His disciples of every generation, but particularly to His disciples, or followers, who would be alive at the end of the age. There has never been a generation in which all signs prophesied for the last days have come as a flood until this generation. In this passage the Lord was telling His disciples who would be living during the end-time period to be watchful and expectant. He promised He will come for them when the signs given in prophecy *begin* to manifest themselves.

Let us consider how near that time must be.

The major symptoms of fallen humanity's end-time societal disorder are given by Paul's prophecy in 2 Timothy. We will look at recent and current issues and events and dissect these matters one at a time, filtering them through the light of God's prophetic Word.

> This know also, that in the last days perilous times shall come. For men shall be lovers of their own selves, covetous, boasters, proud, blasphemers, disobedient to parents, unthankful, unholy, without natural affection, trucebreakers, false accusers, incontinent, fierce, despisers of those that are good, Traitors, heady, high-minded, lovers of pleasure more than lovers of God;Having a form of godliness, but denying the power thereof: from such turn away (2 Tim. 3:1-5).

Symptom #1: Lovers of Self

Today we are told by sociologists and by psychologists that, at the root of practically every personality problem, is lack of self-esteem. Criminals, deprived of equality in society as children, thus grow up feeling left at the bottom of the heap and become angry at the system that rejected them. They rationalize that it is street justice to compensate for what society has done to hurt them and, therefore, society is fair game.

Psychologists say people should be taught to acquire higher self-esteem; then they will become useful, productive citizens. Self-esteem is another expression for self-love, and God's Word says that this inward-turned philosophy is the problem — not the cure. When people think first and foremost of themselves, others whose lives they affect inevitably suffer from their self-indulgence.

One of the most blatant forms of self-love, and one of the greatest detrimental effects of egocentricity is found in the problem of teen-age sex and the havoc it wreaks upon individuals, families, and society at large. Young people are shown by example that it is a natural thing to indulge in sexual activity apart from the bonds of marital commitment. The body is to be enjoyed, they are told by example. They see in movies, TV sitcoms, and their adulterous parents the "If it feels good, do it" philosophy.

Teens are now told by public school systems that sex is a natural act to be enjoyed, just as eating is to be enjoyed. After all, we are but a higher form of animal life, according to public education's adoptive religion, the Theory of Evolution. The only thing to be concerned about, according to a growing number of educators across America, seems to be that teens engage in "safe sex."

A young man, whose glands are inflamed with lust after having been issued a condom by a school-based clinician, impregnates a girl, who is pressured to give in to the boy's egocentric drive. He feels no obligation other than, perhaps, to advise aborting the baby. The girl is harmed physically, socially, psychologically, and spiritually. A baby dies. This tragic reality is played out thousands upon thousands of times each year.

The social engineers tell us the secret to ultimately producing a healthy cultural environment is high self-esteem. A sense of self-worth will make man live up to his own great expectations.

Rather than love of self, however, God's Word tells us to love others, to esteem others more than ourselves, to humble ourselves before God. This generation is obviously doing none of these.

Symptom #2: Coveters

Keeping up with the Joneses is more than a joke in America today, it is symptomatic of a society gone mad with compulsion to acquire not merely as much as one's neighbor, but much more than one's neighbor. Commercials have for years told us that we "deserve the best" and have urged us to "go for the gusto." We continue to have our senses assaulted by advertising slogans that appeal to our human pride — to our love of self.

This materialistic drive has individually, nationally and globally tumbled man into an economic abyss from which he will not be extricated, apart from the unprecedented (and ultimately diabolical) geopolitical and socioeconomic rearrangement prophesied in Revelation 13. Rock star Madonna's hit song, "Material Girl," says precisely what this generation is becoming.

For the United States, the quicksand of opulence began

tugging the first time a general store owner granted a customer the privilege of purchasing merchandise on credit. The credit monster awakened, and the next step was no doubt to bring it to its feet by granting larger loans and expanding the debtor base. Commercial lending thus began in a big way, and usury exploded as did inflation.

The spirit of covetousness is thriving in every facet of life. From young children who desire to out-dress their peers to their parents who overextend to make an impression. From there it moves to governments whose members complain of massive, unmanageable deficits yet vote themselves huge salary increases and other perks, while demanding that the taxpayer tighten his belt and shell out more for congressmen's pork-barrel projects. The greed monster grows!

Coups, revolts, rebellions, and wars have at their sin-blackened centers, Paul's end-time term for greed. Our generation is unparalleled in its covetousness.

Symptoms #3 & 4: Boasters, Proud

Following closely on the heels of covetousness — actually an outgrowth of it — are the dual vanities within the heart of end-time man. These people are boasters; they are extremely proud.

Jesus said, "Blessed are the meek [humble] for they shall inherit the earth [the millennial earth]."

The father of those whose characters exhibit the antithesis of humility is Satan. Lucifer was the greatest boaster of them all. "I shall put my star above the throne of the most high," he said in his supremely prideful arrogance. He seduced Eve in the Garden of Eden with the same prideful boast and promise. "Ye shall be as God," he told her. When Adam yielded, all humankind became genetic heirs to the great pride that first welled in Lucifer's heart.

Again, we see the boasting and the pride in our children. We can remember our own childhood experiences. We made claims, each having to be bigger and better or farther or faster than the boast that went before.

Politicians are living, breathing proof of boastfulness and pride, while they vie for a chance to "serve" us. How quickly the boasts turn bitter and ring hollow when they become inaccessible and self-willed after election time. They become little lords; we become revenue producers for the wastefulness of bureaucracy. The rhetoric of the campaign stump, whether on the courthouse lawn, door to door, or in media propaganda is a strange alchemy of prideful boasting and humble exhortation.

Yet we who are victimized time after time have no room to complain; it is the American political process in action. It is the process we have allowed to stray far from the noble designs of the founding fathers, a process we perpetuate through our acquiescence. This is not cynicism — it is fact.

Such pride has given the Supreme Court a de facto authority. They execute, legislate, and adjudicate such marvelously innovative things as: 1) the forbidding of prayer in public schools; 2) abortion on demand; 3) in effect, evolution as a religion; 4) the softening of the legal system to the extent that criminals now feel they have a green light to plunder, rape, and murder; 5) in some instances, interpreting homosexuality as deserving moral and legal status equivalent to that given heterosexual marriages; 6) made a mockery of the First Amendment by pampering pornographers at every juncture, while at the same time banning Bible reading and all mention of the true, living God from classrooms in public schools.

Like Satan himself, our judiciary over the past three decades has ascended to such heights that it serves as documented proof that we have little to be prideful or boastful about as a people who have allowed it to happen.

In all fairness, there are occasional times of sanity. One such instance involves the 1991 Supreme Court decision regarding abortion and foreign aid to Third World nations. An Associated Press release dated June 4, 1991, states:

> The Supreme Court on Monday let stand a Bush administration rule aimed at making sure U.S. supported family planning programs in Third World countries do not promote abortion.
>
> The court, without comment, rejected a Planned Parenthood challenge to the government ban on federal contributions to health care organizations abroad unless they promise not to use money from any source to "actively promote abortion as a method

of family planning."

Those who would save "Mother Earth" by engineering birth, death, and all facets of life in between those two events, for the entire world, lost one round. They continue, however, to win many others in their drive to set up their version of Utopia. But such an entity would be a global order based on infanticide and would be totally devoid of God Almighty.

Symptom #5: Blasphemy

God's name has been all but officially removed from public education in America — in itself a blasphemous thing. But His name is at the same time in practically every theater in America. Jesus Christ is unmentionable in public forums because His holy name represents a narrow-minded viewpoint and would offend. Religion, if it is to be mentioned, must represent an eclectic view — must encompass an ecumenical theological viewpoint.

In almost every film above the rating of "G," the name of Jesus Christ is repeated frequently. It seems, as a matter of fact, as if screen writers are required to use His holy name blasphemously at least a minimum number of times per scene. Always, the name of God, the name of Jesus, is used in one of two ways: 1) as an expression of frustration, exasperation, or anger; or 2) to portray the fanaticism of one religious zealot or another, usually a character who is dangerously insane.

Is it any wonder that a blasphemous generation of young people reject discipline and self-control, when adults have spent decades producing an anti-God language? Even Christian parents have slowly become desensitized, thereby giving into this blasphemous language's insidious, venomous effects.

Movies such as *The Last Temptation Of Christ*, in which Jesus, man's only hope for redemption, is portrayed as succumbing to sexual immorality, are treated as art form under Supreme Court interpretation. Mention of Christ as the eternal God incarnate in front of a class of public school children, however, has been viewed by that same body as unacceptable. A so-called artist can represent the blessed Saviour by a crucifix submerged in a bottle of urine and receive federal dollars for his blasphemous work! Madonna is looked upon with amusement when she blasphemes, in the most gross fashion, the name of the Lord Jesus Christ! A large audience of Americans pay her millions of dollars for the privilege of watching her do so!

It is perhaps ludicrous to even ask the question: Are we living in a time of blasphemous deportment such as described by the apostle Paul?

A more subtle yet, at the same time, more dangerous indicator of the blasphemous times in which we live is the New Age movement's philosophy that has infiltrated almost every segment of American life. At the heart of the movement is Eastern mysticism and ancient occultism.

New Agers claim the devotee of the movement's methods and agenda has within himself the "Christ consciousness" and can ascend to the apex of God-likeness with meditational effort. All mankind is collectively God, they proclaim. Once laughed at, or shrugged off as merely a weird cult, the New Age is blossoming with unbelievable speed, pervading every part of our lives, including the true body of believers in Jesus Christ.

To claim to be Christ and/or God is blatant blasphemy, and this generation is swallowing the New Age lie that we are all Christs — as they say — hook, line, and sinker.

Symptom #6: Disobedience to Parents

As in the case of blasphemy, we should not be shocked at the rebelliousness of our young when they have watched their parents consume themselves with self-love to a point where the children suffer incalculable damage. There has been for years now a degeneration of respect for anything and everything that smacks of order and discipline.

Children watch adults fly in the face of authority in every aspect of life. In sports, adults curse and all but physically attack referees, umpires, and judges, from the primary level of midget league sports and little girl beauty pageants to the big league competitions. Policemen are almost always unjust, unfair, "stupid cops" when tickets are handed out. Remember a case in 1990 when actress Zsa Zsa Gabor slapped a policeman and flaunted her disdain for law enforcement before the nation?

Teachers are constantly "picking on" the children of parents who refuse to accept responsibility for raising their young in the right way. To these people, schools should be babysitters who never drag them in on their children's problems. When parents are called in to deal with the situations, the school is at fault, no matter what the circumstances.

Likewise, when the children then refuse to follow the laws that govern society, the parents blame "the system" for being unjust and geared only to placate the wealthy and the elite. The parents refuse to accept responsibility — the children follow suit. Each generation thus exceeds the bounds of restraint to an extent greater than the previous generation.

God's Word says there will come a time in human history when children will betray parents. This has already come to pass in one instance. The Hitler youth movement, dissatisfied with the perceived weakness of German parents, removed the children and trained them in Nazi ways for the purpose of properly educating them. The children became tools of the state for spying out those who resisted the regime. When parents refuse to accept responsibility, government, ostensibly to preserve the order of things and promote the general welfare, will.

During the soon-to-come Tribulation, Antichrist and associates will no doubt use the same tactics as Hitler did. It will be relatively easy to institute such a system because uncaring or too-busy parents will have paved the way by handing the most horrendous dictatorship in history a generation of children ripe for the picking.

Jesus said in Luke 18:16: "Suffer little children to come unto me, and forbid them not . . . ."

Sunday school rooms remain more than half-empty while parents selfishly seek other things to do on Sundays. By so doing, they forbid children from coming to the One who can make them truly productive people. A primary command to parents by God is given by the apostle Paul in Ephesians 6:4: "provoke not your children to wrath: but bring them up in the nurture and admonition of the Lord."

Parents who refuse these commands of the living God risk reaping a bitter harvest of disobedience. We can look around us today and see the terrible consequences of rebellion taking their toll on this generation of young people.

Symptoms #7 & 8: Unthankful, Unholy

President Abraham Lincoln officially proclaimed Thanksgiving Day a national holiday in 1863. Thanksgiving, as a concept of thanks for blessings in the land in which we now live, however, was first celebrated in the autumn of 1621, when William Bradford, governor of Plymouth Colony, called for a day of thanksgiving and prayer after the harvest. Other New England colonies gradually adopted the practice.

These godly people, regardless of what revisionist writers of today's accounts of American history claim, escaped England first and foremost for the privilege to worship the one, true God. They knew to whom they were indebted for all blessings they received. Thankfulness and holiness were inseparable in the minds and hearts of our forefathers. They were thankful to the one and only God of heaven because they sought to be holy and righteous in His omniscient eyes.

How far we have come as a nation and as a world from that 1621 autumn Thanksgiving! People are proud of the things they accumulate, accomplish, attain; they are grateful in some instances to other people and to institutions. For the most part, however, they use the word *thankful* interchangeably with the words *happy* and *pleased,* not in the sense of thankfulness to God.

To be truly thankful to God one must be holy, that is, a believer that God is the provider of all things good. This is a generation of unthankful, unholy people. They know neither the God of the Bible nor seek to know Him. The only way to know the Father is to know the Son, Jesus Christ, who said as recorded in John 14:6: "I am the way, the truth, and the life: no man cometh unto the Father, but by me."

The world today views the biblical truth that Jesus Christ is the only way to God as a "narrow" or "close-minded" concept that cannot and will not be tolerated by an enlightened people of the twentieth and twenty-first centuries.

A holy, thankful people in the eyes of God must desire to worship and serve Him. In Joshua 24:15, God commands: "choose you this day whom ye will serve." This subsequent passage records God's command for not only the children of Israel, but for all mankind: "fear the Lord [reverence, worship Him], and serve him in sincerity and in truth: and put away [all other gods]" (Josh.24:14).

One quick glance around us tells the story. Man is obsessed with many things other than the God of the Bible. These are the gods of a truly unholy, unthankful generation.

Symptom #9: Without Natural Affection

We all read with disbelieving eyes accounts of family members killing each other, of babies being sold or discarded by their mothers, of fathers engaging in incestuous relationships with daughters from childhood, until in some cases, the daughter either kills her father or reports the despicable matter to family and authorities.

In Russellville, Arkansas, in 1987, a social miscreant named R. Gene Simmons, killed all his family members whom he had invited for Christmas, including the daughter he had sexually abused since her childhood. It was the worst murderous rampage involving one family member killing other family members in United States' history, and apparently stemmed from the fact a local woman had refused Simmons' romantic advances.

This tragedy punctuated the point that our supposedly civilized nation has reached with regard to familial breakdowns. This was the outer limits of atrocity to be sure, but the numbers of incidents coming to light daily, weekly, monthly, yearly, attest to the fact that such activity is accelerating.

Accounts involving what can only be described as abhorrent behavior that is "without natural affection" stream in from around the nation and world. From Livingston, Montana, a news report of June 26, 1991, reads in part:

> Authorities say a woman, unable to have more children, arranged a rape by her live-in boyfriend of her 11-year-old daughter because she wanted another baby.
>
> The 30-year-old mother of three . . . said that she couldn't have children and she asked the daughter to sleep with the boyfriend.
>
> . . . The girl is pregnant.
>
> "It's one of those things that when you end your shift and you go home, you don't sleep so well that night," said Acting Police Chief Steve McCann.

Abortion

But perhaps no one issue in American society today so fulfills Paul's prophetic end-time characteristic "without natural affection" as does that of abortion. In the great majority of cases in which unborn babies are deliberately exterminated, those doing the killing and those consenting to the murder consider the matter to be no more than medical procedures to solve medical problems.

In most cases, those involved in the abortion process seem to feel no guilt or experience any sorrow over the taking of an unborn child's life. The multiple thousands of victims each year cannot give their views in protest of their impending murders, so they are considered by the abortionists as nothing more than fetal tissue, refuse with which to be done away.

The proposition now has been raised that in some cases the dead fetus be used in the treatment of maladies such as Parkinson's Disease. In that procedure the brain cells of a fetus are transplanted into the brain of a Parkinson's Disease victim. This raises the probability that genetic engineers will some day raise fetuses for the specific purpose of maintaining a bank of tissue for treating humanity's medical problems.

If this seems far-fetched, consider a recent case that has raised moral and ethical questions. A couple conceived a baby specifically so that the baby could donate bone-marrow to another member of the family in order to treat a disease. The couple, of course, claim to love the baby as much as their other children and undoubtedly do so. The point to be made is that such thinking is at the root of what is becoming symptomatic of a generation "without natural affection."

This casual attitude about human life — considering the unborn as non-entities, as nuisances to be eliminated, or as tissue to be utilized — is also precisely the mind set that God's Word says will pervade the generation alive in the era immediately preceding the Apocalypse, Armageddon, and the return of Jesus Christ to earth.

People have been convinced by humanists — the social engineers who claim to want to save planet earth through human effort, apart totally from God Almighty — that these little ones are not people, that the unborn are not yet human. But the God — whom the humanists in their critical thinking, values clarifying, no-moral-absolutes philosophizing consider to be dead — says something diametrically different.

God told Jeremiah the prophet, "Before I formed thee in the belly I knew thee; and before thou cameth forth out of the womb I sanctified thee, and I ordained thee a prophet unto the nations" (Jer. 1:5).

The Psalmist wrote under God's inspiration, "For he knoweth our frame; he remembereth that we are dust" (Ps. 103:14). God's Word records in Luke 1:41-44 that the child within the womb is indeed fully a person. Elizabeth, the mother of John the Baptist, said upon greeting Mary, the mother of Jesus, while both were pregnant with those babies: "For, lo, as soon as the voice of thy salutation sounded in mine ears, the babe leaped in my womb for joy" (Luke 1:44).

God himself tells us that the embryo, the fetus, the unborn child, is every bit as much a living human being as the child who has taken breath.

Paul the apostle says that the last generation before Christ's return will be marked by the trait "without natural affection" — or — without love for the most basic kind of relationship such as the mother for her baby still in the womb. People of that generation will, God's Word says, prefer convenience to responsibility.

Hundreds of thousands of abortions, the vast majority of them nothing less than contraception after the fact, have marked the last several decades as the era of greatest infanticide in recorded times.

Children who *are* born are likewise subjected to atrocity bordering on holocaust. This, the humanist philosophers tell us, is but another reason "unwanted" babies should not be brought into the world. The old bromide, "two wrongs do not a right make," applies. It is analogous to one saying that statistics on cancer project that one out of four people will develop cancer in their lifetime, therefore, we should eliminate one out of four people before they have a chance to develop the dread disease. Only God in His omniscience has the right to decide such things.

Homosexuality

"Without natural affection" means also *unnatural* affection. Homosexuality is rampant; sexual deviation and perversion of every sort is looked upon now as private matters between consenting adults.

One most recent case starkly makes the point. Convicted mass-murderer, Jeffrey L. Dahmer, was confronted by Milwaukee policemen prior to his apartment being found days later to contain body parts from many dismembered corpses. The police, in that first encounter, were called by neighbors who said Dahmer was chasing a nude, bleeding man. The police determined that it was a lovers' quarrel between the two men, and so they did nothing. Later, the bleeding "man" was found to have been a fourteen-year-old boy whose body parts were reportedly found in Dahmer's apartment.

Such perverse activity is more and more becoming private and non-private abominations between adults and children, and even between people and animals. No moral absolutes in the twisted rationale of humanist, critical thinking and values clarification means "*anything* goes."

Symptom #10: Trucebreakers

A report in the *Encyclopaedia Britannica 1990 Book Of the Year* titled "Arms Control and Disarmament" states:

> The most important arms control event of 1989 was Soviet Foreign Minister Eduard Shevardnadze's historic admission that the Krasnoyarsk radar installation in the USSR was a violation of the 1972 ABM treaty. This was the first admission by the Soviet Union that they had violated an arms control agreement; it resolved a long-standing U.S. debate in favour of those who had argued that the Krasnoyarsk was one of several Soviet violations. This argument had been made on successive reports on Soviet noncompliance with arms control agreements by U.S. President Ronald Reagan and had been bitterly criticized by much of the arms control community as being incorrect. However, the Reagan administration's charge was now acknowledged as true by the Soviets.

In actuality, the report grossly understates both the extent of Communist treaty infractions and the extent of protestation of those who knew and know the Communist way of doing business. It also exposes the woolly-mindedness of those who then saw the Soviet Communist leadership and now see the Commonwealth of Independent States leadership as trustworthy citizens of a soon to be New World order.

Communism of the Soviet and Chinese kind, as well as every other variety, presents in microcosm and typifies the last days' characteristics termed by the apostle Paul as trucebreakers. The number of incidents of Communists lying and going back on their word is legendary, though the liberal-minded of the West just don't seem to get it. Perestroika, glasnost, and the USSR under a new name will, in the final analysis, have altered nothing.

But there is an epidemic of trucebreaking in arenas other than geopolitics. It is estimated by some sociologists that as many as one out of two marriages in the United States — that is, people now being married, not necessarily including marriages made in past decades — end in divorce. The most basic truce, treaty, or pact is that made between man and woman to be husband and wife. God ordained marriage to be monogamous and to last a lifetime.

Hollywood has represented the contemporary marriage as a contract to be broken at any time or one to be ignored whenever expediency demands a one-night stand or weekend getaway with someone other than one's husband or wife. Young people now have what seems almost a legitimate excuse to avoid marriage or to at least have an experimental live-in relationship before marriage. "Why have marriage" they can ask, "when the commitment of the marriage vow is so lightly treated in practice?"

Truly, we live in a time when trucebreaking is a way of life for a growing number of people.

Symptom #11: False Accusers

If one wishes to look to a single area within American life where false accusation runs unchecked, it is best exemplified by the political process at all levels. False accusations and false accusers are generally accepted as normal in today's society as a whole, but in politics — as is said of love and war — all is fair.

False accusation is nothing more or less than lying in order to seek and to gain advantage for one's self — to the denigration of the one being accused. Lies, then, are at the heart of that described in 1 Timothy 3 by Paul.

Lying to avoid punishment or to gain advantage has always been the *human* thing to do. Corporations and kingdoms have been built on deception of every sort. The trait of lying — of falsely accusing for personal gains — the Scripture says, is a heart problem. "The heart is deceitful above all things, and desperately wicked . . ." (Jer. 17:9).

It would no doubt be possible for the reader here to recall, in his or her own life, instances when people took advantage of others through deceit, lies, or false accusations. For the purpose of looking at a single event in America that symbolizes or captures the very essence of false dealings, think for a moment on the Watergate affair that brought a president down and very nearly this nation's governmental stability along with him. Most every adult in the United States remembers the series of one revelation upon another — many of which, even at this late date, still serve only to puzzle and confuse.

Politicians in the 1990s still look into cameras and deny wrongdoing even after having the proof of their guilt documented for all to see. Party affiliation makes no difference. Scandals on all sides and at all levels are epidemic.

False accusers, too, are a big part of the political process in America. The very fact that so many public officials are caught red-handed in one ignoble act or another makes the other honest, hard-working public servants vulnerable to innuendo and out-right lies no matter the purity of their record.

Much of the American public can be held responsible for the real and growing evil of false accusation and false accusers. Tabloids thrive on such garbage because their readerships have insatiable appetites for it. We indeed live in an era of false accusers.

Symptom #12: Incontinent

Webster's Third Dictionary defines "incontinent" as: "marked by lacking control; unrestrained evil appetites; inability, disinclination to resist impulse [as in alcoholism]."

Every major civilization in recorded history has ultimately come to a time when the symptoms wrapped up in the term "incontinent" overwhelmed society. Perhaps Edward Gibbons' *Decline and Fall of the Roman Empire* is the most complete account of such a deterioration. The apostle Paul tells us that the last generation of human history will also come to be predominantly incontinent, not only in conduct but in its very character.

A lack of self-discipline and self-control is a growing monster straining at the tethers of law, order, and common sense. These restraints are themselves perpetually under the abrasive, corrosive attacks of Luciferic agencies that seek to replace all traces of godly influence with humanism.

An Associated Press report from Washington, DC, in June, 1991, clearly illustrates this unrelenting strain modern man puts on the leash of morality.

> The National Park Service is "seriously" considering a proposal that would sanction nude sunbathing at one of its facilities in Hawaii, an Interior Department official said Saturday.
>
> . . . (spokesman) Steve Goldstein said three factors the department would consider in making its decision would be local and state laws and normal customs governing "clothing optional" beaches as well as citizen reaction . . . .
>
> . . . He said there has been nude sunbathing at other park service facilities and "there is no federal law governing whether someone can nude sunbathe." But it has never been officially sanctioned by the government, he said.

So even the human governing entities of our nation and world are confused by the author of confusion, Satan. How can we expect our young people to be less confused or more disciplined than the adults to whom they are supposed to look for leadership and example?

A *Knight News Service* report, by Lee Ban, dramatically makes the saddening point that ours is an age of unparalleled incontinence:

> U.S. teenagers are turning increasingly to booze

to relieve stress and boredom, and many may well be on their way to becoming alcoholics, according to a national report released Thursday.

"It's an alarming trend," said Surgeon General Antonia Navello.

More than half, 10.6 million, of the nation's junior and senior high school students are drinkers. Of those who drink, 8 million consume alcohol on a weekly basis, 5.4 million have gone on a binge on occasion, and nearly half a million on a weekly binge, guzzling five or more drinks in a row.

Some drink as many as 33 beers a week, a dozen wine coolers, 24 glasses of wine or 24 shots of liquor, the study said.

. . . The survey, conducted by the inspector general's office of the Department of Health and Human Services found that teen-age students annually consume 35 percent of all wine coolers sold in the United States, about 31 million gallons and 1.1 billion cans of beer, or about 102 million gallons.

Navello termed the findings "shocking" and said they raise questions about alcohol marketing, advertising standards and enforcement of underage drinking laws.

The 1991 survey showed that more than half of the 20.7 million U.S. students in grades seven through twelve who drink alcoholic beverages are, or will become, alcoholics.

The study showed that the highest percentage of drinkers — 54 percent — are among the thirteen to fifteen age group. Imagine! If the percentage holds or increases, in just a few years more than half of all American high school graduates will be users of alcohol. Many will be alcoholics! In some European nations the percentages are even higher. Cultures in several nations are built around wine consumption.

Sexual self-discipline — rather, the lack thereof — is easily observable and able to be documented for anyone caring to open his eyes to facts. We have already addressed this tragedy to some extent. We have seen that lack of control in sexuality has resulted in a significant proportion of this generation of young people emulating adult lascivious and miscreant behavior; teen-age pregnancies and raging diseases continue to follow in the wake of the tidal wave of immorality.

God's Word declares prophetic truth in the 1 Timothy account characterizing end-time man. We live at a time of unbridled behavior. News accounts, such as the case of a former heavyweight boxing champion's rape of a teenage beauty contestant and his subsequent conviction, give vivid testimony of that truth of incontinence.

Symptoms 13 & 14: Fierce, Despisers of Those That Are Good

An incident in 1990, familiar to most Americans, is the report of one teenager dowsing another teenager with gasoline and igniting it simply because the young victim, reportedly a Christian and a well-liked, well-behaved citizen, would not take a drug as the other boy demanded. The teenager who committed the atrocity is allegedly a drug user and small-time dealer.

People of the end time will be fierce, despisers of those that are good.

A newspaper report out of Atlantic Beach, New York, in June, 1991, reads:

> A black teenager was on life-support systems Thursday after being hit by four bat-wielding white men, apparently because he was talking to a white girl.

A June, 1991, AP release from Rome, Italy, reported:

> City councils in 21 towns where officials are suspected of having close ties with the Mafia are slated to be dissolved, reports said Saturday.
>
> Among the towns in Calabria, a southern region, was Taurianova, site of one of the most gruesome slayings blamed on founding clans of the Indrangheta, the Calabrian crime organization likened to the Sicilian Mafia.
>
> A few weeks ago, after shooting to death two merchants who were brothers, gunmen in the main square of Taurianova lopped off the head of one of

the victims and tossed it in the air for target practice as dozens of horrified townspeople watched.

A minor traffic incident in Little Rock, Arkansas, incited one of the men involved in the fender-bender to shoot the other man four times at point blank range while the man sat behind his steering wheel. We expect to read and hear of beastly, murderous individuals like Saddam Hussein, who reportedly once had a member of his body guards killed, then cut to pieces, and the body parts delivered to the front door of the man's widow. But no longer are unbelievably cruel acts done by strange, megalomaniacal individuals in faraway places. Such atrocities are now daily fodder for local news writers. What's more, society is increasingly paralyzed in dealing with perpetrators of these horrible crimes.

The rape of the Central Park jogger is a case well in point in considering the fierceness of modern man. Four young men raped, sodomized, and bludgeoned almost to death a young woman in New York's Central Park. They were on a rampage supposedly akin to a sport they concocted, which they termed "wilding." One of the attackers said in court that another of the men involved had expressed delight during the attack over the force and volume of blood spurting from the woman's cut body. At this writing, the legal system has failed to deal with the accused in a way sufficient to the heinous nature of the brutal attack. Rather than concern for the victim, some lobbyist-like groups seem intent on claiming racial bias against the alleged rapists. These groups apparently see these alleged, would-be murderers as the victims in the matter.

The tide of murderous rampaging seems to have taken a quantum leap during the summer of 1991. It seems as if each serial murderer is bent on breaking records of killers gone before them. As mentioned before, Jeffrey L. Dahmer is alleged to have murdered as many as seventeen people throughout the nation. Body parts of eleven people were found in his Milwaukee apartment.

A confessed killer now is feared to have murdered more than sixty people around the country. An Associated Press report from Gulfport, Mississippi, dated August 16, 1991, reads in part:

Federal and state lawmen, reeling under a barrage of inquiries from 20 states, said Thursday that they will proceed deliberately in investigating claims by a self-professed serial killer that he murdered more than 60 people.

... So far, only three of the killings Donald Leroy Evans claims to have committed have been confirmed, his court-appointed lawyer said.

Mass and serial murders are only at the tip of the mountainous heap of murder cases — solved and unsolved — piling up within society today. Law enforcement must specialize in such areas as mass murders and serial murders, developing expertise in investigating specific types of what were once aberrant crimes but now have become almost standard police work.

There is a pernicious movement among despisers of those that are good today. Texe Marrs gives a masterful, informational presentation in a later essay on this diabolical consortium.

In Luke 18:19, Jesus Christ says "none is good, save one, that is, God." Those who despise good despise God himself, despise Jesus Christ, who was and is God. All people who are redeemed through acceptance of and belief in the fact that Jesus is the One and only way to salvation are good only because they are in Christ Jesus. Only Jesus can change the inner-evil of the fierce and the despisers of those that are good. Only Christ can replace that heart of hatred with wonderful inner peace.

Symptoms 14, 15, 16, & 17: Traitors, Heady, High-minded, Lovers of Pleasures More Than Lovers of God

Reports of military personnel selling secrets or bartering intelligence for sexual favors have become more prevalent in recent years. In some cases we have learned of espionage that involved sabotage for the sake of personal gain. Recently, an FBI agent, and later a CIA agent, were caught in incidents of traitorous activity. These incidents were only the most publicized of the hundreds going on throughout the world.

On the level of industrial and corporate subterfuge, the symptoms point to a plague of betrayal. Fortunes are made and lost yearly, monthly, and weekly by those who step on, or are stepped on, while on the ladder leading to success and/or failure.

This self-uplifting, while ascending on the misfortune of others, is symptomatic of headiness or high-mindedness. Satan was and is the most high-minded of all. He sought and still has the audacity to believe he can lift himself to a position above the one, true, eternal God. Those who reject the truth of Jesus Christ are, through omission, heirs to the fallen one's — Lucifer's — great high-mindedness.

All who seek, through their great intellect, their desire, or their superiority in the realm of power-brokerage, to put themselves upon the pinnacle of god-likeness in the world they have chosen to conquer are inheritors of Satan's pridefulness. They are exhilarated by the cut-throat struggle to vanquish all obstacles, all foes.

The high-minded intellectuals of academia, of the sciences, or of the liberal clergy seek more than at any time in history to erase all mention of God the Almighty, even at the temporary expedient of tolerating many religions and allowing those religions their many various ways to godhood.

With the intellectual exercise of plotting the planet's physical and social salvation, they are sacrificing their eternal souls on the altar of "Evolutional Theory." God's Word tells that the last generation will be as was the generation that perished in the flood of Noah's day. Of that people God says:

> Because that, when they knew God, they glorified him not as God, neither were thankful; but became vain in their imaginations, and their foolish heart was darkened. Professing themselves to be wise, they became fools, And changed the glory of the uncorruptible God into an image made like to corruptible man, and to birds, and fourfooted beasts, and creeping things (Rom. 1:21-23).

What is this, if not a description of modern intellectual man and his attempts to rationalize away all vestiges of the true God? It perfectly describes the writings of Charles Darwin and those who have reworked, reformulated and totally fallen for, in one form or another, the Evolution lie. These, like the antediluvians, "changed the truth of God into a lie, and worshipped and served the creature more than the Creator . . ." (Rom. 1:25). These foolish, soul-darkened "intellects" join forces with those they would once have termed superstitious idiots, the occultists, and New Age adherents, to deify Mother Earth for the sake of ecological purity.

Man seeks to create his own Utopias totally apart from God's moral restraints. Man will go to any lengths that his own intellectual capabilities will permit to satisfy his lustful, ephemeral desires. He seeks, like Satan promised and Eve desired, knowledge, power, and wealth because these things bring temporal pleasures.

Second Peter issues a terrifying indictment and judgment on the heady, high-minded, God despising, pleasure seekers of the last days' generation.

> The Lord knoweth how . . . to reserve the unjust unto the day of judgment to be punished: But chiefly them that walk after the flesh in the lust of uncleanness, and despise government. Presumptuous are they, self-willed, they are not afraid to speak evil of dignities.
>
> But these, as natural brute beasts, made to be taken and destroyed, speak evil of the things that they understand not; and shall utterly perish in their own corruption (2 Pet. 2:9-10, 12).

We live in days such as delineated in 2 Timothy 3:1-5. The evidence is astoundingly abundant to anyone not wishing to be a foolish, deceived, brute beast but rather desiring to seek to be wise unto salvation.

God's desire for you is given a few verses later in 2 Peter 3:9: "The Lord is . . . not willing that any should perish, but that all should come to repentance."

2

The Unmistakable Evidence Mounts: Christ's Return Is Imminent!

by Ray Brubaker

Are we living in the end time? Are we approaching the event we call the Rapture, when Christ will come and take unto himself His own while upon the earth comes great tribulation such as the world has never seen nor shall ever see again?

What signs would reveal that our Lord's return is very close at hand? Why do we believe it is the combination of major signs occurring at our present time that constitutes the one, great signal our Lord's coming is indeed imminent? Please consider the following facts and thoughts, then draw your own conclusions.

Prophecies Being Fulfilled in Our Day

To begin, let us take into account a full page article in the

Jerusalem Post, which states in part:

> These are amazing times . . . The Iron Curtain tumbled . . . Iraq is humbled . . . A tidal wave of Russian Jews reached Israel . . . Nations around the world turn to democracy! Plus, countless other amazing developments that are taking place in front of our eyes.

That article also makes mention of Rabbi Schneerson who foresees events bringing us to the coming of the Messiah. It is further noted, "These remarkable events are merely a prelude to the final redemption."

We can point, almost on a daily basis, to events foreshadowing that universally longed-for peace and security wrapped up in the comforting term "redemption." Is that not a reminder of what Jesus said, "And when these things begin to come to pass, then look up, and lift up your heads; for your redemption draweth nigh" (Luke 21:28)?

What specific things, then, lead us to believe that our Lord's return is near, even at the door? Let us look at some of the astonishing, accumulating occurrences that convince the student of prophecy Jesus Christ's second advent will happen very soon.

I once heard a conference speaker at Calvary Baptist Church in New York City observe, "It is not just a sign here and there, but the combination of these major signs which are the greatest sign to indicate our Lord's coming is close at hand."

Iniquity Shall Abound

According to all pertinent statistics, this year will be the most horrendous year for crime ever. From all indications, we are creating a generation of youth-criminals — many of whom are killers!

U.S. News & World Report, April 4, 1991, notes: "Every 100 hours more youths die on the streets than were killed in the Persian Gulf." It further states: "The reasons why are clear. Today's kids are desensitized to violence as never before, surrounded by gunfire and stuffed with media images of Rambos who kill at will."

A survey by the National School Safety Center suggests

that 135,000 students carried guns to school daily in 1987! That figure is much higher today.

Much of the youth crime is related to gangs and drugs. Some 1.7 to 2.4 million Americans are weekly cocaine users. Gangs, too, are said to be growing like a cancer. Since 1985, in Los Angeles, gangs have doubled from forty-five thousand members to ninety thousand. Gang related killings last year accounted for 690 deaths. About 25 percent of youths who kill are high on alcohol or drugs.

The four major sins of the Tribulation are listed in Revelation 9:21 where we read, "Neither repented they of their murders, nor of their sorceries, nor of their fornication, nor of their thefts."

Jesus said that in the time before His coming, "iniquity shall abound, and the love of many shall wax cold" (Matt. 24:12).

Speaking Evil of Dignities

We are living in a day when there are attempts to tear down and destroy dignitaries. Ever since Watergate, when Nixon was dethroned, the mind-set pervades that all anyone has to do to destroy and/or get rid of someone is to plot against him for whatever reason.

Remember the Iranian controversy with the charge of improper, even illegal, arranging for the release of hostages? Those interrogating Oliver North and other witnesses desperately attempted to incriminate President Reagan in order to force his resignation.

Then came the attempt to determine whether a past president, Zachary Taylor, was assassinated. Seeking to find arsenic in his remains, they had him analyzed in a laboratory, but no evidence was found to substantiate that allegation.

The nation watched as Supreme Court Nominee Clarence Thomas in a media circus faced accusations of some of the most vulgar acts (totally unproven — and even unprovable) ever to be aired publicly. This "high-tech lynching" was conducted by a Senate Judiciary Committee upon which sat *some* men whose moral characters would in more sane times have made them unfit to sit in judgment of anyone.

In the Book of Romans, there is a call to recognize the

position of our government officials. Paul writes,

> Let every soul be subject unto the higher pow-
> ers. For there is no power but of God: the powers that
> be are ordained of God. . . . and they that resist shall
> receive to themselves damnation. For rulers are not a
> terror to good works, but to the evil . . . .
> For he is the minister of God to thee for good.
> But if thou do that which is evil, be afraid; for he
> beareth not the sword in vain: for he is the minister of
> God, a revenger to execute wrath upon him that
> doeth evil (Rom. 13:1-4).

Here, we have a demand of respect for those in authority.
Paul, in writing to Timothy, gives command to pray for those
in authority. In 1 Timothy 2:1-2 we read:

> I exhort therefore, that, first of all, supplications,
> prayers, intercessions, and giving of thanks, be made
> for all men; For kings, and for all that are in authority;
> that we may lead a quiet and peaceable life in all
> godliness and honesty.

Finally, it seems apparent that God has reserved a special
time and place of punishment for those who despise governments. "The Lord knoweth how to deliver the godly out of
temptations, and to reserve the unjust unto the day of judgment
to be punished: But chiefly them that walk after the flesh in the
lust of uncleanness, and despise government. Presumptuous
are they, self-willed, they are not afraid to speak evil of dignities" (2 Pet. 2:9-10).

God's Word is explicitly plain here. There is great danger
in speaking evil of dignities.

The purpose of the broadcast ministry, with which I am
associated, has from the beginning been not to downgrade,
vilify, or assassinate the characters of those about whom we are
reporting. Instead, we seek to deal factually with the issues.
The ethics of the broadcasting profession, as I was taught in the
forties, was to speak favorably of people and individuals.
Madalyn Murray O'Hair, however, is the exception because
she wanted to be known as an atheist who opposes things
spiritual.

The government has sought to deal with such problems by its "fairness doctrine," which demands equal time be given to an opposing view made by someone you quote. If that person wants to clarify their position, the station must allow them free time to answer your vilification of them or their record.

In Jude 7-8 we have a similar picture of warning given. We read,

> Even as Sodom and Gomorrah, and the cities about them in like manner, giving themselves over to fornication, and going after strange flesh, are set forth for an example, suffering the vengeance of eternal fire. Likewise also these filthy dreamers defile the flesh, despise dominion, and speak evil of dignities.

God links those given over to perversions, as in the days of Sodom and Gomorrah, and those who engage in fornication and marital unfaithfulness to those who "despise dominion, and speak evil of dignities." Could it be that those rabble-rousers who carry their banners and signs, who hate the president and want to bring down the government, are these kinds of people?

The warning is ominously clear. We should be careful about those at whom we point the finger of accusation to be sure we don't assume the role of the Almighty. For He alone is the judge of all the earth.

Jude goes on to give an illustration of one who could have had reason to bring accusation but chose not to do so. We read, "Yet Michael the archangel, when contending with the devil he disputed about the body of Moses, durst not bring against him a railing accusation, but said, The Lord rebuke thee" (Jude 9).

Christopher Columbus: Invader or Visionary?

In 1992, the "dignitary" under intense scrutiny is Christopher Columbus, whose character is in the process of being assassinated in some quarters.

A Chicago staff writer says of a grade school teacher:

> She's the one who told us about Christopher

Columbus crossing the ocean blue in 1492, and what a great guy he was. And now it turns out he was a real louse.

Ah! You say you've been reading about the great controversy over the celebration of the 500th anniversary of his discovery of the Americas. Hey, be careful. You said "discovery." Don't let no Indian hear you say that. They say it was an invasion.

I think it is acceptable to say "encounter." Whatever. After he got here, everything fell apart. This was a paradise, where the buffalo roamed and the deer and the antelope played. Then Columbus got the Aztecs killed, and started slavery, and polluted everything, and now because of him, it ain't a natural paradise anymore.

Columnist Mike Royko commented in response to the controversy,

No, I think what the historical revisionists are saying is that by discovering, or encountering, the Americas, he made possible the subsequent invasion by the Spaniards and other Europeans who committed many of the foul deeds you've mentioned.

So, he is asserting that those terrible deeds are not really attributable to Columbus.

When it comes to the matter of examining the life and activities of Christopher Columbus, let us learn the facts before criticizing. Columbus prepared to set sail at a time when Europeans were in despair. The *Nuremburg Chronicle* wrote of "... the calamity of our time ... in which iniquity and evil have increased to the highest pitch." This respected newspaper called upon its readers to forecast the future — to record happenings between 1493 and the day of judgment. In fact, the newspaper gloomily forecast the end of the world soon!

Christopher Columbus had a vision of finding a shorter route to the Indies in Asia. Armed with a letter of introduction to the emperor of China, Columbus set sail in command of the *Nina*, the *Pinta*, and the *Santa Maria*.

A crisis occurred on October 10, 1492, when the sailors

were preparing to mutiny. Only by the grace of God was this prevented. Columbus persuaded them to travel west for three more days. Near midnight the next day, Columbus spotted a dim light ahead. He did not know what it was — possibly a brush fire. On October 12, 1492, the island of San Salvador, in what are now known as the Bahamas, was discovered.

Columbus made three more voyages to the shores of America. He wrote of his travels, "Over there I have placed under their highnesses sovereignty more land than there is in Africa and Europe, and more than 1,700 islands . . . I, by the Divine Will, made that conquest."

U.S. News & World Report (April 22, 1991) quotes Oscar Wilde who wrote, "America had often been discovered before, but it had always been hushed up."

Among those who may have discovered America, mention is made of black Africans in 1500 B.C.; Romans in A.D. 64; Hoei-shin of China in 499; St. Brendan in the sixth Century; Bjarni Herjolfsson in 986 got lost in the fog seeking Greenland and landed in Labrador instead; and Leif Ericson in 1001, who founded a colony called Vinland, which archaeologists claim to have located in 1960 on the northern tip of Newfoundland.

However, this magazine states: "Columbus was indisputably the man who opened the way for European colonization and all that that would mean."

Kirkpatrick Sales, in *The Conquest of Paradise*, pictures Columbus as the leader of an environmental gang rape. The National Council of Churches declared that "what some historians have termed a 'discovery' was in reality an invasion and colonization, with legalized occupation, genocide, economic exploitation, and a deep level of institutional racism and moral decadence."

Peter Marshal, chaplain to congressmen, wrote in *The Light and the Glory* on the evidence of God's divine intervention in American history.

> To begin at the beginning, Christopher Columbus said in his *Book of Prophecies:* "It was the Lord who put it into my mind (I could feel His hand upon me), the fact that it would be possible to sail from here to the Indies. All who heard of my plan rejected it with laughter, ridiculing me.

"There is no question that the inspiration was from the Holy Spirit, because He comforted me with rays of marvelous inspiration from the Holy Scriptures . . . . For the execution of the journey to the Indies, I did not make use of intelligence, mathematics, or maps. It is simply the fulfillment of what Isaiah had prophesied." Columbus believed that his Christian name, which means "Christ-bearer", had been given him by God because that was his calling — to take the gospel of Jesus Christ across the ocean to the heathen in the lands he knew he would discover. Thus the man who opened the Americas was not so much looking for a trade-route to the Indies as he was intent on bringing the good news of Christ into the Western Hemisphere.

What a great heritage is ours. Every day we should thank the Lord for America and our history. How we need to defend our freedom and our liberties.

Separating Church and State

In its next term, the U.S. Supreme Court is scheduled to hear a case as to whether prayer should be permitted as part of graduation ceremonies in public schools. We're told, according to newspaper reports, the court is being asked to decide whether such prayers violate the constitutionally required separation of church and state!

What travesty to try to make the American people believe our Constitution requires the separation of church and state. Those words do not appear anywhere in our Constitution. They were in the now defunct Soviet Constitution — Article 134: ". . . the church in the USSR is separated from the state." Again we're told, "The main decision on such a philosophy is deceptive — it's false — and it's a forced conclusion to which we are driven by those who would like to close the churches."

When this doctrine of separation of state and church is fully consummated, it will mean the closing of churches in America; so, we had better halt such interpretation immediately by writing our congressmen and our justices, urging them not to base their decisions on what is not in the Constitution.

The Communists will tell you that to follow this doctrine to its extreme position is to elevate the state and eliminate the church. This was the policy until Gorbachev's glasnost and perestroika.

In the former Soviet Union, removing the considerable economic allowances that had been given the huge churches under Tsarism caused many of them to close. Likewise, to remove the tax-exempt status of churches and religious organizations in this nation today would cause a majority of them to close. America must wake up before it's too late!

Plans For a United States of Europe

Upon becoming news director for WMBI-WDLM, stations owned by the Moody Bible Institute in Chicago, I was approached by Wendell P. Loveless, who shared his views that plans for Western Europe to unite were one of the great signs that our Lord's coming was near.

Donald Grey Barnhouse once wrote in *Eternity* magazine: "I have not changed my interpretation of Bible prophecy from that which I published as early as 1931." He then predicted, "At the time of the end, the former Roman Empire will have been revived in the ten nations that will come under the domination of the Antichrist. This power will include Egypt but not her Arab allies."

The dream of past visionaries has been for a United States of Europe. In 1971, Victor Hugo cried out, "Let us have the United States of Europe. Let us have continental federation; let us have European freedom."

Later, Lord Salisbury shouted, "Federation is the only hope of the world." Winston Churchill, following World War II, in a dramatic speech, declared, "Our main theme of salvation should be the grand alliance of the European powers."

So, plans for Europe to federate by 1993 are indeed significant in that they not only meet the aspirations and dreams of these noble statesmen, but fulfill one of the great prophecies of the Bible — Daniel's prophecies concerning ten nations uniting within the sphere of the Old Roman Empire. In Daniel 2:44, he declares, "And in the days of these kings shall the God of heaven set up a kingdom, which shall never be destroyed . . . ."

Witnessing nations of the European common market doing away with trade barriers and planning to unite surely leads the thinking, praying Christian to believe we are seeing the coming together of the final Gentile confederacy spoken of by Daniel and further explained in the Book of the Revelation. It will be this confederacy of nations that will bring on the personage we call the Antichrist.

As the late Dr. M. R. DeHaan explained, "After the Church has been raptured, there will arise a world-power, a dictator who will succeed in uniting the nations of the world in a great federation." He notes, ". . . at the same time, the false christ, the Antichrist, the end-time religious leader, will organize all religions into one great world church."

Some see plans for peace in the Middle East as bringing on the Antichrist. The Scripture reminds us, "He will come in peacefully." So, witnessing events transpiring in Western Europe, in conjunction with an urgent call for peace in the Middle East, leads us to believe that time is growing short. Jesus is soon to come!

Plans for Peace

For the first time in history, we have a peace conference in the making involving Israel to which are also invited observers from the United Nations, the European Economic Community, as well as Arab and African nations. The Israeli cabinet approved, by a wide margin, Prime Minister Yitzhak Shamir's formal, qualified, recommendation that Israel attend a Middle East peace conference.

One major question was: "Would Palestinians be willing to attend such a conference?" Secretary of State James Baker said the Palestinians ". . . have more to gain from a viable and active peace process than anyone else . . . and the most to lose if there is no peace process."

Prime Minister Shamir set forth some stipulations he hoped would be followed:

1. Palestinian delegates to the talks will be delegates from the territories, and not affiliated with the PLO.

2. Countries invited will promise to live in peace with Israel; whereas, some are still existing in a state of war.

3. It is requested that the United Nations Security Council will not pass any resolutions about the Middle East peace process throughout the course of negotiations.

4. After the peace conference convenes, there will follow parallel sets of bilateral negotiations on peace between Arabs and Israelis and between Israelis and Palestinians.

A statement issued by Prime Minister Shamir said:

Since its establishment, Israel has sought peace with its neighbors. We have, therefore, expressed our readiness to enter peace negotiations in accordance with the U.S. proposal, subject to a satisfactory solution of the issue of Palestinian Arab representation in the Jordanian-Palestinian delegations.

There have been, and continue to be, of course, meetings of varying dimensions and varying topics. The major sticking point is that Arab insistence of land for peace is not acceptable to Israel. Such a concession was suggested by Egypt's President Hosni Mubarak — that negotiations be governed by the formula "land for peace."

To require Israel to agree to demands that they give up land for peace is tantamount to forcing that nation to relinquish its claim to the land in advance. This is contrary to the terms of the Camp David accords.

What will happen?

Are we not reminded in Psalm 122:6, "Pray for the peace of Jerusalem"? At the same time, as we approach the day of the Lord, we are alerted to the words of the apostle Paul who cautions, "For when they shall say, Peace and safety; then sudden destruction cometh . . ." (1 Thess. 5:3). Plans for peace are an amazing sign that we are approaching the return of our Lord.

Running To and Fro

When we think of Daniel's inspired words telling that "many shall run to and fro, and knowledge shall be increased" (Dan. 12:4), we are apt to think of the automobile and the airplane as helping to fulfill this prophecy.

Nahum surely must have visualized the automobile's appearance at the time when our Lord is preparing to return to earth, for he declares that: "the chariots shall be with flaming torches in the day of his preparation . . ." (Nah. 2:3).

Is this not the day of His preparation? And, we note further, "The chariots shall rage in the streets, they shall justle one against another in the broad ways: they shall seem like torches, they shall run like the lightnings" (Nah. 2:4).

Dr. Theodore Epp once remarked, "Somewhere I recently heard someone say, and it sounds reasonable, that scientific knowledge doubled by approximately the year 1750 over all previous history. Then it doubled again during the next 150 years [up to 1900]. It doubled for the fourth time in the ten years from 1950-1960, etc." Stated Dr. Epp, "Not only is this a sign heralding the near return of the Lord, but it ought to make us really think."

Since the advent of the computer, knowledge has increased as never before.

Robert Jastrow, director of NASA's Goddard Institute for Space Studies, once remarked, "The capabilities of computers are increasing at a fantastic rate . . . . Computer power is growing exponentially; it has increased tenfold every eight years since 1946. In the 1990s, the compactness and reasoning power of an intelligence built out of silicone will begin to match that of the human brain."

Well, here we are in the '90s. One periodical comments: "The miracle [or silicon] chip represents a quantum leap in the technology of mankind, a development that over the past few years has acquired the force and significance associated with the development of hand tools or the discovery of the steam engine."

Author and futurist Isaac Asimov once observed, "We are reaching the stage where the problems we must solve are going to become insoluble without computers. I do not fear computers, I fear the lack of them."

Are Computers a Fulfillment of Prophecy?

In Daniel 12:4 we read again, "But thou, O Daniel, shut up the words, and seal the book, even to the time of the end: many shall run to and fro, and knowledge shall be increased."

The *Second Coming Bible*, prepared long before computers were invented, suggests that the word here means "... to search out and investigate." This is precisely the primary role of the computer.

A computer chip has been developed that is being implanted in dogs and cats. A video produced by Infopet for pet owners states: "In the past four years, thousands of animals have been implanted with microchips. Once implanted, information goes into a computer data bank that can be accessed by a toll-free number from anywhere in North America."

Although designed for animals, it can also be implanted into humans. G. G. Stearman testified, "Students of Bible prophecy will feel a chill, futuristic wind blowing across a sinister horizon. The economic system of the Antichrist will someday call for just such a numeric identification system."

J. R. Church, writing in *Prophecy in the News,* comments: "It looks like the fulfillment of Scripture." He notes: "According to Revelation 13:16-17, a short-lived world government will cause all 'to receive a mark in their right hand, or in their foreheads; And that no man might buy or sell, save he that had the mark, or the name of the beast . . . .' "

Already in the United States, we are able to "tag" released prison offenders and know their every movement. This involves strapping a tamper-proof beeper to the body, a device that alerts authorities when it is moved more than a specified distance from a receiver in the person's home.

It is not difficult to imagine that a computer chip can be placed somewhere in your body, then at a supermarket you would simply pass your hand over a scanner, and your bank account would thereby automatically be accessed and debited. It could also become a universal identification system that would replace credit cards.

The chip, or implantable transponder, is injected under the skin through a hypodermic needle. The Destron Company describes the transponder as ". . . a passive radio-frequency ID reading system." It consists of an electro-magnetic coil and microchip, and the transponder is sealed in a tubular, glass enclosure.

With over thirty-four billion individual code numbers

available, the chip is pre-programmed with a unique ID code that cannot be altered. When activated by a low-frequency radio signal, the transponder transmits the ID code that appears on a screen when the subject is scanned with a computer wand.

Surely we have arrived at the time when the Antichrist could make his appearance, requiring all to carry this kind of electronic identification.

The AIDS Epidemic

When our Lord referred to the coming tribulation in Mark 13:19-20, He said, "For in those days shall be affliction, such as was not from the beginning of the creation which God created unto this time, neither shall be. And except that the Lord had shortened those days, no flesh should be saved . . . ."

An article in *Time,* August 3, 1992 states:

> The World Health Organization says at least 30 million people around the world could be infected with the AIDS virus by the year 2000. Other experts think the number could reach 100 million.

Dr. John Seale, writing in Britain's *Journal of the Royal Science of Medicine,* says AIDS is capable of producing ". . . a lethal pandemic throughout the crowded cities and villages of the Third World of a magnitude unparalleled in human history."

Kimberly Bergalis, who has since died, stated before Congress:

> AIDS is a terrible disease that you must take seriously. I did nothing wrong, and I'm being made to suffer like this. My life has been taken away. Please enact legislation so that no other patient or health care provider will have to go through the hell that I have.

It was reported in *Time,* January 14, 1991, that of the 153,000 reported cases of AIDS, about 4 percent involve health care workers, or 6,436 cases. Of these, 703 were non-surgeon physicians, and 171 were dental workers. In addition, some seven thousand doctors have been reported to test positive for the HIV virus.

President Bush stated, "Here's a disease where you can control its spread by your own personal behavior."

James J. Kilpatrick, news columnist, writes: "AIDS is a serious and expensive problem in public health, brought on largely by people who did it themselves."

Paul Harvey observed, "It is the most devastating disease the world has ever seen, but, also, the most preventable."

The Burning Oil Fields of Kuwait

In Isaiah 34:8-9 we read, "For it is the day of the Lord's vengeance, and the year of recompenses for the controversy of Zion. And the streams thereof shall be turned into pitch, and the dust thereof into brimstone, and the land thereof shall become burning pitch."

Notice, tied in with "the day of the Lord's vengeance, and the year of recompenses for the controversy of Zion" is a picture of burning oil fields such as we've seen in Kuwait. *Newsweek* (July 29, 1991) noted: "The oil fires set by the retreating Iraqis have turned the once pristine deserts of Kuwait into oceans of black glue. Even the camels and the alley cats are tinged a ghostly gray by the muck."

While it was burning, the value of the oil was estimated to be from eleven million to forty million dollars per day, with six million barrels of oil consumed daily. Think of it! Read it again: "For it is the day of the Lord's vengeance, and the year of recompenses for the controversy of Zion. And the streams thereof shall be turned into pitch . . . ."

What is the day of the Lord's vengeance?

Remember when Jesus entered the synagogue and read from Isaiah 61:1-2, He declared,

> The Spirit of the Lord God is upon me; because the Lord hath anointed me to preach good tidings unto the meek; he hath sent me to bind up the brokenhearted, to proclaim liberty to the captives, and the opening of the prison to them that are bound;
> To proclaim the acceptable year of the Lord.

What He *did not* read was, "the day of vengeance of our God . . . ." In Isaiah 63:4, our Lord again states, "For the day of vengeance is in mine heart, and the year of my redeemed is come."

Vultures in Israel

Some years ago, a tract was produced on *Vultures in Israel*. Prophecy buffs who went to Israel, taking their binoculars with them, reported they never saw any vultures there. Then, it was revealed that at certain times migrating birds fly over Israel, including vultures and birds of prey.

The *Jerusalem Post* (September 14, 1991) noted: "The annual migration of birds of prey has started with a flock of over 55,000 honey buzzards and other large birds, tracked by radar from Ben-Gurion Airport, flying over Israel 'en route' from Eastern Europe and Asia to their winter watering grounds in Africa." These birds are monitored so planes can keep clear of them, otherwise, they cause great damage to the aircraft and fatal crashes.

Tens of thousands more honey buzzards and other large birds, including storks and pelicans, are expected to fly over Israel in the coming weeks. Is it possible these birds will fly over Israel during the Russian invasion reported in Ezekiel 38-39? During this battle, we read where the Lord says,

> . . . Speak unto every feathered fowl, and to every beast of the field, Assemble yourselves, and come; gather yourselves on every side to my sacrifice that I do sacrifice for you, even a great sacrifice upon the mountains of Israel, that ye may eat flesh, and drink blood. Ye shall eat the flesh of the mighty, and drink the blood of princes of the earth . . . . Thus ye shall be filled at my table with horses and chariots, with mighty men, and with all men of war, saith the Lord God (Ezek. 39:17-20).

Also, in Revelation 19:17-18, there is a picture of the coming battle of Armageddon. We read:

> And I saw an angel standing in the sun; and he cried with a loud voice, saying to all the fowls that fly in the midst of heaven, Come and gather yourselves together unto the supper of the great God;

That ye may eat the flesh of kings, and the flesh of captains, and the flesh of mighty men, and the flesh of horses, and of them that sit on them, and the flesh of all men, both free and bond, both small and great.

We can't help but ask, "Will these battles be fought at the time these birds of prey fly over Israel?" The *Jerusalem Post* (October 1, 1988) noted:

Each fall, billions of birds around the world, precisely measuring the length of the days with their biological mechanism, rise from their nests at a given hour and head South like retired New York couples heading for Florida after Thanksgiving.

Thomas L. Friedman, in the New York Times, writes: "Each spring and fall, millions of storks, pelicans, buzzards, eagles, and other large birds fly over Israel as they migrate between Europe and Western Asia and Africa . . . ."

Watching the migration patterns of these birds, we can almost tell when the Battle of Armageddon will be fought.

In Revelation 19, mention is made of two different suppers, "the supper of the great God," when the fowl of the air feast on the flesh of men; and "the marriage supper of the Lamb," when the saints are united with their Lord. To which supper are you invited?

What About Nuclear War?

Sometime before the USSR became the CIS, President Bush said, "The prospect of a Soviet invasion into Western Europe launched with little or no warning is no longer a realistic threat."

But, what about the launching of ICBMs upon the United States? How long can we expect friendly faces like former Soviet President Gorbachev and Russian President Yeltsin to run the newly formed government? Marxism thrives on revolution.

President Bush calls his plans for peace, ". . . the most fundamental change in nuclear forces in over 40 years. We can now take steps to make the world a less dangerous place than ever before in the nuclear age. Perhaps we are closer to that new world than ever before."

What concerns us about this proposed new world?

Some point to Scriptures such as Ezekiel 38:14 as indicating the day will come when we will do away with all nuclear weapons and return to swords and spears, even to bows and arrows. We read in verse 15: (during the Russian invasion of Israel) "And thou shalt come from thy place out of the north parts, thou, and many people with thee, all of them riding on horses, a great company, and a mighty army."

Verse 21 states: "And I will call for a sword against him throughout all my mountains, saith the Lord God: every man's sword shall be against his brother."

After the battle, we read of the gathering of the weapons of war in Ezekiel 39:9-10,

> And they that dwell in the cities of Israel shall go forth, and shall set on fire and burn the weapons, both the shields and the bucklers, the bows and the arrows, and the handstaves, and the spears, and they shall burn them with fire seven years: So that they shall take no wood out of the field, neither cut down any out of the forests; for they shall burn the weapons with fire . . . .

President Bush's proposals do not call for the destruction of *all* nuclear weapons. According to those proposals, the former Soviets still have 8,040 warheads scattered throughout the many republics, and we would have 10,821 nuclear warheads. While these may be reduced even further, the overwhelming probability remains that nuclear warfare is ahead for the world.

Are the Four Horsemen About to Ride?

In Revelation 6, we have pictured the four horsemen of the Apocalypse. First, the rider on the white horse, symbolizing a man of peace, appears on the scene. He has a bow but no arrows and goes forth conquering and to conquer.

We hear a great deal about the New World order. We also hear of possible candidates to head up this New World order. Vatican insider Malachi Martin has written a book in which he claims Pope John Paul II, even before he was elected pope, saw himself as controlling the coming New World government. Martin maintains that the Roman Church is prepared to take over this responsibility, for the pope declares such a government must be "Christian." He writes:

> If tomorrow or next week, by a sudden miracle, a one-world government were established, the Church would not have to undergo any essential structural change in order to further its dominant position and to further its global aims.
>
> The Roman Church stands alone . . . as the first fully realized, fully practicing and totally independent geo-political force in the current world arena. And the Pope . . . is by definition the world's first fully-fledged geo-political leader.

Could the pope, following the Rapture, become the rider of the white horse?

The rider on the red horse then goes forth. It is said of this rider in Revelation 6:4 that ". . . power was given to him that sat thereon to take peace from the earth, and that they should kill one another: and there was given unto him a great sword."

What is the great sword? Is it a nuclear missile that is capable of global destruction? Is there evidence that such a sword will be used?

Turn to Jeremiah 24:10 where there is reference to a great sword that God is going to send to the inhabitants of earth. Jeremiah is also told:

> . . . Take the wine cup of this fury at my hand, and cause all the nations, to whom I send thee, to drink it. And they shall drink, and be moved, and be mad, because of the sword that I will send among them. Therefore thou shalt say unto them, Thus saith the Lord of hosts, the God of Israel; Drink ye, and be drunken, and spue, and fall, and rise no more, because of the sword which I will send among you (Jer. 25:15-16,27).

Jeremiah 25:29 records: "for I will call for a sword upon all the inhabitants of the earth, saith the Lord of hosts."

Now, notice verse 31, ". . . he will give them that are

wicked to the sword . . . ." There is evidence to indicate that the Rapture will have taken place and the righteous removed from the earth.

How great a conflagration is seen in verse 33! We read: "And the slain of the Lord shall be at that day from one end of the earth even unto the other end of the earth: they shall not be lamented, neither gathered, nor buried; they shall be dung upon the ground."

The rider on the dark horse goes forth, symbolizing awful famine to come. A voice cries, "A measure of wheat for a penny, and three measures of barley for a penny; [which is a day's wages] and see thou hurt not the oil and the wine" (Rev. 6:6). Think of it! A day's wages required to buy a loaf of bread!

If I were president, I would use every resource, put every plow to work, and profusely sow grain in all the available land in preparation for the bleak days ahead! The farmer is the most mistreated and maligned person today, when he should be the most respected.

In the former Soviet Union there has been severe drought in several of the wheat-producing areas creating the possibility that the harvest will drop 25 percent or more from what it was last year.

We read of the rider who goes forth on the pale horse in Revelation 6:8: ". . . and his name that sat on him was Death, and Hell followed with him. And power was given unto them over the fourth part of the earth, to kill with sword, and with hunger, and with death, and with the beasts of the earth."

It is interesting to point out the name of this pale horse in the Greek is "chloros," from which we get our word, "chlorine." Surely, this must be representative of chemical warfare to be unleashed in the end time.

In Geneva, thirty-nine nations have been negotiating a draft treaty banning production, use, or stockpiling of chemical weapons, but verification is almost impossible. Chemical weapons were used by Iraq on Kurdish dwellers. Such weapons are considered the poor man's atom bomb.

In Zechariah 14:12, we are reminded of a condition that might be attributed to chemical weapons. We read of nations coming against Jerusalem:

And this shall be the plague wherewith the Lord

will smite all the people that have fought against Jerusalem; Their flesh shall consume away while they stand upon their feet, and their eyes shall consume away in their holes, and their tongue shall consume away in their mouth.

What a horrifying way to die!

Officials tell us, "The problems of detecting and stopping production of chemical and biological weapons are nigh to impossible." It is noted: "At present, there are no verification measures, and it is hard to see how any could be made to work. Bacteriological weapons can be produced in very small labs that are easy to hide."

In view of these four horsemen soon to ride, a John the Baptist is needed to warn men everywhere "to flee from the wrath to come" as he did in Luke 3:7.

In 1 Thessalonians 5:9, we are reminded, "For God hath not appointed us to wrath, but to obtain salvation by our Lord Jesus Christ." On the other hand, we are warned that because of "fornication, and all uncleanness, or covetousness . . . . cometh the wrath of God upon the children of disobedience. Be not ye therefore partakers with them" (Eph. 5:3,6-7).

It is time to turn from sin to trust the Saviour. "Therefore be ye also ready: for in such an hour as ye think not the Son of man cometh" (Matt. 24:44).

How Close Is Our Lord's Return?

While we might expect to set a date for Christ's return, we admit to no knowledge of the day and hour when He will come. There have been prophecy students who thought they knew the day our Lord would return and hastened to broadcast the data only to discover they gave out false information.

What we consider to be unique is that we are hearing from the secular world the same ominous message, telling us the hour is late! The end is near! For example, *Newsweek* (November 13, 1989) poked fun at religious zealots who made predictions of the end of the world which, of course, did not come to pass. Now, it is noted men of science and statesmen, especially observers in Western Europe, who are among those recognizing prophetic fulfillment in recent world events.

Newsweek notes: "In the decade before the year A.D. 1000, wild men with shabby hair swarmed across the face of Europe prophesying an imminent apocalypse. Now as the second millennium approaches, another hysterical clamor is descending on the continent. This time prophets are professionals — historians, economists, even military planners . . . . Their concern is the same: What was known hundreds of years ago as the 'Holy Roman Empire of the German Nation'!"

We have had notable men tell us that as God made the world in six days and rested the seventh day, so this world will continue for six thousand years, followed by the Millennium, a time of peace unprecedented in recorded history.

Barnabas, fellow traveler with the apostle Paul, wrote:

> And God made in six days the works of his hands; and he finished them on the seventh day, and he rested on the seventh day and sanctified it. Consider, my children, what that signifies. He finished them in six days. The meaning of it is this; that in six thousand years the Lord will bring all things to an end. For with him one day is a thousand years, as himself testifieth, saying, Behold, this day shall be as a thousand years. Therefore, children, in six days, that is, in six thousand years, shall all things be accomplished. And what is that he saith, And he rested the seventh day; he meaneth this: that when his Son shall come, and abolish the season of the wicked one, and judge the ungodly, and shall change the sun and the moon and the stars; then he shall gloriously rest in that seventh day.

Other early church fathers wrote similar predictions, but let us quote Dr. Oswald J. Smith who wrote,

> The age from Adam to the flood was about 2,000 years; from the flood to Christ was about 2,000 years. And from Christ to the end of the third age will probably be 2,000 years. After that will come the Sabbath Age of 1,000 years, the Millennium, making some 7,000 years altogether. This may, therefore, be the end of the present age!

Draw Your Own Conclusions

Allowing for seven years of tribulation, which we do not expect Christians living at the time of the Rapture to have to endure, we are close to the end of the age. Following Christ's return to earth, the seventh day will begin, the Millennium.

All indicators point to the reality that Jesus is coming again very soon. Do you know Him — personally, as your Saviour, your Lord? Or, will you be told to depart from Him because you are a worker of iniquity?

It is for us to make sure we know God intimately through our acceptance of redemption offered freely through Jesus Christ who came as the revelation of God. As we read in John 17:3, "And this is life eternal, that they might know thee the only true God, and Jesus Christ, whom thou hast sent."

We ask in great concern, "Do you know God? Does He know you?" One day the Lord will return, and to many He will say, "I never knew you: depart from me, ye that work iniquity" (Matt. 7:23).

Repent of sin! Turn from it as you would a serpent, and turn to Christ for salvation and forgiveness. So, "Be ye therefore ready also: for the Son of man cometh at an hour when ye think not" (Luke 12:40).

3

The Computer Messiah Comes Forth!

by William T. James

With continuing and increasing woes in America, such as crime, drug abuse, pornography, and great financial upheaval, concerned people are asking where it will all end. What's more, these multiplying problems are compounded by great crises that engulf the whole world. Technological shrinkage of the planet, due to advances in transportation and in communications, has brought all peoples into what human potentialists would have us accept as the global village.

All such dilemmas are now problems of the world, according to the globalists and humanists; and the world, coming together as one, must solve them.

There is, of course, truth in that premise. There is always an element of truth when the great deceiver, Satan, plants his seed of delusion into the prideful human heart. The formula the father of all lies gives mankind to solve his problems, however, always excludes from the equation the only one who can effect cures. God is no longer needed or even considered in the conduct of human affairs.

Regarding these days in which we live and the problems we face, end-time signs become more apparent every day. Jesus prophesied in Matthew 24:4-8:

> And Jesus answered and said unto them [His disciples], Take heed that no man deceive you. For many shall come in my name, saying, I am Christ; and shall deceive many. And ye shall hear of wars and rumors of wars: see that ye be not troubled: for all these things must come to pass, but the end is not yet. For nation shall rise against nation, and kingdom against kingdom: and there shall be famines, and pestilences, and earthquakes, in divers places. All these things are the beginning of sorrows.

The general order and causes of developing world crises leading to the Tribulation, as given by Jesus, are spiritual, carnal, and economic.

The spiritual crisis results from false theology, through which the deluded seek false christs rather than the true God to save man from calamities of his own making. Thus false christs will arise, and many will follow them.

Because the world system searches for solutions within itself, crimes of passion, hatred, greed, perversions, and wars, great and small, abound and increase. Man rages against man and nation against nation because man refuses to be governed by the God who demands righteousness. All these result from man's carnal nature as James 4:1-2 makes clear:

> From whence comes wars and fightings among you? come they not hence, even of your lusts that war in your members? Ye lust, and have not: ye kill, and desire to have, and cannot obtain: ye fight and war, yet ye have not, because ye ask not.

War, crime, alcoholism, drug addiction, and sinful pleasures are counterproductive activities of mankind. War is the most costly of all.

While defense is essential in this world of predators, tax money invested in bombs, battleships, and all other machinery of war bear the return of human tragedy in war *and* in peace. Weaponry used for defense to deter an aggressor is no less expensive than arms used in actual combat, as eighty years of world wars, conflicts, and the armament races will attest. Man's desire to dominate his fellow man by force continues to contribute to a potential world financial collapse.

World Financial Collapse

The break-up of the colonial powers following World War II resulted in the birth of a number of poor nations. Contributing to economic support of those non-industrialized nations through the World Bank and the International Monetary Fund (IMF) has, as in the case of our own welfare system, caused the proliferation of fantastic waste, corruption, and uncontrollable indebtedness. The United States contributions to the IMF exhausted our gold reserves and adds hourly to our staggering national deficit.

Consider what would happen should there occur a world economic collapse on top of all the other calamities facing the planet. There would be instant unemployment. Starvation and anarchy on a scale the world has never endured would cause global panic.

Although most in the United States believe such world economic catastrophe can and will be avoided, almost all financial experts agree that this nation cannot continue to foolishly drain our own economy by supporting floundering and often tyrannically fraudulent Third World or even so-called super-power economies. To do so almost certainly invites not only national catastrophe but world economic disaster.

The stock market crash in 1929, when the banks failed and fortunes were lost overnight, is still fresh in the memory of some. The resulting depression brought personal and collective tragedies that affected every strata of life in America and stunned the world. Many who had suddenly lost their riches committed suicide. The 1929 economic crash, however, could very well seem merely an unpleasant time of inconvenience when compared to what a world financial collapse would do to the lives of people in the United States, the free world, and the industrialized nations of the Orient today.

The Bible indicates that at the time of just such a future crisis, an international entity will arise to offer a solution that can establish a new economic order. It is certain that such a commission, and ultimately, a man of problem solving genius will arise. We read of the Antichrist in Daniel 11:42-43:

> He shall stretch forth his hand also upon the countries: and the land of Egypt shall not escape.But he shall have power over the treasures of gold and of silver, and over all the precious things of Egypt: and the Libyans and the Ethiopians shall be at his steps.

All problems of humanity involve, in one way or another, money, riches, and the economy. We are told in the Scriptures that the love of money is the root of all evil. Wealth translates into power, power into control of people, nations, and tongues. Society and economics are more intertwined today than at any time in history.

Computer advances combined with breakthroughs in communications technology are more and more being applied to a global perspective. That means more and more power and control will flow through organizations such as the International Monetary Fund and World Bank, creating ominous consequences for the future.

The IMF is the agency most often looked to by the world financial community when the threat of world economic collapse looms. It has been the IMF that has forged autonomous national economies into one gigantic interdependent economic structure. It is probably no coincidence that the IMF is controlled by a block of nations that is in the process of reconfiguring into what will ultimately include ten members. Of that prophesied ten nation end-time power block, we read in Revelation 17:12-13:

> And the ten horns which thou sawest are ten kings, which have received no kingdom as yet; but receive power as kings one hour with the beast.These have one mind, and shall give their power and strength unto the beast.

In Revelation, the term beast is used to describe the end-time despot, who is called Antichrist; and in the realm of world economics, the signs increasingly point to the soon fulfillment of Revelation 13:16-18:

> And he causeth all, both small and great, rich and poor, free and bond, to receive a mark in their right hand, or in their foreheads; And that no man might buy or sell, save he that had the mark, or the name of the beast, or the number of his name. Here is wisdom. Let him that hath understanding count the number of the beast: for it is the number of a man; and his number is Six hundred threescore and six.

A World Prepared for the Antichrist

We are informed in the last book of the Bible that the four horsemen of the Apocalypse will come upon the world scene, bringing with them unprecedented socio-economic chaos and terrors that will cause people of the world to embrace the man who promises relief from their plight. Revelation 6:2 tells us about this "savior."

> And I saw, and behold a white horse: and he that sat on him had a bow; and a crown was given unto him: and he went forth conquering, and to conquer.

Revelation 19:11 informs us that God's Messiah, the Lord Jesus Christ, will return to this planet on a white horse, but the white horse rider of Revelation 6:2 is a false messiah. He will be a pseudo-savior that the nations will choose! This world super-leader's crown, his authority, will be given to him. He will receive his high office by appointment from a council representing ten powerful nations.

After the second rider — the rider on the red horse — comes announcing war, the third rider immediately will bring famine. With his appearance, a new world economic system will go into effect to save the nations from total chaos.

> And when he had opened the third seal, I heard the third beast say, Come and see. And I beheld, and lo a black horse; and he that sat on him had a pair of balances in his hand. And I heard a voice in the midst of the four beasts say, A measure of wheat for a penny, and three measures of barley for a penny; and

see thou hurt not the oil and the wine (Rev. 6:5-6).

A penny at the time the apostle John received the Revelation was a day's wages, and the footnote in the *Pilgrim Bible* that was written more than four decades ago when there was no inflation states: "God is setting a limit on living expenses . . . . During the famine less than two pounds of flour will cost this much." A measure is equal to about one and one-half pounds of grain; therefore, it is evident that there will be a world-wide economic collapse, followed by immense inflation, and then famine.

The words about not hurting the oil and the wine have reference to the need for medical supplies and services during the Tribulation, as oil and wine are the primary medicinal items mentioned in the Bible. When that horrific famine comes, there will be rioting in the streets, revolution, mass murder. Everyone will be fighting over food.

We should also consider the animals of that period, especially the flesh eating predators. What will happen when millions of dogs no longer are fed because all the people have eaten even the dog food and nothing is left?

We read of the aftermath of the economic collapse in Revelation 6:7-8:

> And when he had opened the fourth seal, I heard the voice of the fourth beast say, Come and see. And I looked, and behold a pale horse: and his name that sat on him was Death, and Hell followed with him. And power was given unto them over the fourth part of the earth, to kill with sword, and with hunger, and with death, and with the beasts of the earth.

Most likely, it will be at this desperate moment that the Antichrist will receive his power and will set in motion his ingenious plan to save the world. This global recovery plan will involve a New World economic order that will rearrange or eliminate all existing financial structures and currencies. Business and commerce, from that conducted by the giant corporations to transactions on the personal level, will be carried on through code marks and numbers.

Is this all just the ranting of wild-eyed doomsdayers? These times in which we live aren't so bad, are they? Are there signs of such vicious times to come, based on facts we can examine and analyze? Look around the world, the signs are obvious to anyone who seeks to know the truth.

Famine

Although we can find pockets of poverty here in our own nation — the homeless and the destitute — to really uncover apocalyptic-type human travail, one has only to look at any number of Third World nations.

Human destitution is shown hourly on Cable News Network and other networks. Entire specials are devoted to feeding the starving of Ethiopia, Bangladesh, India, Africa, Middle Eastern nations, and South American countries. No matter which direction the news camera turns, there is human poverty of appalling dimension. Commercials featuring starving children, their eyes bulging, their bellies distended, wrench our hearts while the narrators plead for financial assistance to prevent disease and death.

Though we in the United States often complain about wages not keeping up with costs, for the most part we live comfortably in the safety, warmth, and cool of our own homes. The vast body of humanity does not. Many work a full day for a day's ration; others work in slave-labor conditions to eke out a meager subsistence for their undernourished, often diseased children. Children in India, Pakistan, Thailand, even as near as Mexico, are forced to prostitute themselves in an effort to feed themselves and other family members.

The riders of the Apocalypse are not yet at full gallop across the landscape of our present age, but they are surely mounted. The evidence of their soon coming is everywhere and increasing daily.

A Global Mindset

Although mankind today is consumed with the daily cares of making a living, earning the daily bread, and fighting wars literally around the globe, increasingly there is a humanist spirit that calls the world to unite. Mankind is seaching for a way out of the ominous dilemmas that are closing in on planet earth.

The Persian Gulf War galvanized the one-world spirit,

giving it new impetus in the minds of people who would never have considered such a possibility before. Many even began taking a closer look at prophecy, particularly prophecy about Armageddon.

But, with the mobilization of American-led coalition forces and then the complete rout of the over-estimated Iraqi army, human thinking and human solutions to man's problems again attempted to push God and His solution aside. God's answer is Jesus Christ. It is He alone who changes the hearts of men and replaces war with a peace that surpasses human understanding.

A New World order appears on the horizon to shine on a glorious new age of cooperation and enlightenment. Humanists from all walks of life — economics, science, politics, and religion — urge us to meet on common ground and unite as one so that the world's problems can be solved through working together.

These "enlightened ones," who wish to lead us into such a glorious future, ignore one important fact: not only can nations not get along with other nations but political factions within countries are at each others' throats and refuse to cooperate for their peoples' own good. Neighborhoods within cities adamantly disagree on even insignificant matters. Families are literally murdering each other because of disputes among themselves. And individuals are committing suicide in record numbers because of violent inner-conflicts.

The humanists, however, will not face the facts and accept the pathway to true peace required by God. Instead, they are more determined than ever to resolve all of mankind's onrushing ills by human effort alone. Humanism seeks salvation for Earth, but rather than looking to Jesus Christ, who *is* God, they intend to create the gods of their own choosing, made in their own image.

The AIDS Plague

Jesus said in Matthew 24:7 that one of the signs of His coming would be pestilences. Since the day Jesus returned to heaven in the spring of A.D. 30, there have been many terrible disease epidemics. Smallpox, bubonic plague, cholera, typhoid fever, influenza, and other killer diseases have literally swept continents, killing millions. But Jesus, in that prophecy, must have been forewarning of a disease that would come upon mankind at the end of the age which would be more terrifying than any recorded in medical history.

AIDS is a pestilence of unprecedented virulence and is sweeping across the planet unchecked. It is 100 percent fatal; there is no cure. On March 30, 1987, Surgeon General C. Everett Koop stated that "no cure is possible within this century, and it is probable that none will ever be found." The outlook is no brighter today.

A May, 1991, news report stated findings that estimated one in every four males between the ages of twenty-four and forty-five in New York City has the HIV virus. The possibility for exponential growth in numbers of people who will become infected with the AIDS virus is a real danger. While some victims survived the plagues of the past, no one who has developed AIDS has survived it, and the number dying from this disease is more than doubling every year.

As far back as 1987, an Associated Press release reported: "Grim message on AIDS scares Australians; 50,000 Australians are now infected. Women are now giving birth to children with AIDS, and these children are called the living dead." More recent reports, following the astounding collapse and break-up of Communist domination over Eastern Bloc countries, tell of the same problem. For example, Romanian children by the thousands suffer from the disease.

The AIDS virus is diversifying. The virus now killing thousands in Africa is different from the virus in the United States. An Associated Press release reported that AIDS victims are now dying in Russia. Former Soviet propagandists at one time claimed the virus was originally leaked from a U.S. Army experimental laboratory.

In many countries AIDS is now being called "The Grim Reaper."

Again, as far back as April 6, 1987, *US News & World Report* carried an article entitled "And Now, A Worldwide War Against AIDS." The article stated: "There is a global epidemic of AIDS that leaves no country untouched. We can't stop AIDS anywhere until we stop it everywhere." It was an international battle cry long overdue. The words came from Dr. Jonathan

Mann, director of the World Health Organization's AIDS program. WHO estimates that as many as ten million people are now infected with the acquired immune-deficiency syndrome virus.

Newsweek, of that same year, reported that Europeans were demanding that foreigners take a test for AIDS. An AP news release of April 7, 1987, stated that foreigners were banned from Japanese bath houses to prevent the spread of AIDS. At that early date, there were already ten thousand cases on record.

One example of the fear that gripped the minds of people in a dramatic way was seen when the initial attempts were made to sell Rock Hudson's home in Beverly Hills following the actor's death. The price dropped dramatically, and at the time no one would buy the property, apparently considering it too great a risk.

The Humanist Approach

The anti-God obstinacy is seen in the humanists' approach to the AIDS pestilence about to consume mankind. Do they demand that governmental authorities make illegal the perverse acts that perpetuate this 100 percent lethal disease? No, of course not. Instead, they scream with one voice for legislation that would force society at large to embrace those perversions as a legally protected, alternate lifestyle under the banner of freedom of choice.

Homosexuality is at least as normal as heterosexuality, they proclaim. In fact, they want us to believe that, in many ways, it is preferable because it helps with, for example, unwanted pregnancies and overpopulation of "Mother Earth." Homosexual relationships, they argue defiantly, are nobody's business but the people involved. But, are the rest of us involved in this impending holocaust called AIDS?

AIDS is primarily a disease contracted and spread by male homosexuals. History, however, indicates there have always been homosexuals. There were homosexuals in Moses' day, and God's law expressly prescribed death for those who engaged in it. Alexander the Great, Nero, and many other well-known men in history, were either bisexual or homosexual. So, why has it suddenly erupted and spread wildly in this generation?

An answer to this question may possibly be found in Jesus' statement: "As it was in the days of Noah, so it will be at the coming of the Son of Man" (Matt. 24:37;NIV). And, from the description that Moses gave of the moral condition of mankind in those days, we know that men and women were committing every evil abomination of which they could conceive.

The apostle Paul writes in Romans that, before the flood, both sexes had given themselves over to sexual perversion. In 2 Peter 2:4-9, the reason for God's destroying the antediluvian world is explained as the same as why He destroyed Sodom and Gomorrah — primarily sexual perversion. Jude, in his epistle, also refers to the days of Noah and Sodom and Gomorrah as examples of God's judgment when the human race sinks to the bottom of immoral conduct.

God's Word informs us in Genesis 6:8-9 that Noah was perfect in his generation. He was not without sin, of course. He had to be saved by the grace of God just like everyone else. The logical meaning here is that Moses and his household were the only ones not contaminated by the sexual perversion that had infected the whole human race. AIDS, or a similar contamination of the blood of men and women, had apparently so infected mankind before the Flood that it became necessary for God to destroy all the people on earth with the exception of eight souls.

On May 20, 1991, the American Red Cross announced its latest approach to the AIDS plague. Elizabeth Dole, American Red Cross president, announced the organization was instituting a new computer system. Dole said, "The first step is to install a computer network that will run within the entire Red Cross system . . . . One national registry of ineligible blood donors will guarantee that only the healthiest blood donors will contribute to our system."

But how do they know who has AIDS and who doesn't? It has been reported that an organ donor, who did not test positive for AIDS before the donation, may have infected as many as fifty-two organ/tissue recipients. Even after his premature death, postmortem tests again showed his body to be HIV free. This donor, however, was apparently the one link common to the victims later found to be HIV positive.

Not even a computer can track this deadly disease with its many hidden traits and constantly growing resistance to even the most powerful drugs.

Computer Worship

As with the AIDS plague, humanists believe the solution to all mankind's problems is in the computer.

Computer scientists maintain that within less than a decade the computer will control every facet of man's life. This awesome power that is predicted to guide the destiny of the human race is causing many experts in the field to wonder if man is not now in the process of creating his own god. Amazingly, it is not primarily the leaders and spokesmen for religion that are expressing concern, but the computer makers themselves.

Some try to justify the neo-godly aspects of the new computers by rationalizing that it really makes no difference, because God, like all things of importance to man, is in the computer. For example, on page 94 of the book, *The Fifth Generation*, the writer says, "As the philosopher and logician Alfred North Whitehead observed, God is in the details."

The May, 1984, edition of *Science*, page 40, presents an in-depth article titled "Computer Worship." The piece contains a colorful full-page picture of a computer on a church altar, a beam of light streaming from above as if from heaven itself. Obviously, the computer is the centerpiece for a worship service.

The authors of the book present the position taken by computer authorities who say that future students will need not bother becoming proficient in reading, writing, or arithmetic. To meet future challenges in life, young people will need only to learn how to operate the new generation of computers.

The apostle Paul said that in God we move and have our being. Some today say the same about the computer.

A computer controls the traffic lights through which we pass on our way to and from work. Computers instruct us when we can move and when we cannot. Computers control our banking, our working, our buying, and selling.

One theologian said correctly that modern man fears a computer failure more than God's wrath against sin. Christian organizations themselves are becoming increasingly computerized. National religious conventions, for example, conduct highly specialized computer workshops. Mailing lists are computerized into many specific categories. Sophisticated computers determine the type of letters donors receive, the kinds of envelopes, the gifts asked for, the designs on stationery, and how often individual donors are to be contacted.

The perfect fifth generation computerized man is envisioned in a *US News & World Report* article titled, "What Next? A World of Communications Wonders":

> A phone in every pocket, a computer in every home: That and more await consumers as astonishing Information Age techniques start to pay off. A global telecommunications revolution is poised to bring astonishing changes to virtually every American — especially anyone who picks up a telephone, switches on a television set or logs on to a computer. Growing out of the marriage of communications links with modern computers, the new technologies are spreading lightning fast. Experts say that the upheaval won't end until anyone, anywhere can reach out and touch anyone else — instantly and effortlessly — through electronics. Among the extraordinary possibilities in store for consumers by the end of this century, electronic information technology will have transformed American business, manufacturing, school, family, political and home life.

In that *US News & World Report* article dated April 9, 1984, the story was very wrong in its predictions. Rather than at some distant time in the future, most of the technology is already in use today! Not only in America, but such technology now links most of the industrialized world.

At Babel man's intelligence convinced him he could reach into heaven, symbolically usurping God's throne. God short-circuited this humanistic power play by changing their common language into many languages and totally confusing that destructively prideful generation. When a man asked for a brick, he was given something other, and the tower project failed.

Man's new god, the computer, is today reversing that ancient communications breakdown. Soon the computer will be able to instantly translate what anyone speaking in a foreign language is saying. Revelation 13 clearly tells that everyone in the world will go to their knees and worship the image of Antichrist.

Today, computerized communications technology is capable of transmitting images of the world's political leaders into our living rooms — even in three dimensional form. Holography research and development technology promises that soon those leaders will seem to be in our living rooms in a physical sense.

Daniel 12:4 tells us that in the last days knowledge, travel, and communications will greatly increase. The computer is fulfilling this prophecy in astounding detail and with amazing swiftness. Ultimately, all commerce and banking will be done through electronic funds transfer via the computer terminal. Every person will be required to conduct his or her transactions at a computer terminal, using personal computer code marks and numbers.

We are warned, "And that no man might buy or sell, save he that had the mark, or the name of the beast, or the number of his name" (Rev. 13:17).

The Fifth Generation Computer

Fifth generation computer technology has been on the drawing boards since 1978. The American computer industry, which has led the world in computer development, was hesitant to bring in the fifth generation age because of uncertainty about how it might affect human societal interaction in economics, education, military defense, politics, and religion. Japan changed all that, forcing computer scientists in the United States to produce these new machines, which some contend will not really be machines at all, but organic, thinking entities.

If the United States computer industry fails to fully develop the fifth generation computer, Japan and the emerging European community behemoth will conquer the world market. The potential is there for a computer Pearl Harbor.

The authors of *The Fifth Generation* quoted Japanese sources who claim that the new biocomputers will solve the world's unemployment, energy shortages, medical costs, problems that come with old age, industrial insufficiencies, food shortages, and economic crises from troublesome currency exchange rate fluctuations to full-blown depressions. One computer expert estimates that every piece of data that is stored in the memory banks of all computers in the world at present could be stored in a space no larger than a sugar cube within a fifth generation computer.

Major credit card companies and commercial companies are already bringing us, they say, into "a new age . . . an age in which computers make miracles happen . . . ." Inviting us ". . . to step over that threshold and accept the credit card for a new age in shopping."

More than nineteen hundred years ago, the apostle John wrote in Revelation 13 that the day would come when all the world would worship the image of the beast who would command all to work, buy, and sell through a system of marks and numbers. According to fifth generation computer experts, that day may be very near — perhaps less than a decade away.

Governments are among the biggest users of computers, which are rapidly eliminating or taking over jobs once performed by people. This increasingly ominous intruder into all aspects of human existence is quickly merging all nations into a single economic system.

The computer is making its presence known in outer space. Computer and laser breakthroughs have combined to make human war possible in the heavens. The phenomenal success of America's remarkable futuristic weaponry during the attacks on Saddam Hussein's war-making facilities and armaments was spectacular proof that the technology is already here! Critics of Reagan's Strategic Defense Initiative (Star Wars) suddenly were forced to acknowledge, in amazement and praise, the accurate and effective results rendered by the new tactical weaponry. Much of the technology used in the Persian Gulf were by-products, off-shoots of, or precursors to SDI planning.

The fourth generation computer age was made possible by the discovery and/or invention of the silicon computer chip, which is made from quartz or sand. However, the silicon chip has no defense against outside power sources. Even lightning will burn a silicon chip to a crisp, and it is theorized that a single fifty-megaton air blast over Chicago would knock out every computer in the United States and Canada.

The next generation of computers, however, will have biochips, that will be capable of repelling outside interference and would only be destroyed by a very close nuclear blast. According to authorities on the subject, biochips are made from antibodies that are prevalent in the human body for the purpose of fighting disease germs. These antibodies have a short life span, but through an induced fusion between them and cancer cells, the result is ". . . a wildly reproducing cancer cell [which] results in a unique inheritance: an immortal hybrid cell, or hybridoma, that externally manufactures antibodies, one after another, each identical."

The fifth generation computer will, in effect, be a living entity. It will reproduce and program itself, and theoretically, one super computer could indeed control the total activity of every human being on earth.

It's Alive!

To us who know the Bible to be God's inerrant Holy Word and accept the Genesis account of creation as truth from the mind of God Almighty, we are convinced that the Theory of Evolution is a great satanic lie designed to keep mankind from accepting and worshiping the Lord as Creator. With the Theory of Evolution having done as much damage as it can in accomplishing demonic chaos in public school systems, it now stretches its sinister tentacles toward a new victim.

This new evolutional assault is so secretive and mysterious that it is usually referred to with cryptic terminology or hidden in veiled phraseology. There are a few scientists, however, like humanist Dr. Robert Jastrow, who are bold enough to explain, in words we can all understand, just what kind of "being" the synthetic computer evolution will ultimately produce.

Dr. Jastrow, founder of NASA's Goddard Institute, has few peers, if any, in scientific research, writing, and teaching. In his book on the subject of the emerging super-human intelligence, Dr. Jastrow writes:

In 1975, the Goddard Institute installed the first fourth-generation computer .... I stood there, looking at the giant third generation machine purring through its sums, and then at the little fourth-generation computer off in the corner. Suddenly, I became aware that powerful forces were at work. Because compactness leads to greater speed in computers ... computer designers are already under pressure to turn out more compact models. If these trends in computer evolution continued, a machine that occupied a floor in our institute would soon fit into a thimble, and its circuits would be as densely packed as the electrical circuits of the human brain. If it became possible to wire those circuits so that they worked in the same way as the circuits in the brain, man would be able to create a thinking organism of quasi-human power — a new form of intelligent life.

That was an earlier assessment by Jastrow. He now says that biochip breakthroughs "... change all that" (limitations by intricate wiring problems). Jastrow said:

... in these chips there are no wires; the connections are microscopically small. This development ... is a breakthrough in computer evolution, because it makes it possible to build a computer with gates that work like gates in the human brain. Such computers will come into existence in the 1990s .... They will match the human mind in many respects, and will possess attributes of intelligent life — responsiveness to the world around them, the ability to learn by experience, and quick grasp of new ideas. Will they be living organisms? Most people would say that a computer can never be a living organism, because it has no feeling or emotion; it does not eat, or move, or grow .... Most of these attributes could easily be built into computers if they were desired .... If its batteries run low, it can be programmed to move over to an electrical outlet and plug itself in for a snack .... Feelings and emotions also can be built into the computer .... I believe that in a larger cosmic perspective, going beyond the earth and its biological creatures, the true attributes of intelligent life will be seen to be those that are shared by man and the computer — a response to stimuli, absorption of information around the world, and flexible behavior under changing conditions. The brain that possesses these attributes may be made of water and carbon-chain molecules, and housed in fragile shell of bone, as our brain is; or it may be made of metallic silicon, and housed in plastic; but if it reacts to the world around it, and grows through experience, it is alive.

The era of carbon chemistry life is drawing to a close on the earth and a new era of silicon based life — indestructible, immortal, infinitely expandable — is beginning. By the the power of the machine . . . . This hybrid intelligence would be the progenitor of a new race . . . a bold scientist will be able to tap the contents of his mind and transfer them into the lattices of a computer. Because mind is the essence of being, it can be said that this scientist has entered the computer, and that he now dwells in it. At last the human brain, ensconced in a computer, has been liberated from the weaknesses of the mortal flesh . . . . Man need not wait a thousand years to reach the stars; the stars will come to him.[1]

In Genesis 11:6, Moses recorded that when man first reached for the stars, God said, "this they begin to do: and now nothing will be restrained from them, which they have imagined to do."

The Point of No Return

We read about the beast that will take control of the earth before Christ returns.

And he had power to give life unto the image of the beast, that the image of the beast should both speak, and cause that as many as would not worship the image of the beast should be killed. And he causeth all, both small and great, rich and poor, free and bond, to receive a mark in their right hand, or in 'their foreheads; And that no man might buy or sell, save he that had the mark, or the name of the beast, or the number of his name (Rev. 13:15-17).

Humanist computer scientists and experts have themselves given veiled warnings. For example, the author of *The Organic Computer*, warns that inasmuch as computers are already deified, the fifth generation computers may become man's god.

Dr. Robert Jastrow addressed himself to this danger in *The Enchanted Loom*.

> As these nonbiological intelligences increase in size and capacity, there will be people around to teach them everything they know .... If this forecast is accurate, man is doomed to a subordinate status on his own planet .... What can be done? The answer is obvious: Pull the plug. That may not be so easy. Computers enhance the productivity of human labor; they create wealth and the leisure to enjoy it; they have ushered in the Golden Age. In 15 or 20 years, computer brains will be indispensable .... If someone pulled the plug, chaos would result. There is no turning back.

If all computers were to be silenced, traffic lights would not function, airplanes would not fly, banks would not open, and people in this nation would stand at the supermarkets in lines longer by far than those endured by citizens of the former Soviet Union. The present generation has passed the point of no return.

Man — Satan's Robot

Major computer companies have worked hard and long and have spent millions of advertising, promotional, and marketing dollars to make people accept the computer as a helpful "user friendly" work saver. They've made it out to be man's companion, friend, counselor, and playmate.

Remember how the two computerized robots in the movie *Star Wars* were given distinct personalities? Audiences identified with the two main machines' characters more than with the actors.

Xerox produced a commercial several years ago in which a chubby, lovable little monk apparently found his personal computer to be more proficient and reliable than God in solving problems. The term "personal" implies that the individual has his own personal slave to do his every bidding — a thing few can resist at least contemplating.

Promises made to men of god-like power is in fact seductive delusion of the most destructive sort. The Serpent's tactics have not changed since the time he told Eve, in the Garden of Eden, that, when she and Adam ate of the forbidden fruit of the tree of the knowledge of good and evil, they would be "as God."

The awesome power within the computer appeals to man's pride, seemingly offers him a way out of his mounting pressures and dilemmas. Humanism, the belief that man, totally apart from a disciplining God, can solve all of man's problems, grasps greedily for what seems the infinite possibilities promised by the computer. But the power of the computer will not serve man, ultimately. In the hands of Antichrist, the computer will almost totally control people, will cause man not only to serve, but to worship the god it will satanically spawn.

Homer wrote in the *Iliad* that the god, Hephaestus, made splendid robots to relieve the gods and goddesses of mundane chores in looking after the human race. From Genesis 6, we can understand how much of mythology is based on the true biblical accounts of Satan's all-out attempt to subvert the human race and claim God's creation, including man and the earth for himself. The fifth generation computer, it appears, will be part of the wicked one's relentless, continuing effort.

A Marriage Made In Hell

Humanism is demanding answers to the problems exploding on every front. Scientists are working feverishly to fulfill man's demand for more intelligent computers. God said what man has imagined, he can eventually do. There is one thing no computer can do for humankind, however.

We read about that in the article titled "Computer Worship," which appeared in the May, 1984 edition of *Science* magazine. "Massachusetts Institute of Technology computer scientist Joseph Weizenbaum suggests, 'Take the great many people who've dealt with computers now for a long time ... and ask whether they're in any better position to solve life's problems. And I think the answer is clearly no. They're just as confused and mixed up about the world and their personal relations and so on as anyone else.'"

Satan's end-time tyrant, Antichrist, will use the computer to confuse and delude mankind; he is the author of confusion. That evil, super-genius linked to human technology will be a marriage truly made in hell.

With these many things coming together and flooding our world with uncertainty, we must consider them in the light of Bible prophecy. Is the dreadful day, when every person in the world will be commanded to receive the mark of the beast or be killed, nearer than most Christians dare believe?

The apostle Paul's divinely inspired instructions are given more so for this generation of Christians than for any in history.

> And the Lord make you to increase and abound in love one toward another, and toward all men, even as we do toward you: To the end he may stablish your hearts unblameable in holiness before God, even our Father, at the coming of our Lord Jesus Christ with all his saints (1 Thess. 3:12-13).

Humanistic attempts to make life heaven on earth are not working. Can we not see the truth of that statement in our daily newspapers and on our TV screens? The computer is not a magic box from which the leaders of this world will extract the solutions to mankind's proliferating problems. Rather, God's Word tells that such an instrumentality in the hands of Satan's super-tyrant, the Antichrist, will cause to be enslaved and/or killed all who are alive when the beast receives full power to do his diabolical work.

Before that horrendous time is allowed to come, God's children — those redeemed by the blood of Christ — will be taken out of this sin-cursed world to safety in the arms of Jesus, their Lord and Saviour.

Only Jesus Christ can give peace of soul and of mind. Only Jesus can provide forgiveness of sin. He, and He alone, can remove the agony of guilt that dwells within and marvelously, wonderfully fill the void — the emptiness that cries out for the one, true God.

If you are not now a Christian, receive Jesus Christ right this moment as your Saviour and your Lord, and thereby receive the peace and joy you so desperately want and need.

"For God so loved the world, that he gave his only begotten Son, that whosoever believeth in him should not perish, but have everlasting life" (John 3:16).

[1]Dr. Robert Jastrow of Goddard Institute, *The Enchanted Loom,* excerpt from *Gospel Truth,* June 1982.

4

The Rise of Babylon

by Joseph R. Chambers

The climax of all the ages is at hand. Everything must be in order. Judicial excellence must be perfectly satisfied. The Creator is ready to conclude the period within eternity that we call time.

Human systems of religious and civic order have failed. Out of that failure, however, God has redeemed a remnant of godly men and women, and it's time for their vindication. They will be His new kings and priests and will reign under His complete holiness and perfect government forever and ever.

The only biblical fulfillment in our generation that surpasses the rebuilding of ancient Babylon is the regathering of Israel to their God-given homeland. Babylon represents to the world system what Israel represents to biblical ideas and Christianity. Babylon was the worldly system that popularized the vices of paganism and government control over the masses.

Man was created to be the Creator's family and to live under His sovereign and spiritual lordship. When our early fathers rejected His commandments, they accepted control by an evil system designed by Lucifer and carried out by the basest of men.

Satan has always sought base men to be his emissaries. That's why carnal and worldly persons are found in high places of government. An evil system will lift the shrewd into positions of power to gain control over their lives. That's what the liberalism of America represents today. The ultimate struggle is between good and evil, godliness and godlessness.

William Buckley, one of America's foremost conservative thinkers, said the same in his book, *God and Man at Yale.*

> But there was a nice rhetorical resonance and an intrinsic, almost nonchalant suggestion of an exciting symbiosis, so I let pass: "I believe that the duel between Christianity and atheism is the most important in the world. I further believe that the struggle between individualism and collectivism is the same struggle reproduced on another level" (Yale University, page xviii).

Babylon of the Past

The Babylonian wickedness introduced three major systems in opposition to God's rule of His creation. All three of these systems have continued from that day and have been the means of great evil and human catastrophe. Every cruelty known to man has sprung from one of these systems. They were expressed in earlier towns of Sumer, Assyria, Persia, and Egypt, etc., but were made fashionable by Babylon. Understanding these systems is imperative to this article and the rise of Babylon.

1. The Religious System

Babylon made pagan religions fashionable. They took the base and deplorable idea of pantheism (matter as a series of gods representing every act or expression of nature) and elevated all of it to an art form. They incorporated art, drama, and music until the pagan ideas were beautifully represented in the highest expression of their culture. It literally overwhelmed the populace, and they gave it their soul.

Then, they added sexual and carnal satisfaction with great feast days, celebrations, and pleasurable religious expressions, including sexual orgies and temple prostitution. The religious life became the center of the cultures, and the king was transformed into a god.

The whole idea is a perfect picture of the New Age religion

so popular today. It is religious Babylon seen in Revelation, Chapter 17, and being joined by every religious system of our present world.

2. *The System of Government*

Babylon took the ideas of the city-states, as known in Ur, Uruk, and many other small cities, and gave it a philosophical and intellectual form. They raised government to a system of bureaucracies that permanently established control over the populace. They brought in representation from conquered small states, trained them to serve as their bureaucrats, and then used them to control their own people.

Building giant forms of bureaucracies, they made the people dependent on government. As government met human needs, it took on a god-like form. The state became all powerful, and the people gave up their independence.

3. The System of Education

Iraq today brags about the kind of educational system and inventions it gave the world through the Sumerian and Babylonian periods. Here is their own description:

> What is known is that they were a tremendously gifted and imaginative people. Their language, linguistically related to no other, ancient or modern, is preserved for us through the thousands of clay tablets on which they inscribed and developed the first writing as yet known to man. Fortunately, the Sumerians were prolific writers and meticulous record-keepers: these tablets richly describe their existence. With the invention of writing, the simple village life could evolve into complex civilization. They developed schools for an educated elite and for the many scribes who were needed for all the record-keeping and letter-writing they liked to do. Not only business records were written down, but also the first numbers, calendars, literature, laws, agricultural methods, pharmacopoeias, personal notes, maps, jokes, curses, religious practices, and thousands of lists and inventories of all manner of human interests (*Historical Iraq*).

They made education a responsibility of the state and

used it to promote state control. The educated elite came to claim authority and wisdom above the common people. Through the elitist educational system, they were able to control thought and intellectual development.

When government operates the educational program, you have the fox in the hen house. It takes on the form of the all-powerful state and squelches independent thinking so intrinsic to personal responsibility and true faith in God.

These three systems are destined to be judged in the very geography of their origination. That is why it is absolutely imperative that Babylon be rebuilt and once again heralded as the great city.

God's final judgment cannot be complete unless the judgment equals the offense. It is not acceptable for Him to judge something that symbolizes the offender. His judicial excellence requires perfect justice in complete harmony with the sin and rebellion that is judged. He cannot judge you for someone else because you favor them. Babylon will be judged for her sin and stubbornness against the government and holiness of God.

Babylon Rises Again

A recent booklet published by the Iraq government best describes their dream for rebuilt Babylon. The booklet's title itself is quite revealing: *From Nebuchadnezzar to Saddam Hussein, Babylon Rises Again.* Let me quote the first six paragraphs.

> Babylon rises again. Glorious in a glorious time. She is the lady of reviving centuries. Rising dignified and holy. Showing the great history of Iraq. Adding to its magnificence. And emphasizing its originality. The Phoenix of the new time rising alive from the ashes of the past to face the bright present that places it on a golden throne and bringing back to it its charming youth and unique glory.

> Babylon was not a city made of rocks and bricks and full of events. It was not a forgotten place of the ancient past. In fact, Babylon is something else. Since its birth Babylon has stretched its arm to the future to be the place of wisdom and to represent the civilization and to remain as a glittering lighthouse in the dark nights of history. Here is Bab-ilu . . . .

It survived the ages, defied all times and over-
came whatever threatened its existence. It won the
battles by virtue of its great heritage and the formi-
dable men, who carried that heritage, and defended
it throughout the ages that produced unique heroes
who know the originality of their city as it rises and
revives to add to human civilization something new
in writing, law, astronomy, medicine, arts, literature,
commerce, agriculture, education, and mathematics.
So history can start with it so that it remains the
compass throughout the ages.

When Babylon consisted of small city-states
and separate dynasties, Hammurabi waged succes-
sive wars to unite these city-states so that Babylon
remains as one city, as the bright light of civilization.

However, it suffered more and more from repeated attacks until Nebuchadnezzar came to power
and reconstructed it. He built temples and high walls
as he realized it was the pulpit of the first Iraqi
civilization.

Today looks exactly like yesterday. After long
periods of darkness that enveloped the land of
Babylon and concealed its characteristics, Saddam
Hussein emerges from Mesopotamia, as Hammurabi
and Nebuchadnezzar had emerged, at a time to
shake the century old dust off its face. Saddam
Hussein, the grandson of the Babylonians, the son of
this great land is leaving his fingerprints everywhere.

When you couple this dream of the Iraqi president, Saddam
Hussein, with present facts, it makes an impressive picture.

World Press Review did a story in their February, 1990,
edition. Here's how they described ancient Babylon:

And yet, for almost two millennia, Babylon was
the most important city in the world. It was the
commercial and financial center for all of
Mesopotamia — the link connecting the Orient with
the Mediterranean, Egypt with Persia. Its scribes and
priests spread the cultural heritage of Sumeria,

Chaldea, Assyria, and Ur — the arts of divination, astronomy, and accounting; private commercial law; and even the chariot — through the ancient world.

Then they gave a description of what is actually happening now.

Today, thousands of workers are reconstructing the ancient city of Babylon in the middle of the Iraqi desert. More than that of Marduk or even of Nebuchadnezzar, the new Babylon, expected to be finished in 1994, will be the city of Iraq's President Saddam Hussein. Though he has not had the martial successes of his distant predecessors, he is having his name stamped into the bricks with which the city is being restored. Every six feet along the new walls, there is a brick with an inscription in Arabic provided by the Iraqi president: "The Babylon of Nebuchadnezzar was reconstructed in the era of Saddam Hussein." Sixty million bricks have been laid so far.

It is very clear from this article, in *World Press Review*, that archaeologists (at least outside Iraq) think this is an unjustifiable adventure. They called it a "megalomaniacal Disneyland." Regardless, the Iraqi ruler continues. The progress was described in these words,

Besides the palace of Nebuchadnezzar, which is almost complete, he plans to rebuild the summer palace, the Temple of Hammurabi, the Greek theater, the processional way, and even the controversial Hanging Gardens, which many historians believe never existed. Three artificial hills, each almost 100 feet high, are being built on the plain. They will be planted with palm trees and vines. At the foot of the hills will be restaurants and perhaps a casino.

It is certainly exciting to preach a prophesied biblical truth for over twenty years, and then watch as the great God of this universe fulfills all that you have preached. That's exhilarating, but the glory goes to God who has proven himself so completely faithful that every nuance of His Word is to be perfectly fulfilled.

Living in a day of religious intellectualism, most ministers and teachers have given Bible truths relative interpretation. We are not searching for those hidden gems of revelation as the great Reformers and Revivalists of the past. We are satisfied with warmed-over religious grits.

The rebuilding of Babylon has caught the church leaders of our day by surprise, and the ones I know are still denying that there is any significance. Very soon, there will be no doubt.

Here are some things you can watch for that will help strengthen this powerful biblical truth:

1. Iraq will be increasingly in the world news.

2. This small nation will become a sore spot in the Middle East and will gain political dominance.

3. The rhetoric between Iraq and Israel will intensify.

4. Watch for a peace initiative between Iraqi leaders and Israeli moderates (this will eventually lead to a covenant of peace).

5. Don't set a timetable on what's happening; leaders could well come and go before the ultimate events in this nation of destiny.

The Mystery Babylon — Mother of Harlots

The eighteenth Chapter of Revelation is the picture of Babylon's revived *political* system.

Chapter 17 describes Babylon's pagan system of *religion*. The harlot decked with gold and precious stones and pearls, arrayed in purple and scarlet, represents the ecumenical religious crowd. Every religious idea from the crudest paganism to the pomp of Rome will be united in lust for wealth and political power. They will serve the political system and gain the allegiance of the multitudes.

Religion is the most powerful unifying force on this earth. The Antichrist will use the harlot and then destroy her.

Here is the picture of the Babylonian political system destroying her pagan ally, the harlot.

> And he saith unto me, The waters which thou sawest, where the whore sitteth, are peoples, and

multitudes, and nations, and tongues. And the ten horns which thou sawest upon the beast, these shall hate the whore, and shall make her desolate and naked, and shall eat her flesh, and burn her with fire. For God hath put in their hearts to fulfil his will, and to agree, and give their kingdom unto the beast, until the words of God shall be fulfilled (Rev. 17:15-17).

Just as Babylon, under Hammurabi and Nebuchadnezzar, used pagan religion to unify their control, revived Babylon will do.

The Revived Political System of Babylon

Now, we come to the actual rebuilding of this original city and her establishment as the leader of the world nations. Here are a few pertinent verses from Revelation.

And after these things I saw another angel come down from heaven, having great power; and the earth was lightened with his glory. And he cried mightily with a strong voice, saying, Babylon the great is fallen, is fallen, and is become the habitation of devils, and the hold of every foul spirit, and a cage of every unclean and hateful bird. For all nations have drunk of the wine of the wrath of her fornication, and the kings of the earth have committed fornication with her, and the merchants of the earth are waxed rich through the abundance of her delicacies.

How much she hath glorified herself, and lived deliciously, so much torment and sorrow give her: for she saith in her heart, I sit a queen, and am no widow, and shall see no sorrow. Therefore shall her plagues come in one day, death, and mourning, and famine; and she shall be utterly burned with fire: for strong is the Lord God who judgeth her. And the kings of the earth, who have committed fornication and lived deliciously with her, shall bewail her, and lament for her, when they shall see the smoke of her burning. Standing afar off for the fear of her torment, saying, Alas, alas, that great city Babylon, that mighty city! for in one hour is thy judgment come. And the merchants of the earth shall weep and mourn over her; for no man buyeth their merchandise any more: The merchandise of gold, and silver, and precious stones, and of pearls, and fine linen, and purple, and silk, and scarlet, and all thyine wood, and all manner vessels of ivory, and all manner vessels of most precious wood, and of brass, and iron, and marble.

And a mighty angel took up a stone like a great millstone, and cast it into the sea, saying, Thus with violence shall that great city Babylon be thrown down, and shall be found no more at all. And the voice of harpers, and musicians, and of pipers, and trumpeters, shall be heard no more at all in thee; and no craftsman, of whatsoever craft he be, shall be found any more in thee; and the sound of a millstone shall be heard no more at all in thee; And the light of a candle shall shine no more at all in thee; and the voice of the bridegroom and of the bride shall be heard no more at all in thee: for thy merchants were the great men of the earth; for by thy sorceries were all nations deceived. And in her was found the blood of prophets, and of saints, and of all that were slain upon the earth (Rev. 18:1-3; 7-12; 21-24).

To read these passages leaves little doubt that the Holy Spirit is talking about a literal city. When Babylon is cited, the language is not symbolic language. To create symbolism by interpretative fiat is a horrible method of scriptural exegesis. It leaves the Holy Bible open to many intrusions that weaken its message. Once you accept the premise that this city is literal, then supportive truths emerge to strengthen the facts.

Babylon — Yet to Be Destroyed?

A few brave souls have preached that the prophesied destruction of Babylon is yet future. Most Bible scholars have chosen the least controversial route of the convenient interpretation. They have taught that the great prediction of her destruction was complete, and this city would never have a future. They cited such passages as,

And Babylon, the glory of kingdoms, the beauty of the Chaldees' excellency, shall be as when God overthrew Sodom and Gomorrah. It shall never be inhabited, neither shall be dwelt in from generation to generation: neither shall the Arabian pitch tent there; neither shall the shepherds make their fold there (Isa. 13:19-20).

It certainly sounds convincing on the surface.

As we pointed out earlier in this chapter, Babylon is the human source of every foul institution that Satan has developed to control men. The pagan institutions of religion, the design of a governmental bureaucracy to control civil institutions, and state-controlled educations are Satan's methods to establish his own government.

God created men to be ruled by His theocracy. The invasion of sin changed that. Satan didn't just induce men to slip up. Man fell into his arms, and Satan became the god of this world. Every true believer has been a pilgrim and remnant since that day. We are not of this world nor of its systems.

Such debauchery, as described, must be judged. To think that judgment is complete in the past is to ignore many great biblical principles. Not only do we have direct scriptural proof that Babylon's judgment is future, the very idea of a final hour of restitution and revelation demands it.

When the reconciliation of all things is at hand, both systems, God's and Satan's, must be seen in contrast. It will be forever indelibly etched in man's mind that evil doesn't pay. Satan and sin will be seen in the light of eternal purity and justice, and the elect will never desire the opposite of the Creator. There will never be another "Garden of Eden" catastrophe.

"Babylon the Great Is Fallen, Is Fallen"

This is an incredible statement. If it appeared only once in the Bible, it would be powerful and dependable. But it's more than a statement; it's a theme.

Babylon is destined for a specific act of God that will cause the whole earth to wonder. No doubt will be left that God the Creator had the last word. Look at the expression in this statement, "And he [angel] cried mightily with a strong voice, saying, Babylon the great is fallen, is fallen ..." (Rev. 18:2). Our God intends to show this act to the whole world.

Again in Revelation, we have almost the exact words. The setting of this expression is an overview of the time of judgment. The exact words are, "And there followed another angel, saying, Babylon is fallen, is fallen, that great city, because she made all nations drink of the wine of the wrath of her fornication" (Rev. 14:8). This statement was made in conjunction with the worship of the Antichrist and his image, the mark of the beast given to Satan's initiates, and to God's great wrath against those who worship the devil and his cohorts.

What is striking is that these same words appear in Isaiah's treatment of the judgment of Babylon.

> And behold, here cometh a chariot of men, with a couple of horsemen. And he answered and said, Babylon is fallen, is fallen; and all the graven images of her gods he hath broken unto the ground (Isa. 21:9).

Everywhere in Scripture that such exact phraseology is used, we know that the Holy Spirit is arresting our attention. The wording is powerful proof that Isaiah and John are talking about the same judgment. We cannot ignore this fact.

Jeremiah made a similar statement by saying, "Babylon is suddenly fallen and destroyed: howl for her; take balm for her pain ..." (Jer. 51:8).

In all four of these predictions of destruction, suddenness is clearly a factor. Babylon is to be destroyed in a devastating blow of judicial expression.

Historical facts clearly demonstrate that this has never happened. Babylon's finely baked bricks have been used for centuries to build other buildings in the vicinity. A large town within visible sight named Hilliah is almost completely constructed of bricks with the name "Nebuchadnezzar" stamped in them. The area is a lively community of businessmen, professionals, educators, farmers, herdsmen, and Iraqi governmental functions. God's Word is specific when describing the final and complete judgment. It has not happened.

Even Saint Peter, when writing his first epistle, made

mention of the church at Babylon. He said, "The church that is at Babylon, elected together with you, saluteth you" (1 Pet. 5:13). Some have tried to establish that he was talking about Jerusalem or Rome, but such language would have been utterly foreign in Peter's day. If he had meant spiritual Babylon, the Holy Spirit would have inspired him to say that. That's the kind of confidence we can have in our verbally inspired, infallible Word of God.

The Arabs to Be Judged in Babylon

The Holy Scripture clearly states that Arabians will be the occupants of this nation in the final hour of judgment. Previous times when Babylon was attacked and defeated, it was by Sumerians, Assyrians, Chaldeans, Persians, or Grecians, but never Arabians.

In fact, it was in A.D. 637 that the first Arab empire was established in Mesopotamia. The northern city of Hatra was built and inhabited by Arabs about the time of Christ, but it was never more than a city-state. The first Arab government in Iraq was called the Abbasid Empire.

Another great evidence of biblical prophecy stating names and places hundreds of years in advance was spoken by the Holy Spirit through Isaiah when he prophesied,

> And Babylon, the glory of kingdoms, the beauty of the Chaldees' excellency, shall be as when God overthrew Sodom and Gomorrah. It shall never be inhabited, neither shall it be dwelt in from generation to generation: neither shall the Arabian pitch tent there; neither shall the shepherds make their fold there (Isa. 13:19-20).

Isaiah even called Babylon the beauty of the Chaldees yet saw it occupied by the Arabians. This clearly puts the final judgment of this evil city after A.D. 637, and no such event has taken place in these intervening years. Another example of a small jot or tittle awaiting fulfillment in God's pre-established hour.

Israel to Possess the Babylonians

The judgment of Babylon goes beyond the destruction of

the city itself. Very important details can be overlooked as we view the larger picture. Those small details give specific information. Israel is destined to possess the Babylonians as servants even as the Israelites themselves were once possessed. Isaiah said,

> For the Lord will have mercy on Jacob, and will yet choose Israel, and set them in their own land: and strangers shall be joined with them, and they shall cleave to the house of Jacob. And the people shall take them [Babylonians] and bring them to their place: and the house of Israel shall possess them in the land of the Lord for servants and handmaids: and they shall take them captives, whose captives they were; and they shall rule over their oppressors (Isa. 14:1-2).

This has never been fulfilled. The golden kingdom of Israel is immediately after the tribulation of the last days when Babylon will be destroyed. Israel will possess the promise land stretching all the way to the Euphrates River, and those whom she served will then be her servants and handmaids. Not one promise of God's Word can fail, and this prophecy, too, will be fulfilled.

Companion Prophecies (Isaiah 47, Revelation 18)

Chapter 47 of Isaiah is his most vivid description of Babylon's judgment. It is filled with clear details and descriptive events. Revelation 18 is equally descriptive and similar beyond accident. There is no comparison in the two Testaments more striking than here. Many quotes from the Old Testament by New Testament writers are far less similar than we see in this contrast. Neither should be doubted because the New Testament is the completion of the Old Testament.

Let's compare several passages. We will list the Isaiah text on the left and the Revelation on the right.

Isaiah Text	Revelation Text
Come down, and sit in the dust, O virgin daughter of Babylon, sit on the ground: there is no throne, O daughter of the Chaldeans: for thou shalt no more be called tender and delicate (47:1).	For all nations have drunk of the wine of the wrath of her fornication, and the kings of the earth have committed fornication with her, and the merchants of the earth are waxed rich through the abundance of her delicacies (18:3)
Therefore hear now this, thou that art given to pleasures, that dwellest carelessly, that sayest in thine heart, I am, and none else beside me; I shall not sit as a widow, neither shall I know the loss of children (47:8).	How much she hath glorified herself, and lived deliciously, so much torment and sorrow give her: for she saith in her heart, I sit a queen, and am no widow, and shall see no sorrow (18:7).
But these two things shall come to thee in a moment in one day, the loss of children, and widowhood: they shall come upon thee in their perfection for the multitude of thy sorceries, and for the great abundance of thine enchantments (47:9).	Therefore shall her plagues come in one day, death, and mourning, and famine; and she shall be utterly burned with fire: for strong is the Lord God who judgeth her (18:8).
Thou are wearied in the multitude of thy counsels. Let now the astrologers, the stargazers, the monthly prognosticators, stand up, and save thee from these things that shall come upon thee (47:13).	And the light of a candle shall shine no more at all in thee; and the voice of the bridegroom and of the bride shall be heard no more at all in thee: for thy merchants were the great men of the earth; for by thy sorceries were all nations deceived (18:23).

Behold, they shall be as stubble; the fire shall burn them; they shall not deliver themselves from the power of the flame: there shall not be a coal to warm at, nor fire to sit before it (47:14).

... and no craftsman, of whatsoever craft he be, shall be found any more in thee; and the sound of a millstone shall be heard no more at all in thee; And the light of a candle shall shine no more at all in thee ... (18:22-23).

I suggest that you read these two chapters several times and do a verse by verse study. They will yield many more similarities.

Babylon — The Seat of Sorceries and Paganism

This infamous city has provided the world with Satan's clever duplication of the true faith and the one true God. The account of Genesis' creation is matched with the Epic of Creation, Babylonian style. The flood of Noah has its counterpart in the Epic of Galgamesh. Even the biblical jurisprudence given by God to Moses has its contrast in the Code of Hammurabi.

All of these Satanic counterparts are far inferior and always filled with theological, moral, and philosophical distinctions that leave no doubt to their origin. Satan is certainly not very smart. He is the idiot god that rebelled against the Holy God.

Satan is having his last fling. Babylonian style mythologies are experiencing worldwide interest. America has its New Age religion with multitude expressions of the occult. From the Cabbage Patch doll to the metaphysical Charismatic churches, our nation is on a binge of pleasure, riches, and superstition.

Even jewelry is no longer simply worldliness. It is now an intimate part of the seduction scheme. New Agers are producing the Babylonian spirit in every conceivable way. The very "elect" will be deceived if possible. The words "if possible" means if you do not have the guards of the "Word" upon the frontlets of your spiritual eyes.

BABYLON RISES AGAIN!

5

Is Silence Golden?

by Joseph Carr

Sometimes It's Blood Red, and Sometimes It's Just Plain Yellow

I am often reminded of the TV commercial in which a Jewish diamond cutter is shown sitting at his workbench about to split a magnificent 100-carat, blue-white stone. With the knife edge firmly placed against the $1,000,000 rock, he swings his hammer and — wham! — a rough diamond worth a fortune shatters into a pile of industrial diamond dust worth about ten bucks.

The Jewish man slowly takes off his yarmulke and, looking very forlorn, laments: "Oy Vey! Am I gonna get hollered at."

I don't smash prized diamonds, but sometimes my writing does hammer equally prized prejudices, errors, and bigotries. There have been times recently that I have said — as I stripped copy off the word processor — "Oy Vey! Am I gonna get hollered at when this is published."

Since 1968 I have published 57 books, more than 300 magazine articles, and several monographs, tracts, and booklets. My first two Christian books were published within a few months of each other early in 1985. I received more mail during that time than I had from all my other writings combined.

The Twisted Cross is about the occultic New Age religion of Adolf Hitler, while *Christian Heroes of the Holocaust: The Righteous Gentiles* is about the pathetically few Gentile Christians who helped Jews during the Holocaust. What a storm these books have unleashed!

Meeting Hatred Face to Face

The first personal assaults over these books occurred only a few weeks after *The Twisted Cross* was published.

During the National Religious Broadcasters (NRB) Convention, my publisher gave away hundreds of books in hopes of gaining author interviews and book reviews from the broadcasters attending the convention. On the second day, a cold, steely-eyed gent bellied up to our table and asked me for ". . . that Hitler book." After telling him I was the author, I read his name tag and realized he was one of America's leading anti-Semites — a vile man who is widely known among Jew-haters.

Looking into the bigot's face was chilling for he reminded me of SS-Reichsfuehrer Heinrich Himmler — Hitler's SS chief. If I believed in reincarnation, then I would have thought this fellow was ol' "Reichs Heini" himself. In fact, his hairstyle, mustache, and pince-nez glasses were close enough to Himmler's to suggest that it was an intentionally affected image.

"Reichs Heini II" listened to my nervous description of the book, read the blurb on the back cover, and then venomously hissed, "The Fuehrer was a Christian!"

Another fellow came by the booth and contested my identification of Hitler's victims as "Jews." This man is a radio evangelist with a following in the East and South. He argued that the Holocaust never happened and pressed some of his tracts "proving" his assertions into my unwilling hands. With his lips tightly pursed, jaw set tight, and eyes narrowed into hostile slits, he nonetheless almost shouted at me, "The Holocaust is a hoax! And the people who call themselves 'Jews' today are counterfeits!"

My protests that he was wrong caused him to shake his fist at me! His face became contorted, his eyes blazed with hatred, and he practically snarled, "The Jews are the 'Seed of the Serpent,' and you're doing the Devil's work by supporting them."

At one time, such statements about the Jewish people, especially coming from a professing Christian, would have shocked and outraged me. "Don't you know your Bible?" I would have shouted. "Where did you get such stupid ideas?"

But I didn't question the shaking fist because, after years of research, I knew the source of his hatred and the deception that fosters it.

Christian Anti-Semitism

About eight years ago I heard about Stan Rittenhouse's book, *For Fear of the Jews*, through a critical review in an issue of *Israel, My Glory* magazine. The article indicated that the book was distributed through The Exhorters Foundation in Vienna, Virginia.

I ordered a copy of *For Fear of the Jews* and read it. There was little in Rittenhouse's book that appeared new to me, it was the same old Nazi world Jewish conspiracy, anti-Israel rubbish that has been disseminated for generations. Unfortunately, Rittenhouse claimed to be a "fundamentalist" Christian.

During the summer of 1984, a plain, brown mailing envelope arrived by U.S. Postal Service at my home. It contained an anti-Semitic newspaper named *The CDL Report* from the so-called "Christian Defense League" and a booklist from some related group called the "Sons of Liberty." The letter accompanying the material indicated that Stan Rittenhouse told them I might be interested in their material; apparently, Rittenhouse shared his mailing list with them.

In order to investigate this obviously anti-Semitic group, I ordered a number of their books and back issues of the newspaper. Again, it was the same old anti-semitic rubbish; they weren't even clever enough to invent new material.

I also received (apparently from the same group) a newspaper named *The Christian Vanguard*. The masthead of that newspaper indicated that it is the "Official Publication of the New Christian Crusade Church" of Metairie, Louisiana. Again, the same old anti-Semitic claptrap.

Finally, Christian Defense League sent me a copy of a form

letter to their supporters indicating they are planning to set up a Washington, DC lobbying group to be called the America First Lobby. Can you imagine the implications of a band of anti-Semites lobbying Congress in the name of "Christian patriotism?"

A common ploy used by these groups is to deny the Holocaust ever happened; claim that the 6,000,000 dead Jews did not really exist; and preach that the State of Israel is some kind of satanic creation (despite biblical prophecy!) that furthers the interests of some mysterious international World Zionist Conspiracy. Of course, *The Protocols of the Learned Elders of Zion* are high on their list of proofs.

There are also many people out there offering spurious theories about the Jewish people. Some claim that one race or another — who were the ancestors of the people we call Jews today — invaded ancient Israel and usurped the place of the biblical Jews. Others claim that the present day Jews are the bastard sons of Eve and Satan through Cain and that the real Jews (usually "Aryan" white men) were descendants of Abel. Again, the "real" Jews were somehow displaced by the evil "pseudo-Jews."

Still another myth claims that modern Jewry are not Semitic descendents of the biblical Jews but rather are descended from the Khazars who ruled southern Russia from the fifth to twelfth centuries A.D. The Khazars converted to Judaism in 740 A.D., and that supposedly permitted them to usurp the place of the Jews.

Will there never be an end to such foolishness? The history of the Jewish people is well known and traceable — so why the great mystery? Make no mistake about it, the Jewish people we know today are the direct descendents of the Jewish people of the Bible — God's chosen people.

Getting Shot At!

I *expected* the anti-Semites to crawl out of the woodwork in response to my books. But what surprised me most was the number of Catholic haters who attacked me. People almost routinely come to me bearing supposed "proof" that Pope Pius XII "owned" or controlled Adolf Hitler. They usually give me the same old printed rubbish, the same poorly reproduced photographs, and the same vile anti-Catholic comic books. (I have quite a pile now, so no more please.)

When I counter their arguments with a dose of confirmable historical facts, these "Christian" Pharisees explode, shake their fist at me, and shout that I am some sort of Jesuit sympathizer or Fellow Traveler. Somehow I doubt that the haters of either the Jews or the Catholics are driven by the Holy Spirit.

During that same National Religious Broadcasters Convention, I stopped by a booth manned by several nuns who publish Catholic Sunday school curricula. One of the sisters showed me a box behind her counter that must have contained 300 anti-Catholic comic books.

"How did you get all those?" I asked.

Before she could explain, a pastor came up to the booth, handed the nun a comic book, and said: "Sister, I'm a Protestant, and I have a lot of problems with Catholic teachings, but I'm ashamed and embarrassed that a 'Protestant' puts out this rubbish!"

The nun took the comic book that we recognized as the one being passed out to convention-goers by a certain group.

"That's how I get most of my comic books," the nun told me with a smile. "I intend to use them to start the woodburning stove back at the convent."

It made me feel better to know that most Protestants are decent folks who do not promote hate and the literature that fuels it.

Still, I pondered the power of the written word and how as Christians we can use it to spread evil or oppose it. When a writer opposes evil, he can expect heat. But, I must admit, I was shocked by the searing intensity of the blasts that were coming my way.

These issues were much on my mind when I later traveled to Chicago for the Christian Writer's International conference. There I met journalist Dan Wooding.

Dan, who now works for Brother Andrew's Open Doors News Service was once a Fleet Street (England) reporter writing show business pieces (much to the dismay of his missionary parents). A fellow Christian journalist had challenged Dan to stop writing "show business junk" and "go to Uganda to get shot at." Dan accepted the challenge and wound up in Entebbe writing about the persecution of the Church under Idi Amin. He now specializes in covering the Church in those areas of the world where believers suffer and die.

During the writer's conference, Dan related to me how he once confronted another talented writer, a man well known for his work but whose writing is shallow.

"Although he is commercially successful," Dan said, "he has little impact on the world. After all, who really needs to know all *Twelve Ways to Reuse Air Sickness Bags?*"

I knew Dan was telling me, in a round-about way, to write about significant subjects. "If you've got to slave over a word processor," he said, "then at least write about something worthwhile!"

He was right — time and talent are simply too precious to waste on trivia.

Seeing 20/20

After I appeared on a television talk show, one man wrote and made a thinly veiled threat regarding my "kosher throat" (and I'm not even Jewish!). Another man wrote to call me a "Jew-loving . . . (expletive deleted)." Taking a cue from Rev. Frank Eiklor of Shalom Radio, I wrote the man back: "Sir, you are only half correct — my parents were married."

My appearance on Marlin Maddoux's live radio broadcast, "Point of View," resulted in nearly 200 letters. About 20 percent either made anti-Semitic claims or asked questions that indicated they have been listening to such claims. The bulk of those letters came from the American heartland where thousands of farmers and others have been suckered into a vile anti-Semitic hatred by the so-called "Christian Identity" movement (Neo-Nazis).

While I was in Portland, Oregon to appear on the "Gary Randall Program," the show host held a party for me at the home where I was lodged.

Gary told me "Don't worry . . . ."

I quickly thought, *There's something to worry about?*

"Security at the studio is pretty good," he said in passing.

At that, I nervously asked him, "Why does it have to be so good?"

"A few weeks ago, the station showed the Raoul

Wallenberg docu-drama. After the show went off the air, a rifle bullet crashed through the station's plate glass window," Gary told me. "That's when we hired a bodyguard to sit in the audience during the show."

For several weeks thereafter, it perplexed me why they felt an armed guard was needed. Then, on August 15, 1985 the ABC-TV "20/20" show ran Geraldo Rivera's investigative piece titled "Seeds of Hatred." Rivera exposed the venomous Jew-hatred currently running amuck in the Midwest and throughout the USA. He also pointed out the religious nature of this "Christian" Neo-Nazism called "Christian Identity."

When I heard people saying they were going to kill "evil, Zionist Jews" in the name of Christ, I recalled how my books had been received and felt a little like a Christian Scientist with appendicitis.

Frank Eiklor of Shalom Radio has fought anti-Semitism for almost a decade and comes under attack regularly. An associate of Frank, who is now himself on the frontline in Ethiopia with World Vision, told me, "Frank doesn't think his ministry is effective unless he gets at least one death threat a week."

The morning after the "20/20" broadcast, I stopped in the office of a Jewish colleague at my secular job and asked him if he'd seen the show. He replied that he had and politely listened to my shocked statements on the content of the program. He looked at me with a polite, sad, knowing but slightly condescending expression and said, "Those Neo-Nazis may surprise you, Joe, but we Jews have known what Christians are really like for centuries."

That is why I won't waste my time on "Air Sickness Bag" stories.

Low-Grade Fevers in the Church

Not everyone should go to Uganda or Kansas to get shot at, but I am challenging you to break out of your warm "fortress church" and make a significant contribution. There are, after all, important issues in your own neighborhood. All aspects of our culture involve critical issues, some of which affect the very basis of our religious freedoms and moral fiber.

A hand-lettered sign in my seventh grade homeroom

proclaimed, "Silence Is Golden!" That slogan made sense to a harried teacher, but is it valid for the Church?

Isaiah 21 admonishes us to place a watchman on the wall. Interpreted in modern terms this advice could mean informing ourselves about the dangerous trends and critical issues in our culture and then speaking out on them where appropriate. After all, of what use is a silent watchman on the wall?

As Christians, we are faced with many tremendous challenges today: Secular Humanism, Liberal Theology, the New Age movement, and the Neo-Nazi "Christian Identity" movement. Anti-Semitism is also once again raising its ugly head. All of these movements are threats to the Church of the 1990s.

We must not think that Christian anti-Semitic groups are merely a lunatic fringe that can be safely tolerated until they go away. That was the position taken by the minority of German Christians who were not Nazis during the 1920s and 1930s, and you see what good it did them. It is necessary that the Christian churches be aware of the evil they are permitting if they allow Christian anti-Semitism to exist in their congregations without checking it.

Unfortunately, even Christians who are not overt anti-Semites frequently harbor a mild anti-Semitism that acts like a low-grade fever in the Church body. That form of anti-Semitism is even more hideous because it sets an attitude that will easily succumb to more virulent forms of the disease.

We need to stop using the word "Jew" as a prerogative; we should not talk about "Jewing down" someone's price; we should not make assumptions regarding Jews or Jewishness; we must guard against telling "Jewish jokes."

I recall one young Christian who tried for a period of many months to get a Jewish friend to come to church with him. On the Sunday when the Jewish friend finally relented and came to church with the Christian, a speaker from a missions board was guest preacher. He told a simple-minded Jewish joke from the pulpit.

That Jewish man knew what he would find in Christian churches, and that missionary proved to him that his beliefs were correct! Never before or since had a Jewish joke been told in that pulpit, at least in the three years I attended that church. Only on the day when a Jewish guest was in the Sunday service did such a thing happen.

Satan has a perfect sense of timing, and uses the most righteous among us in his work. I hope that the Jewish friend of the young Christian will forgive us.

Surely telling Jewish jokes and using the word "Jew" as a prerogative fall under the category of "doubtful things." Anti-Semitism is a recurrent cancer in the Church body that must be eradicated.

Jews — Rich and Power Hungry?

Anti-Semites routinely charge that Jews control the wealth of the country and, thereby, control the economy and politics as well. Even non-anti-Semites and some Christians accept this generally held belief, making it easy for them to think there might be something to the "world Jewish conspiracy" myths.

The magazine of the American Board of Missions to the Jews (ABMJ), *The Chosen People,* for March 1985 discussed the question of anti-semitism. In an article titled, "Even Your Best Jewish Friends Won't Tell You," they gave us a few facts regarding the Jews and wealth.

First, believe it or not, only a few Jews are wealthy. A study done in New York City, with one of the largest and most varied Jewish populations in the United States, found that 20 percent of the Jewish people lived below what the U.S. Government considers "lower income level," and 15 percent were at or below the official poverty level. I suspect from this statistic that a disinterested, objective study will show approximately the same distribution of wealth throughout the Jewish population as among the Gentile.

Second, Jews do not run American business! In fact, the proportion of Jewish top corporate officers is so low compared with their percentage of the population that I suspect Jews have a legitimate complaint under discrimination laws! In fact, the Episcopalians and Presbyterians are most abundantly represented. *The Chosen People* magazine used the word "over-represented," while Jews (and Baptists and Catholics) are under-represented.

The article cited a study that showed, of the fifty-six major American companies that could be controlled by only 5 to 10 percent of their stockholders, only three have any substantial number of Jewish stockholders.

Third, the claim that a cabal of Jewish interests controls the media to benefit a supposed Jewish conspiracy is pure rubbish. Although it is true there are a lot of Jewish people in the media, and in responsible positions, one need only look at how "favorably" the media treats the nation of Israel. The distortions and half-truths that stream forth from the "boob tube" daily is proof that the supposedly Jewish media doesn't favor Israel in any conceivable way. If "the Jews" control the media, then how come they cannot keep their employees from slandering the world's only Jewish state?

It's clear the anti-Semitic assertions that the Jews either control, or seek to control, the world are pure rubbish. These claims simply stand on the edge of a logical chasm that is too broad for the healthy mind to leap.

Could It Happen Here?

During the Holocaust many millions lost their lives because of Christian silence. Could Christian silence bring on a Holocaust in this country? I know a lot of Jewish people who fear that it could happen here — in the United States of America.

A Jewish woman told me that her grandmother advocates keeping $2,000 in cash and some gold coins in the house all the time in order to finance a flight to Canada or Mexico when Americans start killing Jews. Extreme? I would hope so, but maybe not.

With the Christian Identity movement preaching a message that amounts to racial holy war and elimination of the Jews, it is more than possible that Jews are in danger in "Christian America."

Could it happen here? You better believe it can! After all, Germany was one of the leading civilized nations of the twentieth century; it "couldn't happen" there, either — but it did!

What can you do? First, become informed about Naziism, Nazi religion, Christians Identity, the New Age movement, and anti-Semitism in general. Shalom Radio and its founder Rev. Frank Eiklor have been fighting anti-Semitism for almost a decade. Frank broadcasts daily on ten or twelve stations nationwide and offers a newsletter and tapes on anti-Semitism.

You can also work to get the Jew-haters off the air. Some of these preachers of hatred broadcast their vile message over the radio — even on Christian stations. Let the advertisers who buy time on those stations know you are boycotting them because evil hatred is being broadcast on their dollar.

You might also contact the Christian programmers who buy time on that station and tell them your complaints. Let them know that your support for their ministry will be discontinued unless they either change stations or convince the station manager to stop airing programs that promote hate and violence.

Finally, if you hear a Neo-Nazi (or anyone else) threaten violence against the Jews, Catholics, blacks, or any other group, then complain to the FCC (1919 M Street NW, Washington, DC, 20037) — surely it's illegal to threaten physical violence on the airwaves!

You should challenge anti-Semites in your own church or circle of friends. God is not amused over either "Christian" anti-Semites or those who tolerate them (see Genesis 12:3). That is why challenging the Jew-haters is absolutely essential — it is not optional.

While Scripture encourages us to fellowship with non-believers in hopes of winning them to Christ, it also requires us to break fellowship with believers who fall into sin and refuse to repent. If there are Neo-Nazis in your church, then the only course open is the Matthew 18 process. Those people must be required to either repent or leave. Again, no other option exists.

To paraphrase a famous quotation: "The only thing needed for evil to triumph is for decent people to say nothing."

Tearing a Hole in the Night

Confronting Christian anti-Semites, New Age Jew-haters, and Neo-Nazi pseudo-Christians can be uncomfortable; it can even be dangerous. Sure, these people are tough, but fear must not stop us from speaking out against their hatred and violence.

To quote Rev. Frank Eiklor of Shalom Radio: "Silence isn't always golden, sometimes it's just plain yellow."

Christian silence in this matter will send the wrong message to non-believers, especially Jews. It will also set the stage for eventual success of the Christian Identity movement, as it did for Nazi success in Germany 50 years ago.

The righteous Gentiles, like Corrie ten Boom and her family, who aided Jews during the Holocaust were not previously heroes — almost all of them were very ordinary people like you and me. But they tore a hole in the Nazi night by their simple actions.

The Israeli government operates the Yad Vashem memorial on a hillside in Jerusalem to honor the murdered six million of the Holocaust. On the same site is the Avenue of the Righteous. There Carob trees are planted in honor of individual righteous Gentiles who helped the Jews escape Nazi terror — and paid for it with their own lives. One account regarding the selection of the Carob tree says that "its fruit is sweet and nutritious, but its tough, leathery leaves do not wilt in a hot, dry hostile desert environment."

What is needed in the Church today are people who will not wilt in a hostile environment! With an anti-Semitic darkness settling over our country, I am calling you to tear a hole in the Neo-Nazi night.

If the watchman on the wall is silent, if he fails to cry out when danger approaches, then no one will hear his laments when barbarous hordes pour through the city gates.

To paraphrase anti-Nazi pastor Martin Neimoller: "First the Nazis came for the Jews, but I wasn't Jewish so I remained silent. Then they came for the Communists, but I wasn't a Communist so I didn't speak up. Then they came for the trade unionists, but I wasn't a trade unionist so I remained silent. Then they came for the Roman Catholics, but I was a Protestant so I said nothing . . . then they came for the Protestant clergy, and there was no one left to speak out."

Is silence golden? No, sometimes it's blood red.

6

Night Cometh!

by Texe Marrs

A man wrote me to say, "I read your book, *Mystery Mark of the New Age,* and I didn't believe the things you reported could be possible. I decided to prove you wrong, Texe."

He spent an entire week at one of the largest libraries in a major American city, researching what I had written and examining all the various magazines and books to see if what I had said was true.

What did he discover?

His letter continued, "Texe, you didn't say enough! It's worse than you wrote in your books. Much worse!"

It *is* much worse. Whatever I say to you in this book today, it's much worse. Words cannot express the horror of the New Age movement and what it plans to do.

The Bible clearly tells us that in the last days, people will fall victim to seducing spirits and doctrines of demons. "But evil men and seducers shall wax worse and worse, deceiving, and being deceived" (2 Tim. 3:13).

The New Age world religion is based on spiritism — communication with the dead. These seducing spirits are evident in every New Age book, every New Age church, organization, group, or cult. False spirits, some of whom actually claim to be Jesus, "communicate" their doctrine of demons to those who have opened their minds to believe anything but the Truth of God's Word.

> . . . they received not the love of the truth, that they might be saved. And for this cause God shall send them strong delusion, that they should believe a lie (2 Thess. 2:10-11).

People who were involved in the New Age have told me, "You know, I listened to the New Age leaders say the very things you quote in your books, and I didn't understand. There seemed to be some kind of blindfold over my eyes."

If you don't know Jesus as Saviour, you will believe the lie. You *will* believe the lie!

If you are reading this and you say, "Hey! I'm a smart man or woman! I've got an education. I'm not going to fall for the lie."

If you reject the truth that is Jesus Christ, you *will* believe the lie. Why? Because, the Scripture warns that God is going to send strong delusion, and you will believe the lie.

How can we fortify ourselves against this powerful, spiritual lie? By knowing what our enemy, the adversary of our souls, has planned for those who are true followers of Jesus Christ. The plan is already unfolding, and Satan's mouthpieces have made their intentions clear.

I do not want you to be ignorant or taken by surprise. Some of the things you are about to read will shock you, but they must be told so you can be prepared.

Jesus said we must work while we still have the day because the night cometh when no man can work. The night surely is coming.

The New Age Explosion

The New Age is the fastest growing religion on earth today. An estimated sixty million Americans are involved in some facet of the New Age. Sixty million! Its tentacles are everywhere — in politics and religion, in the economy and business, in education, in the military, and in the Church.

New Age signs are everywhere in symbols: the satanic triangle, the upside-down crescent moon, the splotch of blood on the Striper album cover, and on and on.

I recently saw in *Parade Magazine* a full-page ad for a crystal necklace, and it very clearly said in the ad that this was a sign of the New Age. We see these occult symbols in TV shows and commercials and in magazines and newspapers. I describe many of these symbols in my book *Mystery Mark of the New Age*.

We are experiencing an occultic explosion today. It's everywhere — in satanic rock music, on MTV, in books. Even our children are being brought into sorcery by cartoons, comic books, television, and movies. Experts say there are six to ten million witches across America. Devil worship is dramatically on the increase today.

Probably one-third of Americans, or more, believe in reincarnation, even though Hebrews 9:27 very clearly states that it is appointed unto a man once to die and after death, comes the judgment. Reincarnation is a lie of the Devil, a New Age doctrine of demons.

We are enduring an explosion of New Age music, New Age movies, New Age books, all promoted by the idols of stage, screen, and television. Stars like Michael Jackson, Tina Turner, Patrick Duffey, Oprah Winfrey, Ally Sheedy, John Denver, and Shirley MacLaine make no bones about their New Age religion. In addition, Hollywood directors and producers like George Lucas and Stephen Speilberg promote their New Age philosophy through their popular movies. And the list goes on and on.

These people are victims. Our Bible warns that in the last days, men will go about deceiving and being deceived. These, who are victims, are themselves victimizing others, thereby perpetuating and increasing in intensity the vicious cycle of satanic delusion.

In Places of Power

Many powerful, influential people in the United States, boldly advocate the New Age religion, including U.S. Senators Claiborne Pell and Terry Sanford. Former U. S. Senator from Colorado, Gary Hart, says he believes in native American Indian magic. Former astronaut Edgar Mitchell is now a highly dedicated New Ager devoted to New Age principles. Even George Shultz, secretary of state under Ronald Reagan, has called for a New Age and says that, whether we know it or not, it has already occurred; it is already here.

Remember Barbara Marx Hubbard, who a number of years ago received several hundred votes for president at the Democratic Party Convention? She now says the people of the New Age are the horsemen of Revelation 6 and that Christian fundamentalists will have to change or die!

A prominent member of the Better World Society, who is pushing pro-Soviet philosophies, has called for a New Age president of the United States.

Mikhail Gorbachev, the former Soviet leader, says the world peace movement will bring the whole world together in a one-world system. Gorbachev, an atheist, is more than willing to accept a man as god. He will not, of course, accept the true God.

Prince Charles of Great Britain, a great believer in holistic medicine, practices the eastern mystical religions and accepts New Age philosophies. Willie Brandt, the former Chancellor of West Germany, is today a strong peace advocate and a determined New Ager.

New Age in the Church?

In the Christian World, New Age teachings are being introduced into many churches that once taught a solid biblical message. Moreover, many leaders once highly respected by evangelicals now commonly parrot New Age dogma.

Norman Vincent Peale, a man who believes in reincarnation and the Hindu philosophy of Karma, recently endorsed a book called *The Jesus Letters* by Jane Palzier. Apparently, a demon spirit, who identified himself as Jesus, told Ms. Palzier to write this ungodly book. Although it totally opposes and contradicts the teachings of the Bible, Norman Vincent Peale recommends that everyone read it. He says that God is simply an energy force, a consciousness, and that it doesn't matter whether you believe in the Jesus of Nazareth or the Jesus of Jane. We are all God, he says.

Harold Sherman, a dedicated occultist and New Ager, also received Norman Vincent Peale's endorsement for his book,*The Dead Are Alive. They Can and Do Communicate With You.* Peale called it "a masterpiece."

Dr. M. Scott Peck, author of *The Road Less Traveled,* a book on the Christian bestsellers list, went to India and worshiped the Hindu gurus. Although he is a dedicated Zen Buddhist meditation advocate, Peck has been invited to many Methodist, Presbyterian, and even Baptist churches and others across America. Dr. Peck, a psychiatrist and an M.D., says it is heresy to emphasize the divinity of Jesus Christ.

Richard Foster, who wrote *Celebration of Discipline,* used a quotation in the book that included the words "we of the New Age." In a later edition, however, he altered the quote, evidently after he began to receive criticism.

The Dominion theologians today, who call themselves The Kingdom Now, claim they are reconstructionists when they are actually dedicated New Agers. Many today say they are Christians, but instead they are deluded victims, adhering to theologies sired by the father of all lies.

Positive Thinking?

Gerald Mann, who calls himself the "pastor" of the multithousand member Riverbend Baptist Church in Austin, Texas, does not believe in the Bible as the inerrant Word of God. He says that his is a church not of *holiness* but of *wholeness.* Wholeness is a New Age term.

Dr. Mann, a New Age advocate — though he would most likely deny it — wrote a book, published by Harper & Row, called *Commonsense Christianity.*

What an insult to our most holy God! There is no such thing as "common sense" Christianity. The things of God are marvelous, miraculous, unfathomable. Our God is imbued with *uncommon* sense because the mind of God is not the mind of men. His thoughts are as high above man's thoughts as the heavens are above the earth. God gives us the peace that surpasses all understanding; it flows like a river once a person accepts Jesus.

Preachers like Robert Schuller and Norman Vincent Peale say we must be positive thinkers.

Let me introduce you to the world's greatest positive thinker, the world's greatest positive confessor, the person who made the greatest positive affirmations. He was and is the world's greatest positive thinker. His name is Lucifer.

Lucifer said, "I will ascent into the stars. I will control. I will seize dominion. *I will, I will, I will.* I will be above the Most

High." What a positive thinker! Read all those positive confessions he made! But, in the end, he will be thrown down and cast into the pit.

New Agers say Christians are negative because we proclaim that bad times are coming. Therefore, negative thinking, as the New Age terms it, is *truth* as God foretold it in the prophetic Scriptures.

Negative thinking is *not* to believe that Jesus Christ is Lord and the only way to God the Father. Nothing is more negative than that. You can make positive confessions and be a positive thinker in your head all day long. But God's Word says, "There is a way that seemeth right unto a man, but the end thereof are the ways of death."

The Coming One

As Christians we pray the Lord's Prayer, which Jesus gave us: "Our Father which art in heaven, Hallowed be thy name. Thy kingdom come. Thy will be done in earth, as it is in heaven" (Matt. 6:9-10).

The New Agers have a counterfeit prayer called the Great Invocation. People in the Unity Church, the Universalist Unitarian Church of Religious Science, and many New Age churches across America in the Lucis Trust are promoting this satanic prayer.

I recently talked to a woman who had been a victim of the New Age for 18 years. Jesus Christ came into her life and cleansed her of all unrighteousness, and she now worships Him as Lord. She said, "Texe, I used to recite this Great Invocation."

Every Sunday the members of the New Age church to which she belonged would meet and begin their "service" by reciting the "Great Prayer." Each member of the congregation was also given a copy of the prayer and instructed to recite the words at least a dozen times every day.

"I read those words and didn't even know what I was saying," she told me. "At the time, my eyes were blinded by Satan, and the words sounded great to me. In fact, I couldn't wait to recite them."

The Great Invocation reads: "Let the lords of liberation issue forth. Let the rider from the secret place come forth, and coming, save. Come forth, O mighty one. Let light and love and power and death fulfill the purpose of the coming one."

We know who the New Age's "coming one" will be — that man of Satan, the man of lawlessness, the man of rebellion, the son of perdition, the Antichrist, the Beast.

The Beast of Revelation 13 will be a political leader whose number will be 666. The false prophet, a religious leader who is the other Beast, will create an image of the first Beast, and everyone will be required to worship the image or be put to death.

What does God's Word tell us about this plan of the Antichrist and his world Mystery Babylon system?

The prophet Daniel records what God wants us to know about the end times, as spoken by the angel Gabriel: "Behold, I will make thee know what shall be in the last end of the indignation: for at the time appointed the end shall be" (Dan. 8:19). This speaks of the end of time, the last days just before this world — controlled by Satan, the lord of this world — comes to an end. God wants us to know what is going to happen.

Daniel 8:23-25 says,

> And in the latter time of their kingdom, when the transgressors are come to the full, a king of fierce countenance, and understanding dark sentences, shall stand up. And his power shall be mighty, but not by his own power: [This man's power is going to come from Satan.] and he shall destroy wonderfully, and shall prosper, and practise, and shall destroy the mighty and the holy people. And through his policy also he shall cause craft to prosper in his hand; [This means witchcraft and the sorcery of the Devil!] and he shall magnify himself in his heart, and by peace shall destroy many: he shall also stand up against the Prince of princes; but he shall be broken . . . .

Satan's plan is to destroy God's holy people — all those true believers who refuse to worship the Beast's image. How will the Devil accomplish a task of such great magnitude? Where will the manpower come from to carry out such widespread persecution? The groundwork for his diabolical, bloody scheme is being laid right now in the United States and throughout the world.

Revelation 17 tells us that in the last days, a church of Satan will be so widespread over this planet, that it will encompass peoples and tongues and nations. All the rulers of the world will become involved in this worldwide, satanic church known as Mystery Babylon, Mother of Harlots, and Abominations of the Earth.

> And such as do wickedly against the covenant shall he corrupt by flatteries: but the people that do know their God shall be strong, and do *exploits*. And they that understand among the people shall instruct many: yet they shall fall by the sword, and by flame, by captivity, and by spoil, *many* days (Dan. 11:32-33; KJV).

This Mystery Babylon, this worldwide church of Satan, will be so wicked that she will have the blood of the saints and the martyrs of Jesus on her hands. Moreover, God's Word says that in her cup is the filthiness of her fornication. She is actually drunken not on wine, not on alcohol, but is intoxicated on a most gruesome substance — the blood of the saints and martyrs of Jesus! She is the woman who personifies the church of Satan. I call her Satan's mistress.

What is this Mystery Babylon? I believe it is the false religion of the New Age that is sweeping across America and the world.

A Great Falling Away

When will all these things take place? Jesus told us that no man knows the day nor the hour, but He also said that when you see certain signs, you can look up because you know redemption is drawing near.

The whole purpose of Bible prophecy is to let us know that the time is short — to let us know that night cometh when no man can work. But some people today refuse to believe the prophecies of Scripture.

The apostle Peter wrote that in the last days scoffers would come walking after their own lusts, "And saying, Where is the promise of his coming? for since the fathers fell asleep, all things continue as they were from the beginning of the creation" (2 Pet. 3:4).

My friends, when someone mockingly asks you where is the sign of His coming — saying, in effect, I don't see these signs; I don't believe Jesus is coming again for the saints; I don't believe in the Rapture; I don't believe in Bible prophecy — they are in reality bringing to pass Peter's prophecy that in the last days scoffers would come on the scene.

Because this sign of prophecy — the scoffers — is so prevalent today, we know that Jesus Christ is coming soon. Where in the history of the Christian church has prophecy been so scoffed at and scorned? God warned us that this would be so.

I can understand how unbelievers can be skeptical. But how can Christians, who say they believe God's Word, refuse to accept the one-third of the Bible that consists of prophecy? Maybe they don't want to know what the future holds.

Some preachers are saying that Christians will rise to a place of prominence across this nation, and there will be a great revival involving tremendous numbers of people. They will tell you that, as a result, a one-world religion based on Christianity will emerge.

That is true, in part, because there will come a time when every knee will bow and every tongue confess "that Jesus Christ is Lord to the glory of God the Father" (Phil. 2:10-11). But, before that great and wonderful day when Jesus Christ comes to rule and reign, there will come a ghastly tribulation. Jesus himself said in Matthew,

> "For then shall be great tribulation, such as was not since the beginning of the world to this time, no, nor ever shall be. And except those days should be shortened, there should no flesh be saved: but for the elect's sake those days shall be shortened" (24:21-22).

The bloodshed, the horror, of those days will be so great that if it were not for Christ's personal return, no flesh would be spared.

In 2 Thessalonians 2:3, the apostle Paul told us that just before Jesus comes to gather up the saints, there will be a great falling away. That great falling away has already happened, and it continues today.

Another word for "a great falling away" is *apostasia* or apostasy, which is the lie that Bible prophecy has either already happened or is not true or is merely allegory — a fantasy to be accepted only by the gullible. Be careful, my friends, when someone devalues the importance of biblical prophecy.

God's Word says "a strong delusion" will fall on those who reject Jesus, so that they will believe the lie. These deluded ones will be eternally damned. Don't believe the lie. Do not believe the Antichrist's agents who are all around us today. Choose to believe, instead, the Word of God.

When Jesus was tempted three times by Satan in the wilderness, He answered the Devil with Scripture. Remember, the Word of God is "quick, and powerful, and sharper than any two-edged sword . . . a discerner of the thoughts and intents of the heart" (Heb. 4:12).

The night is surely coming. It's almost here. We need to understand that the New Age could well be the last age.

The Devil's Timetable

We don't know if Jesus Christ is coming next month or next year or in the next few minutes, but we do know that these undoubtedly are the last days. God has His own timetable, and all this could begin winding up this year, next year, or tomorrow.

It could wrap up by the year 2000, which is, by the way, the year the Devil proposes to bring his plan to fruition. Satan's New Agers and the occult world today are planning that by the year 2000, their New Age occult kingdom will be fully in place on planet earth and the New Age messiah will be in charge of this world. But, that's the Devil's timetable, not God's.

We need to know more about God's timetable. Let us understand that all these events, the wrapping up of human history, will not take place until God so decides. Regardless of what Satan wants — and Satan apparently wants to wrap it all up by the year 2000 — he might or might not get what he wants.

The New Age religion is based on a "force" god, a "universal consciousness," and on false bibles like the *Satanic Bible*, *The Keys of Enoch*, the books *God Calling*, *The Aquarian Gospel of Jesus Christ*, and many others.

Of this Antichrist, the Bible answers the question, "Who shall this evil one, this last days' dictator honor?" He shall "honour the God of forces: and a god whom his fathers knew not shall he honour with gold, and silver, and with precious stones, and pleasant things" (Dan. 11:38).

We see today an explosion of signs and wonders and miracles, some by God, many by Satan. God help us and give us the spirit of discernment — the gift of discernment — so we can determine which is which.

The New Age religion promotes world unity — a one-world government and a one-world religion. New Agers tell Christians, "Forget your doctrines; let's all have unity." Unity without Jesus, however, is unity under Lucifer. There can only be peace on earth, goodwill, harmony, justice, and sharing when Jesus Christ comes to rule. Any other unity, man-made or Devil made, will bring us under the control of Satan.

What is the New Age Plan?

Vera Alder, in her book *When Humanity Comes of Age* — a prominent New Age document — says, "There is actually a plan. World unity is the goal. The world plan includes a world organization, a world economy, a world religion."

John Randolph Price put together the World Instant of Cooperation, also called World Healing Day and World Meditation Day. He says 875 million New Agers meditated simultaneously to invoke the New Age kingdom to materialize. According to Mr. Price, the revolution has begun and, throughout the world, men and women are coming forward to be counted as part of a new race — a new race that will someday rule the universe. Price then eloquently states: "Now we can co-create the future according to the divine plan."

Benjamin Creme is a self-styled John the Baptist for a New Age christ called the Lord Maitreya. According to Creme, the plan includes the installation of a new world government and a new world religion under Lord Maitreya.

A satanic plan to deceive and to seize dominion of planet earth is in the works. A far greater plan — the great divine plan — to bring forth the most wonderful kingdom that has ever existed, the kingdom of Jesus Christ, is also coming soon.

But, there is more to the New Age plan — something more ominous and dangerous than the formation of a world religious system. The plan calls for the death, killing, and mass murder of every Christian believer.

Low Life Forms

Moira Timms, who has written a prophecy book for the New Age, says: "The stormy channel from this age of sorrows to the New Age cannot be navigated by life forms of unrefined vibrations. This is the law."

Who are these "life forms of unrefined vibration?" Christians, of course. Unable to acknowledge that we are human beings created in the image of God, Timms believes we cannot be allowed to exist.

According to those in the New Age, Christians are of a lower spiritual race. That's why the Maharishi Mahesh Yogi, grand guru of Transcendental Meditation, has told his followers, "There has not been, and there will not be, a place for the unfit. The fit will lead, and if the unfit are not coming along, there is no place for them."

The Maharishi Mahesh Yogi then says, "In the age of enlightenment, there is no place for ignorant people. Nonexistence of the unfit has been the law of nature."

Christians are apparently the unfit because we believe that Jesus was correct and truthful when He said, "I am the way, the truth and the life." If that makes us life forms of unrefined vibrations, ignorant and unfit, let us tell those in the New Age to do whatever their master, Satan, requires that they do. As for us, we will follow and serve Jesus Christ.

New Age Christian Haters

Ruth Montgomery, who has been called the "Herald of the New Age," said that great chaos is coming. She says there is going to be a shift about the year 2000, and those who survive the shift will be a different type people from those today. The souls of those people who help to create the chaos of the present century will have passed into spirit, in which state they will have to rethink their attitudes. There is going to come, as she calls it, "a cleaning process for Mother Earth."

Ruth Montgomery's demon spirit guides told her that certain people, such as fundamentalist Christians, are negative — that is, not attuned to the philosophies of the New Age. We, therefore, must pass into spirit to rethink our attitudes. She says, "Millions will survive and millions won't. Those who don't will go into the spirit state."

Ms. Montgomery is right about one thing: Christians will go into the spirit state. Those who know Jesus Christ as Saviour and Lord are going right up into heaven to be with Jesus, according to 2 Thessalonians. We won't be here. Christians will indeed leave this judgment-bound planet. But, she's wrong about the rethinking of our attitudes. In fact, we'll be more convinced than ever when we see and know Jesus as He is and reign and rule with Him forever!

Why would a New Age leader tell millions of followers that we Christians will not survive? Ruth Montgomery's opinion of Christian fundamentalists provides the answer. She says, "So many are ignorant, with closed minds and little education, that they fail to realize the close relationship between ancient Eastern religion and that which Christ brought to the world. They fail to understand that we are all one." And, she says of you and me as Christians, "Unless they can accept that basic premise, they will continue along their bigoted, ever-narrowing path that leads to nowhere."

Montgomery is not the only Christian-hater involved in the New Age. There are many who sound a continual drumbeat of bigotry. Just as in Hitler's day, a particular group has been selected for persecution — today it's the group known as fundamentalist Christians.

Hate Without Cause

Jesus himself was no stranger to persecution or the fanatical hatred of Satan's followers. In John 15:18-19, the Lord Jesus Christ says:

> If the world hate you, ye know that it hated me before it hated you. If ye were of the world, the world would love his own: but because ye are not of the world, but I have chosen you out of the world, therefore, the world hateth you.

Christians, the world hates you. You say you want to be loved, you want to be liked? No, my friends, we are at enmity with the world. Jesus said that if the world hates Him, it will certainly hate you, too. In John 15:20-25, Jesus says:

> Remember . . . that I said unto you, The servant
> is not greater than his lord. If they have persecuted
> me, they will also persecute you; if they have kept my
> saying, they will keep yours also. But all these things
> will they do unto you for my name's sake, because
> they know not him that sent me. If I had not come and
> spoken unto them, they had not had sin: but now
> they have no cloak for their sin. He that hateth me
> hateth my Father also. If I had not done among them
> the works which none other man did, they had not
> had sin: but now they have both seen and hated both
> me and my Father. But this cometh to pass, that the
> word might be fulfilled that is written in their law,
> They hated me without a cause.

People in the New Age today deny Jesus Christ, and, thereby, they hate Him without a cause. Because they hate Him, they will hate you, for the servant is not greater than the master.

Jesus tells us in John 16:2-4:

> They shall put you out of the synagogues: yea,
> the time cometh, that whosoever killeth you will
> think that he doeth God service. And these things
> will they do unto you, because they have not known
> the Father, nor me. But these things have I told you,
> that when the time shall come, ye may remember that
> I told you of them . . . .

Yes, Jesus told us that these things would come upon the world. They would come upon Christians. He told us they would happen, and they will happen because God's Word is always true.

The night is coming.

The Coming Persecution

My fellow Christians, there is coming a dreadful and horrible time when people will be put to death for their faith in Jesus Christ. As a matter of fact, people in some areas of the world are being persecuted today for that very reason. And, the people who are brutalizing and killing actually believe they are doing God a service.

Be assured by this, however: Jesus promised that we who belong to Him are not reserved for the wrath that is to come. He alone is our salvation. God has always come to the rescue of His children.

This does not mean that we will not suffer persecution. But we do know, from the prophetic Word, that the great wrath that is to come will fall upon people who have rejected Jesus Christ as Saviour and Lord. During a seven-year period of unprecedented tribulation, God will send His righteous judgment on a world that has rejected Him. If you have accepted Jesus Christ, if you know Him as Lord and Saviour, God is not going to punish you. You are His child for eternity.

As the New Age Kingdom's influence and power increase and this world system swiftly transfers into the hands of the New Age messiah who institutes the Mystery Babylon religion, God will rain His wrath upon this satanically-controlled planet. I believe that as Satan's people begin their campaign — their brutal purging of Christians — the great anger of God Almighty will be kindled.

God loves us, and when He sees persecution beginning to overtake His children, I believe the Rapture will take place. When Christians are gone from earth, then God's great judgment and punishment will fall on this world.

Revelation 13 tells us very clearly that in the last days, all the world will worship the Beast and the Beast will war with and overcome the saints. But, we are assured of this one wonderful Truth: Just as this world religion, this one-world economy, this one-world political system emerges and solidifies and begins a chaotic period of intense persecution of the saints of God, Jesus Christ himself will come like a whirlwind from heaven. We are told in the Bible that He will come in the clouds and that He will rapture up the saints.

> In a moment, in the twinkling of an eye, at the last trump: for the trumpet shall sound, and the dead shall be raised incorruptible, and we shall be changed (1 Cor. 15:52).

In the twinkling of an eye, all believers will be caught up — the Rapture! My belief is based on the wonderful, inerrant, powerful Word of the Living God. You can count on His promises.

> For the Lord himself shall descend from heaven with a shout, with the voice of the archangel, and with the trump of God: and the dead in Christ shall rise first: Then we which are alive and remain shall be caught up together with them in the clouds, to meet the Lord in the air: and so shall we ever be with the Lord (1 Thess. 4:16-17).

The dead will rise from their graves, and then we who are alive on earth will be caught up in the air with them. We will meet Jesus in the air and will forevermore be with Him.

Let me repeat. I'm not saying you won't go through any persecution at all. But, I do believe this: We who are Christians today are not going to be here during that seven-year period of horror when the Antichrist comes to full power.

During that time, the world will go through an awful purification and cleansing process as the Antichrist makes an all-out attempt to stamp out any and all vestiges of Christianity. This most terrible tyrant in history will persecute those who will not worship his image — the image of the Beast. I believe Scripture tells us that we who are now Christians will be with our Lord while these genocidal atrocities are taking place.

In spite of the horrendous persecution, many will accept Jesus even during the Great Tribulation period.

If you are reading this, and you haven't put your faith in Jesus, it is just possible that you will turn to God in those terrible days, having remembered things we are now talking about. I want to repeat some wonderful words of Jesus:

> "I am the resurrection, and the life: he that believeth in me, though he were dead, yet shall he live: And whosoever liveth and believeth in me shall never die . . ." (John 11:25-26).

Putting a Stop to Christianity

How do New Agers view Christianity? Do they take a passive, complacent attitude toward believers who consider Jesus Christ the only way to God? Read what they have to say.

Timothy Leary, a New Age expert whom you may remember as the LSD guru, says, "Many problems we face today are caused by fundamentalist religion. Middle East crises, terrorism, the current war-like atmosphere based on fanaticism — this is the familiar position taken by the right-wing Christian." He says that we are, "psychopathic, paranoid, weird."

Bhagwan Shree Rajneesh, a Hindu guru and New Age leader has said: "The fundamentalist Christians are the worst Christians. They are the most fanatic people. They believe that Christianity is the only religion. All other religions are wrong, and they believe that the whole world should be turned toward Christianity. These are very primitive ideas."

Jesus Christ said:

> "Enter ye in at the strait gate: for wide is the gate, and broad is the way, that leadeth to destruction, and many there be which go in thereat: Because strait is the gate, and narrow is the way, which leadeth unto life, and few there be that find it" (Matt. 7:13-14).

The path that leads to God is not broad. It is very narrow. No wonder, in terms of the world, we must, indeed, appear "weird."

Psychologist Robert Anton Wilson, author of the books, *The Illuminati Papers; Sex and Drugs;* and *Cosmic Trigger,* roundly denounced Christian fundamentalists in a recent interview. If you are a moderate or a liberal Christian, however, you are perfectly acceptable in the New Age.

The problem is, however, there is no such thing as a moderate or a liberal Christian. To be a true disciple of Jesus Christ, you must believe the fundamentals.

What are those fundamentals? Jesus Christ came to this earth. He cloaked himself in humanity, yet He was God. He is God, today. Just as He ascended to heaven, He is going to return to this earth. He loves us. He died on the Cross for us.

Those are the fundamentals of the faith. So, I am a Christian fundamentalist. I am proud of it and praise Jesus Christ that, even though I was wicked and corrupt and undeserving, He loved me enough to die for my sin. And He loves you, too. If that makes me "weird," then I am weird. I do believe Jesus Christ is the only Way.

Robert Anton Wilson says: "Fundamentalism of all sorts is conducive to stupidity. And, it interferes with the proper functioning of intelligence, creativity, and joy and having a good time." In his book *The New Inquisition*, Wilson accuses Christian fundamentalists of being extremists and says that to correct this extremism, the more enlightened people of the planet — as he calls them — "... might have to rise up and put a stop to it." He says: "I think the 90s are going to bring back radical change."

Their intention is to "put a stop" to us witnessing about Jesus Christ! What will happen to Christians if the New Agers have their way? The New Age leaders have made their goals and intentions clear.

Heaven on Earth?

A man who calls himself "Pastor" Roger Hight of the New Age Assembly in Corpus Christi, Texas, believes in the occult, yet calls himself a Christian. He says, "We have been given a black eye long enough by ignorant and superstitious people," meaning fundamentalist Christians. He goes on to say, "I pray most heartily that during this, the Aquarian Age, people will mature, understand the laws that govern their being, and begin to live by them so that the race-consciousness will reach a state whereby heaven and earth shall become one."

You see, they don't believe in the Rapture, when true believers go to be with Jesus in heaven. Instead, they think their "christ" is going to come, put his feet on planet earth, and that heaven and earth will become one. Of course, their heaven is Satan's demon world; their christ is the Antichrist.

That is why my good friend, Dave Hunt, has written a book called *Whatever Happened to Heaven?* Heaven is our hope. The apostle John told us in the Book of Revelation about the sea of glass and the beauty of heaven, the dwelling place of Almighty God and His true saints.

New Agers say that this earth will become heaven because heaven and earth will become one. It is true that eventually God will reconcile all things to himself. He will bring things to consummation, not the New Age way, but exactly the way He has foretold in His Holy Word.

The New Age believes you are a dangerous rebel against the world, Christian friend. Why? Because you believe that Jesus Christ is going to come and reign a thousand years on the earth.

Margot Adler, a pagan advocate who promotes witchcraft, says: "The fundamentalist impulse coupled with the inevitable rise of apocalyptic millennialism, these things, as we approach the year 2000, are, along with nuclear waste, the most dangerous things facing the human race. Most fundamentalists," Adler says, "are at war with the diversity of life and ideas."

You are at war with the diversity of life because you believe in the narrow pathway to God and the millenial rule of Jesus Christ on the earth. When you accepted Jesus, you made yourself a rebel in the deluded eyes of the world. They intend to put down the insurrection they believe Christians are causing.

Eliminating Christians

Djwhal Khul, a spirit guide who has been called the "Tibetan Master," has dictated twenty-four books to Alice Bailey of the Lucis Trust, formerly known as Lucifer Publishing Company. Khul said this about the New Age goal concerning Christians: "The fetus of the new humanity is already stirring in the womb of time, and like the human mother, humanity must learn to eliminate its waste materials and poisons."

In his dictation to Alice Bailey, Khul further says, "A violent streptococcic germ and an infection makes its presence felt in infected areas of the bodies of humanity."

Then, this demon chieftain, who is dictating books, articles, and even music to New Agers today, says something very significant. "Another surgical operation may be necessary to dissipate this infection and get rid of the fever." What does he mean when he suggests the likelihood of need for *another* surgical operation?

Others have tried to eliminate Christianity: Nero's persecution of the early church; the Great Inquisition by the Catholic Church; Hitler in Nazi Germany; Communist leaders in China and the former Soviet Union. Church history is replete with accounts of the torture and massacre of believers.

Adolph Hitler, an occultist (in effect, a New Ager), who frequented occultic bookstores in Nazi Germany, formed the S.S., which was nothing less than a satanic cult group. Hitler wanted to kill the Jews primarily because he wanted to prevent Bible prophecy from coming to pass. God in His omniscience and omnipotence, however, turned the Third Reich's attempt to wipe the Jews into fulfillment of prophecy.

At the close of World War II, the world was so aghast at the Nazi atrocities against the Jews that there arose a universal outcry. As a result, the Jews were allowed to regather and re-establish their nation in their rightful homeland. Because people felt so sorry about what had happened to the Jews, the nation of Israel exists again today. In attempting to thwart and defeat Bible prophecy, Adolph Hitler actually was instrumental in bringing Bible prophecy to pass.

Hitler's surgical operation was not sufficient. Therefore, this demon, Djwhal Khul, is telling us that another such surgical procedure may be necessary.

All such satanic attempts have failed. Why? Because God's Word, His influence, and His power are always brought to pass on planet earth regardless of the efforts of Satan, his legion of demons, and his human agents. They cannot stamp us out, friends; there will always be the influence of the Holy Spirit on earth.

Djwhal Khul goes on to say, "When a life form proves inadequate or too diseased, or too crippled, it is, from the point of view of the hierarchy, no disaster when that life form has to go."

In their estimation, Christians are too diseased and too mentally and spiritually crippled to be of use. So, the hierarchy — that is, the demon hierarchy — believes it will not be disastrous when we have to go. They are talking about killing us.

Deciding Who Dies

Is death something good in the New Age? Let us examine what Djwhal Khul says about the subject. "Death is not a disaster to be feared. The work of the Destroyer is not really cruel or undesirable."

Think about that for a moment, friends. Djwhal Khul, demon author of twenty-four books that have sold in the millions around this globe, bestsellers in New Age bookstores, said this: "The work of the Destroyer is not really cruel or undesirable; therefore, there is much destruction permitted by the custodians of the Plan, and much evil turned into good."

That quote says quite a lot about New Age philosophy,

does it not? Death is okay as long as it fits into the plans of those who have the power to decide who lives and who dies. But such a philosophy is nothing new to the Eastern religion of Hinduism, the source of New Age teaching.

Well over 150 years ago, when the British in effect colonized India, a British officer wrote to his government about certain, despicable practices among the Hindus, especially the Khans people: "The Khans are keeping men and women as we keep pigs. They raise and fatten them until the time comes for a sacrifice. Then, the victims are cut to pieces while alive, and their flesh offered to the Earth Goddess. These victims, called Mariahs, are allowed to marry and have children, who themselves become victims in their turn."

This officer forced the Hindu Khans sect to end the keeping of men and women, the Mariahs, as pigs, and stopped the ritual of offering them up for sacrifice to their Mother Goddess.

Friends, the Mother Goddess has returned. You see bumper stickers that read: "Heal Mother Earth." They call it the Gaea Politics. Yes, the Mother Goddess has indeed returned, and that is why ungodly, liberal feminism runs rampant in America today. This Hindu, Babylonian Mother Goddess, is back!

In ancient Egypt, she was called Isis. Rome had its Venus, the goddess Demeter. You remember Diana of the Ephesians from accounts given in the book of Acts. They still worship Mother Kali today in India. She is pictured with a necklace of skulls because she is the Mother Goddess of life and death. We are witnessing today the return of Mystery Babylon in Mother Kali as well as in many other manifestations of this Mother Goddess.

Blood, Disruption, Chaos

Christopher Hyatt, head of the Order of the Golden Dawn — whose symbol is a satanic triangle combined with a satanic circle — is saying Christians must be annihilated before the New Age can come to full power! Because the fundamentalist forces of Christianity are attempting to enforce their dogma, he says, they must be overcome. According to Hyatt, there is going to be a changing of the guards.

The guards of the ancient era [Christians], the

ones dying right now, are not willing to give up their authority so easily. I foresee, on a mass scale, that the New Age is not going to come into being as so many people believe and wish to believe. I see it as requiring a heck of a lot of blood, disruption, chaos and pain for a mass change to occur.

How did Christopher Hyatt, this prominent New Age leader, propose this changing of the guards take place? He said: "I see that the earth still requires some blood before it is ready to move into new and different areas."

According to New Age doctrine, bloodshed is going to come and be used to heal and cleanse Mother Earth of negative Christian influences.

Djwhal Khul has said of this cleansing: "Your earth's immune system is now critically dysfunctional. And, it is not inaccurate to describe the consciousness of your earth as that of victim. Therefore, toward its own survival, the earth seeks a cleansing, a transformation into health."

In *Parade Magazine*, August 9, 1987, writer B. J. Williams did an article titled "Head Trip." Quoting New Age spokesman Ken Ires, he writes: "Those who cannot be enlightened will not be permitted to dwell in this world."

Where are we going to go? Ires' answer: "They will be sent to some equally appropriate place to work their way to understanding."

I think I understand! He is saying we are not going to be permitted to dwell in this world. And no wonder! Because this is going to be Satan's domain.

What Mr. Ires does not know is that God's wrath is going to fall on a wicked, unrighteous, and unrepentant world when the saints of God are raptured. Christians will be long gone, living in eternal bliss in the presence of our Holy and Righteous God. And we won't have to return to this world until Jesus Christ comes to reign for a thousand years.

Why Us?

You might be asking, "Why us? Why Christians? Why has Satan and his New Age leaders targeted Christians for destruction?"

Why would John Randolph Price's spirit guide, Asher, say that two and one-half billion people might have to be slaughtered, wiped off the face of the earth? Why would Djwhal Khul say that one-third of humanity must pass away by the year 1999 for the New Age kingdom to come to pass?

And, why is it always the Christians — the *true*, Christian, fundamentalist believers — who are targeted for destruction by the New Age? Incidentally, the Jews are also targeted, because Satan has always hated the Jews. Today, Satan considers Christians and Jews in the same malicious way. He seeks to destroy both groups.

There is a revival of Nazism today in the New Age. Their beliefs coincide with Hitler's because they are led by the same spirit that has been with the Hindus and other Eastern religions throughout history.

Maharishi Mahesh Yogi, who has tens of thousands of supporters in America, has said that "nonexistence of the unfit has been the law of nature." We know that nature itself needs to be redeemed by God, but that's not what Maharishi meant.

Karl Binding, the German pre-Nazi guru, a man with a Doctorate of Laws who inspired Adolph Hitler, said the same thing: "As society progresses in a spiral, we will again come to see the higher morality of destroying the unfit."

Is there a difference between the philosophy of Binding and Hitler and that of the Maharishi Mahesh Yogi? Aren't they both saying that the unfit must not be on planet earth — that there is no place for them?

Jesus said they would kill us and "thinketh that they do God a service." To kill Christians or Jews is a holy act, Satan tells New Agers.

You see, in terms of the New Age, we are not the children of light, despite the fact that Jesus said we are the light of the world and He is the light of this world. According to the New Age, we are not the light but the darkness.

Satan turns everything around. He turns truth on its head. Truth becomes lie, and lies become truth. The Devil is the "author of confusion." I show in *Mystery Mark of the New Age* that the New Age believes we fundamentalist Christians are the sons of darkness.

One New Age leader, for example, has said there will be

wars between the sons of light (those of the New Age) and the sons of darkness, and from these wars will come a New Age on this planet.

John Randolph Price belongs to the Planetary Commission, a primary New Age group. Price, who has been led by his spirit guides, Asher and Quartus, was asked in one of his books: Who is the Antichrist? He answers that the Antichrist is "any individual or group who denies the divinity of man."

If you, fellow Christian, say that God alone is divine and that man is His servant, according to John Randolph Price's definition, you are of the Antichrist!

Our Bible applies a completely different definition to Antichrist. John, the Apostle, told us this in God's Holy Word: "He that denieth that Jesus is the Christ is of the Antichrist."

People of the New Age believe that Jesus was a christ. Mohammed was *a* christ. Buddah was *a* christ. The people of the New Age say that we are all christs, that we all have the "christ consciousness." But, they refuse to admit and confess and profess that Jesus is Lord of all — that He is *the* Christ.

They hate us because, as Christians, we know we are not gods. We serve the one, true God. And, the Bible tells us very clearly that Jesus is the name above every name.

> Wherefore God also hath highly exalted him, and given him a name which is above every name: That at the name of Jesus every knee should bow, of things in heaven, and things in earth, and things under the earth; And that every tongue should confess that Jesus Christ is Lord, to the glory of God the Father (Phil. 2:9-11).

The Aquarian Race Theory

Those of the New Age believe Christians should be exterminated for another reason. According to their Aquarian Race Theory, we are spiritually inferior.

The New Age doctrine promotes the idea that man has been transforming over the centuries through evolution. The last great stop of evolution will be, they proclaim, when man takes a quantum leap in consciousness, and, through his own mind-powers, becomes a god. As a god, he no longer needs the other God. Man *is* god.

All of mankind, they believe, is collectively god under the Aquarian Race. The highest race of man to this point in history, they say, has been the Aryan race. Sound familiar?

You will remember that Adolph Hitler also elevated the Aryan race above all others and believed that Aryans alone were fit to become the Aquarian god-men. The Fuehrer, therefore, decreed that those who were not of Aryan race be exterminated.

New Agers believe that man can finally evolve, leap into a new consciousness, catapult to a man-god status, and become a member of the new Divine Species known as Aquarian Man.

If one is not fit to become an Aquarian, if one is not ready, if one is not spiritually prepared, one is unfit for the New Age kingdom and considered a spiritually-inferior species.

✝ The World's Troublemakers

The New Age philosophy says killing Christians would be a holy act because we are said to be the world's troublemakers.

Jesus said we are the peacemakers and that the meek shall inherit the earth. What is a "meek" person? In Jesus' definition, it is a person who is willing to yield his or her will to Him. We become meek, and in becoming meek and receptive to the will of Christ, God works through us to do mighty things to His honor and His glory.

New Age leaders blame Christians for the problems facing the world. The Middle East crises, terrorism, war — all are attributable to the fact that fundamental Christianity claims to be the only way to God. They consider us the bigoted troublemakers of the world because we believe Jesus Christ is *the* way, *the* truth, and *the* life, and that no one comes to the Father but by Him.

In the *Satanic Bible,* Anton LaVey, head of the Church of Satan, says that human sacrifice is wrong except in one instance: if somebody makes trouble for you. And, the New Age believes, of course, that we are troublemakers.

Because we as Christians confess Jesus and Him exclusively, we set ourselves apart by living lives of holiness and righteousness in the midst of "a crooked and perverse nation." We who love the Lord Jesus with all our heart and seek to obey

His commands do not straddle fences. But as His disciples, we can expect hatred and persecution from the world. The apostle Paul told Timothy, "All that will live godly in Christ Jesus shall suffer persecution" (2 Tim. 3:12).

Christians, it is time to stop straddling the fence. God tells us in the Old Testament, if He is God, then serve Him. If Baal (the false god-system) be God, then serve him. Jesus said a person is either for Him or against Him. You must choose this day, this moment, whom you will serve.

Salt and Light

Satan is the lord of this world, but we are the representatives of Jesus Christ. When we let Christ's light shine through us, we praise and worship and witness to those in darkness about God's love for them. It is understandable that Satan is desperate to stamp us out. His one ravening desire is to destroy and extinguish that Light.

Because God's Holy Spirit dwells within believers, Jesus said His disciples are the "salt of the earth." Salt preserves, by preventing decay and corruption. It delays the onset of decomposition.

Satan and his New Age system of delusion want to keep the souls of fallen mankind from the Light of Jesus Christ. The preservative against total evil must, therefore, be removed before Satan can freely do his deadly work. The "salt of the earth" must be exterminated.

How is it possible that Satan could actually inspire people to kill Christians, Jews, and others? It seems incredible! Many in the New Age say they are for peace and love and harmony. How could these people be transformed into mass-murderers when this New Age kingdom and the New Age messiah come to power?

Because the New Age is based on satanism, there comes a point when New Agers are no longer in control of their minds. When God withdraws His influence, their minds become reprobate. That is why there will come a time when they will believe the number 666 is a holy and sacred number.

You say, "Hold it! You mean the number 666 will be considered a holy number?!" In *The Mystery Mark of the New Age,* I quote many in the New Age who believe that 666 is the number that will be used to do good in the world.

Many in the New Age believe they will be given a mark in their forehead or in their right hand that will be, not the mark of eternal damnation, but a good, holy sign. Satan is warping the minds of these people just as God's Word told us he would.

All shall worship the Beast, the Bible says in Revelation 13 — all but those who refuse the mark and whose names are written in the Lamb's Book of Life.

An Angel of Light

The New Age video, *Invocation of my Demon Brother*, also goes by the name, *Lucifer Rising*. With the help of Mick Jagger of the Rolling Stones, this demonic production surges with mystical, evil power. Film makers have referred to it as "The shadowing forth of Lord Lucifer as the powers gather at a midnight mass."

Another New Age authority praises this remarkable production and says, "It's a film about the love generation — the birthday party of the Aquarian Age — showing actual ceremonies to make Lucifer rise."

How do you think Lucifer is presented in *Lucifer Rising?* As the god of hate and anger and murder that he is? Of course not. Instead, he is presented as the god of light.

The Bible tells us Satan will come not as the evil god, but he will come as an "angel of light." His agents here on earth, his followers, will appear to be ministers of righteousness.

In the book of Jude, we are told to anticipate these people coming on the scene. Described as "spots in your feasts of charity" who are like clouds without water and trees without fruit. They look good, but they have no substance and produce only death, disobedience, and destruction.

Few people willingly serve Satan. How then does he attract his followers? By deception. Many in the New Age today simply do not realize they have been deluded. Because they do not know God's Word, they actually think they are serving the true God. Many would be appalled to learn they are serving the father of all lies — Satan himself!

Shock Troops

Foster Bailey of the Lucis Trust, who wrote the New Age

book *Things To Come,* has a name for those who will participate in the coming New Age kingdom — shock troops. He says, "You can become part of the now forming, inner group, which has been called Christ's own people. This special group, in training now, are the shock troops of the coming Aquarian Age."

Hitler called his blitzkrieg wave of soldiers "shock troops."

Through Benjamin Creme, Lord Maitreya has declared: "My army of light is assembled. It is ready. Banners flying, eyes uplifted, they march forward into the future, into the light."

This false christ promises to burst forth at any moment to proclaim that the New Age kingdom has arrived. His army is on the move, and he beckons people, saying: "Join those who are on the side of light, who are on the side of truth and freedom and justice. Join my vanguard and show the way. My army has made its plan, and soon will follow results. A new hope seizes mankind."

Why does Satan want his army of darkness to fight? What is it being summoned to do? Why will they kill and pillage and plunder?

Here is what Lord Maitreya reveals: "Will you take your place in this great work and fulfill the world's need? There is no higher call than that to serve the world." This great army of darkness is going to fight to serve the world and Satan, the lord of this world.

We know by Maitreya's own words that they serve Satan and not the true God. He said there is no greater calling then to serve the world. Satan is the prince of the power of the air, this earthly realm. But, Jesus Christ, God himself, told Pontius Pilate, "My kingdom is not of this world."

This "Rainbow Army of the New Age" will attempt to put together the one-world order and one-world religion of the New Age. By killing the Christian resisters, they will be serving the world for the lord of this world.

Why would a person willingly enlist in Satan's army of darkness? How can one possibly put on the Devil's uniforms and serve him without resistance? What kind of people are they?

Many of those who killed the Jews in German concentration camps were apparently considered good people at the outset of World War II or before. They didn't start out as butchers, murderers, executioners, and torturers. Satan confused their minds, subtly, insidiously. Led by Adolph Hitler and his henchmen, their minds became clouded through delusion given by Lucifer.

The Bible tells us this genocidal madness is going to happen again. Look at the soldiers of darkness, and see how Satan is inspiring his army to come forth and seize this world. Their purpose is to help his New Age dictator form a one-world government and a one-world religion. Like Hitler's S.S., the Beast's soldiers of darkness will vilely persecute those who refuse to worship his image.

The Cosmic Secret Service

A demon spirit, who calls himself "Orion," came to Elizabeth Clare Prophet, one of the primary New Age leaders and head of the Church Universal and Triumphant.

In order to stir up the spirit of the New Age believers, Orion said: "I am a devotee of freedom, and I am proud to be called a patriot of life. Patriots, I summon you into the service of the light. In my house of light, you will find mementos of patriots of every nation who have won for the cause of the great white brotherhood, some noble gain for the Aquarian cycle, for the soul of humanity."

Reading in depth what Orion has said to the world through Elizabeth Clare Prophet leads one to realize that his master is the lord of this world. He also says he is Sanat Kumara, a code name the New Agers use for their lord and master, Satan.

Elizabeth Clare Prophet says there is yet another spirit, an ascended master, that has come to her and who uses the code name K-17. Sounds 007 James Bondish, doesn't it? And, even more coincidentally, K-17, this ascended master from beyond, has said through Elizabeth Clare Prophet that he serves in the Cosmic Secret Service.

Such statements would be laughable were it not for the fact that Elizabeth Clare Prophet has built an international organization reportedly with more than 300,000 devoted, deluded followers. She takes in millions of dollars, operates a national TV ministry, and publishes books that sell hundreds of thousands of copies and can be found in all the major bookstores across America. These books have such blasphe-mous titles as *The Lost Teachings of Jesus.*

The successful ministry of Elizabeth Clare Prophet is a classic example of how the coming Antichrist is going to be able to manipulate, to mesmerize, to control men's minds through mass hypnosis just as Hitler did a few decades ago.

K-17, this agent of the Cosmic Secret Service, says he is going to help raise the feminine ray in this age. I am convinced he will do so. The feminine ray apparently activates the Mother Goddess, Mystery Babylon, Mother of Harlots, Abominations of the Earth. Ultimately, it will become the worldwide Church of Satan described in Revelation 17.

K-17 says, "Also with me are angels of light, angels who guard the secret destiny of every nation, the destiny of America and the destiny of the soul."

Infiltrating America's Armed Forces

New Age authority Donald Keys, a United Nations lobby-ist and a top official with a New Age group called Planetary Citizens, co-authored the New Age Manifesto called *Planetary Initiative for the World We Choose.*

In his bestselling book, *Earth and Omega,* Keys makes this statement, "We must go forth and planetize the earth." He says you can become a steward of earth, a mid-wife of the new era, a warrior for peace. You can become a *change agent.* Keys also says, "The call is out for world warriors similar to the union blue, bereted U. N. peacekeeping soldiers. Their perimeter is the globe."

Another New Age authority has said: "We are a team, a united team, working together for personal and planetary awakening. Why? To bring forth the larger plan," he says.

Yes, there is a New Age army, the Devil's army, the army of the adversary. They will come forth fully supported by Satan's demons so that the Great Invocation of Satan can be fulfilled. "Let light and love and power and death fulfill the purpose of the coming one."

Dr. Michael Aquino, who led a San Francisco group called The Temple of Set and now heads the Church of Satan is a Lt. Colonel in the U.S. Army. Michael Aquino admits he is a Satanist, yet he has a top secret government clearance! In fact, he oversees the Federal Records Center in St. Louis, Missouri, where the records of all military personnel are stored. It's frightening to think that a man of his background and present status should have such a nationally vital and sensitive responsibility.

How about a New Age Army? The very prestigious Army War College, looking to move in that direction has formed a First Earth Battalion, led by Lt. Col. Jim Channon.

Many military men and women have written me about the sinister, diabolical things going on in the U.S. military. Buddhist priests have become chaplains in our Armed Forces. Witches in the military are now demanding their rights, saying chaplains should be provided for their contingent.

As a former regular Air Force Officer, it distresses me to say I believe the United States military will be used someday, perhaps very soon, for evil purposes. I wish it could be otherwise, but I cannot deny the facts or the prophecies of Scripture.

Satan wants to control our Armed Forces and apparently believes that, if he can do so, eventually he can use our military to terrorize, torture, and persecute the people of God. We must pray diligently for our men and women in uniform and those who lead them.

I love the United States of America and believe this nation is the last great hope of mankind, in human terms. Because we have been so blessed with the gospel of Christ in this land, we, who are Christians in America and other free democracies, have the responsibility to witness to the entire world about our Lord.

We must work while there is still day, my friends. Night cometh when no man can work.

Fight to Win

Should we as Christians fight back? Yes, we should fight back. But what should our weapons be?

As the apostle Paul instructed, let us put on the whole armor of God, which includes prayer and God's Word. Let us make our testimony count for the Lord. And, if they come at us, if they begin to persecute us, don't get your guns, my friends. No, don't go off to the mountains and form a paramilitary unit to become guerrilla fighters.

I'll tell you the way to fight and to win. Simply wield God's Word, the sword of the Lord. Let that be your shield.

Jesus Christ won the victory on the cross, and, because of His sacrifice, we are the victors today! We cannot be destroyed. We are eternal beings because we have placed our faith and trust in the one, true Lord and God, Jesus Christ. All the weapons of the world mean absolutely nothing when compared to His omnipotence.

The New Age, indeed, portends frightening things for this planet. What should be our response in light of all we have learned? This is a most important question. How would God have us respond to this New Age challenge?

More than three hundred prophecies in the Old Testament pointed to the coming of Jesus Christ, the Messiah. He came, precisely as prophesied. There are many prophecies pointing to the second coming of Jesus Christ. And every one will be precisely fulfilled.

Revelation 13 and 17 and numerous passages in Daniel and Ezekiel tell of the horrors that are certain to come to pass. The bloodshed will be incredible.

Watching prophecy coming to pass just as God foretold should strengthen, not diminish, your faith. The more I study about the New Age and see Satan at work, the more I am strengthened in the knowledge that he is a pitiful, defeated foe.

For instance, why would Satan choose the number 666, the exact number the New Age is beginning to promote now as a good and holy number? The apostle John warned Christians about the man of sin and his number 666 nearly two thousand years ago. Apparently, Satan has no choice but to have the number attributed to him.

He is already defeated because of the atoning work on the cross by Jesus Christ. Think on these things and know that we who believe in Him are victors in Christ. God is in control, and He cares for and delivers His own.

Have faith in almighty God.

Some would say, have faith in your faith, but the Bible says we must have the kind of faith *in God* that moves mountains. Our faith doesn't move the mountains. God moves the mountains when we have faith that He knows and does what is best for us. Our faith must reside in Him and Him alone.

Have No Fear

God doesn't want us to constantly wring our hands and say, "Oh, woe is us, all these terrible things are happening. They hate us. They are making movies like *The Last Temptation Of Christ* and other New Age-inspired, anti-Christian propaganda. O, woe! Woe is us!"

Despite the evil of the hour in which we live, we are not to have fear.

> Fear not them which kill the body, but are not able to kill the soul: but rather fear him which is able to destroy both soul and body in hell (Matt. 10:28).

Jesus himself told us not to fear those who kill the body, rather, we are to fear Him who can destroy the soul. Only God can decide the destination of your eternal soul — not Satan, only God.

In Romans 8:35:37-39, the apostle Paul tells us:

> Who shall separate us from the love of Christ? shall tribulation, or distress, or persecution, or famine, or nakedness, or peril, or sword?
>
> Nay, in all these things we are more than conquerors through him that loved us. For I am persuaded, that neither death, nor life, nor angels, nor principalities, nor powers, nor things present, nor things to come, Nor height, nor depth, nor any other creature, shall be able to separate us from the love of God, which is in Christ Jesus our Lord.

Think of it; absolutely nothing can separate us. I'm moved by these words. Tears should come to the believer's eyes when he or she reads this majestic, powerful promise of God. Have no fear, Christians, nothing can separate us from the love of God, which is in Christ Jesus our Lord.

Prayer Changes Things

"What good does it do to pray?" you might ask. To begin with, God commands us to communicate, to speak with Him, to worship Him, to praise Him.

> Be careful for nothing; but in every thing by prayer and supplication with thanksgiving let your requests be made known unto God. And the peace of God, which passeth all understanding, shall keep your hearts and minds through Christ Jesus (Phil. 4:6-7).

We pray in simple obedience as an indication that we love God and want to speak with our Heavenly Father. And, despite the fact that God is omniscient — knows all things — His word tells us that "Prayer changes things." Believe me, *prayer changes things*.

We can tell him our fears and our anxieties about the future, asking Him to help us and give us the strength

> Let us therefore come boldly unto the throne of grace, that we may obtain mercy, and find grace to help in time of need (Heb. 4:16).

Do you remember the man in the Bible who said, simply, "Lord, I believe. Help thou mine unbelief?" Many times I have gotten on my knees and said, "Lord, please give me more faith." And, you know what? He does. We can actually pray for and get greater faith. You can ask God for more faith. He will give it to you.

Even when we don't know how to pray, the Holy Spirit will pray for us! We must speak with God. If we draw near to God, He will draw near to us.

You do not want to go through the terrible times that biblical prophecy tells us is surely coming, do you? But how should we pray? Jesus said we should pray that we may be able to escape all that is about to happen. (See Luke 21:36.)

Christian brothers and sisters, I really believe some of us are going to suffer persecution. Even now, believers in some parts of the world are suffering because they love God and believe in His Son, Jesus. I recently read about and saw a picture of a man from Nicaragua. Because he believed in Jesus Christ, the Nicaraguan Communists, the Sandinistas, tied him up and cut off both his ears. Even though they horribly tortured this man, he is still a fervent, dedicated believer in Jesus Christ.

Throughout the world — in Communist China and in certain Moslem-controlled countries — Christians are suffering for the sake of Jesus. Some day soon, though, the time will come when God will put an end to Satan's attacks against God's people. I believe that prayer changes things. We must pray.

We also need to pray for those in the New Age. I honestly do not hate those in the New Age movement; in fact, I have great sympathy for them and pray for them constantly. If they do not acknowledge Jesus Christ as Lord, they will spend eternity in suffering and pain because they have rejected Him. Jesus Christ himself told us:

> Love your enemies, bless them that curse you, do good to them that hate you, and pray for them which despitefully use you, and persecute you (Matt. 5:44).

We must ask God, by His Holy Spirit, to move in the hearts of those who are deceived by Satan's lies. Even though they may do vile, hateful things to us, we should not respond in kind. The best Christian witness you will ever have is when you pray for those who hate you and despitefully use you. I believe that many of these people can be won to Jesus Christ through prayer and by the love and compassion of Christians.

Let Your Light Shine

One pastor told his church that they did not need to be informed about the New Age or what is going on in the occult. He said to study New Age teachings would be doing God a disservice.

I cannot understand that reasoning because the Bible distinctly commands us to be sober and vigilant, for our adversary, the Devil, walks about like a lion, seeking whom he may devour. We are instructed not to be ignorant about Satan's devices. In Ephesians 5:11, we are told to have no part with the works of darkness, but we are to expose and reprove them.

I believe in being an activist in love, witnessing to others about Jesus Christ and His salvation. As we go about our daily lives, we are to warn and to educate others about the dangers of New Age thinking.

We desperately need to witness to those in the New Age. Don't give up hope. They may revile you and laugh at you and call you uncouth and ignorant because you believe Jesus is the one and only way. Just keep witnessing. Let them scorn and scoff. When the Holy Spirit draws one of these New Agers, He will do the work. Our job is simply to witness.

We must let our own light so shine that we glorify our Father in heaven. We are the light of this world because we have Jesus in us. That does not make us Christ; it doesn't make us little gods; it doesn't make us collectively the planet of God. We don't have the Christ consciousness, but we do have the mind of Christ. Even though we still struggle with the flesh-nature, we have become totally new creatures in Christ Jesus.

God expects us to let our light shine in an ever-darkening world where Satan reigns, where the New Age seems to be taking giant leaps of success, where all about us godly restraints seem to be crumbling and hope seems to be almost extinguished.

Hope still lives, my friends. There is still light because the Light of this world cannot be snuffed out. Jesus is that inextinguishable Light who illuminates heaven itself. Let each of us, as mirrors, reflect and project the glorious, heavenly light of Him who indwells us and who will soon return to wipe darkness from earth with His brilliant appearing.

Beyond night, there is the dawn. Jesus said when you see these signs, look up, for your redemption draws near.

Section Two

God's
End-time
Plan

7

Israel:
The Clear Signal

by William T. James

Sixth century B.C. prophet, Zechariah, spoke words that pierce today's ears in thunderous decibels.

> Behold, I will make Jerusalem a cup of trembling unto all the people round about .... And in that day will I make Jerusalem a burdensome stone for all people: all that burden themselves with it shall be cut in pieces, though . . . gathered together against it (Zech. 12:2-3).

Jerusalem is a city as ancient as any still in existence, yet it is as contemporary as today's front page headlines. It is a city destined to become the center of the world's most volatile geopolitical conflict ever and, ultimately, the precise spot on the planet where God's own foot will touch down to put an end to man's genocidal madness.

The beginning of the end of human history is traceable to a general geographical area of the Earth, portions of which the world watched the United Nations Desert Storm coalition forces decimate with unprecedented military might. It has been termed "Mesopotamia" by the geographers and the "Cradle of Civilization" by historians and anthropologists.

According to the Bible, it is the region where the Garden of Eden was home for the first human beings. When Adam and Eve broke fellowship with the Creator by yielding to the serpent's temptation, the end-time clock began ticking for the present Earth.

The first murder followed, setting in motion the blood-drenched record upon which we now look back. Such dynamics will produce the indescribable carnage and gore that is prophesied to take place during man's last seven years of this dying, decaying age.

What Are the Signs?

Apocalypse and Armageddon loom just ahead. But, can we know if those long talked about, worried-over events will even come to pass, much less within our own lifetime? Have not doomsday prophets for centuries been predicting such things? Most of them have been predicting those end-time events would occur during their lifetimes. What makes predictors and predictions today any different from then?

Perhaps to begin answering such questions — good questions at that — questions of another kind are in order. Why are you reading this treatment of the subject of the biblically prophesied Apocalypse and all it will entail? Something has piqued your ears, your eyes, your attention.

Why the suddenly increased fascination with things to come — with that once hazy, most generally presumed-to-be-mythical matter called Armageddon? Something has happened. Something drastic, almost irresistible, calls people to begin looking more seriously at what the immediate future holds for their world.

Jesus found himself surrounded by a group of people who asked what the signs of His return to earth and of the end of the world would be. As He always did, Jesus spoke to the heart of the subject with precision and truth, outlining the major signs that would immediately precede the Second Advent.

His followers asked in Matthew 24:3, "... what shall be the sign of thy coming, and the end of the world?" Jesus gave them more than they asked for as He answered,

Take heed that no man deceive you. For many shall come in my name, saying, I am Christ; and shall deceive many. And ye shall hear of wars and rumors of wars: see that ye be not troubled: for all these things must come to pass, but the end is not yet. For nation shall rise against nation, and kingdom against kingdom: and there shall be famines, and pestilences, and earthquakes, in divers places. All these things are the beginning of sorrows. Then shall they deliver you up to be afflicted, and shall kill you: and ye shall be hated of all nations for my name's sake. And then shall many be offended, and shall betray one another, and shall hate one another. And many false prophets shall rise, and shall deceive many. And because iniquity shall abound, the love of many shall wax cold. But he that shall endure unto the end, the same shall be saved. And this gospel of the kingdom shall be preached in all the world for a witness unto all nations; and then shall the end come (Matt. 24:4-14).

In these few passages, Jesus swept the entire panorama of world history from His time on earth forward, using specific word pictures of things in the future. These signs were given and are recorded in God's Holy Word to be understood by each and every person, of each and every generation that the prophecies involve.

God's Word has many levels of meanings pertaining to the truths given. However, one must seek to know what is given. We do not simply absorb these truths as a sponge absorbs liquid, nor can we through osmosis assimilate God's holy ways as a plant draws nutrients.

If we want to know God's instructions, information, and truth, we must "know" the Bible for ourselves. This "knowing" begins with the heart of the gospel, John 3:16. To know God is to know Jesus Christ.

The Beginning of the End

Each of the signs Jesus expounded upon in the foregoing passages of Scripture will be dealt with in future essays. For now, we will concern ourselves with the one sign Jesus gives that seems most directly to signal the beginning of the end. We have been living a part of that most dramatic sign since 1948, when the nation of Israel was born in a single day — May 14.

Of that time of Israel's rebirth, Jesus — speaking in parabolic language to His disciples — said,

> Now learn a parable of the fig tree; When his branch is yet tender, and putteth forth leaves, ye know that summer is nigh: So likewise ye, when ye shall see all these things, know that it is near, even at the doors. Verily I say unto you, This generation shall not pass, till all these things be fulfilled (Matt. 24:32-34).

Jesus, in speaking to His disciples in the Olivet Discourse, looked down through the eras of future man; He spoke to future disciples — to the generation that would be alive at the time of His second advent.

The nation Israel, in the symbolic language sometimes utilized in God's Word, is likened at times to a fig tree in that God intended the children of Israel to be fruitful, a blessing to all the world. Such references to Israel as a fig tree are found in Judges 9:10-11, Joel 1:7-12, Habakkuk 3:16-17, and in many other passages.

Jesus clearly used the fig tree parable to tell the last generation of believers that the re-establishment of the nation Israel would be a key sign of His nearing second advent as well as a sign of the end of the world system. All other signs given by Jesus would accompany this major sign as the end of the age approached.

Since Jesus had told of the destruction of Jerusalem — and implied the dispersion of the Jewish people — just prior to giving the parable of the fig tree, He spoke most pointedly of the time when Israel would be regathered and begin to "shoot forth" its leaves. The golden summer of His millennial reign would be near when this came to pass. His coming again would be imminent.

First, however, the black winter clouds of Apocalypse would have to storm upon a world gathering to commit collective suicide.

Possessing the Land

The prophet Ezekiel spoke of the Diaspora and rebirth of God's chosen nation — the same nation that made the world tremble nervously in anticipation of its reaction to Saddam Hussein's Scud missile attacks during the Persian Gulf War.

> And I scattered them among the heathen, and they were dispersed through the countries: according to their way and according to their doings I judged them. For I will take you from among the heathen, and gather you out of all countries, and will bring you into your own land (Ezek. 36:19,24).

God's promises to this beleaguered, precariously perched nation, the nation most prominent in the process of pursuing world peace, are numerous throughout the Scriptures.

Consider the profound assurances given through Moses:

> That then the Lord thy God will turn thy captivity, and have compassion upon thee, and will return and will gather thee from all the nations, whither the Lord thy God hath scattered thee.
>
> And the Lord thy God will bring thee into the land which thy fathers possessed, and thou shalt possess it . . . (Deut. 30:3,5).

And,

> . . . Shall the earth be made to bring forth in one day? or shall a nation be born at once? for as soon as Zion travailed, she bought forth her children. Shall I bring to the birth, and not cause to bring forth? saith the Lord . . . (Isa. 66:8-9).

The exodus of Jews from the Soviet Union, since the supposed benevolent institution of glasnost and perestroika, has been staggering. The dissolution of much of Eastern Europe's communist superstructure has freed many more to migrate to Israel. They stream from Ethiopia and from around the globe to the Land of Promise. We are witnesses to God's promises to Israel in ways unthinkable a few years ago. God is indeed making manifest, through the Jews, His great prophetic truth in this generation!

Dry Bones, Live!

Put yourself in the prophet Ezekiel's place for a moment. While you do so, think of the things you know about the Jews in the day in which we now live. Think for a moment on the blowing sands of the Palestinian region and of the empty, desolate places, void of human life for the most part.

Now, remember the stark black and white images of starving, dying people you've seen on documentary footage of the death camps called Auschwitz, Buchenwald, Dachau, Mauthasen, Sachsenhausen, Treblinka. Remember the trenches, the bulldozers, the skeletal forms beneath loose, pasty-white skin. See again the corpses, intermingling and meshing together — rolling over each other as the bulldozers did their work of pushing the bodies into the ditch-like, common graves.

Recall the scenes of the allied commander, Dwight D. Eisenhower, as he and his staff walked among the pathetic, stick-like, human figures following the liberation of the concentration camps. See again the German people, robust, well-fed, even though bone-weary of war. Picture them in your mind's eye as they held handkerchiefs to their noses, some of them weeping, others retching, and some trying to leave the lines in which they were forced to walk while viewing the rotting bodies of the dead Jews.

Remember all this as you put yourself, for one moment, in the place of God's prophet, Ezekiel.

The hand of the Lord was upon me, and carried me out in the spirit of the Lord, and set me down in the midst of the valley which was full of bones, And caused me to pass by them round about: and, behold, there were very many in the open valley; and, lo, they were very dry. And he said unto me, Son of man, can these bones live? And I answered, O Lord God, thou knowest. Again he said unto me, Prophesy upon these bones, and say unto them, O ye dry bones, hear the word of the Lord. Thus saith the Lord God unto these bones; Behold, I will cause breath to enter into you, and ye shall live: And I will lay sinews upon you, and will bring up flesh upon you, and cover you with skin, and put breath in you, and ye shall live; and ye shall know that I am the Lord. So I prophesied as I was commanded: and as I prophesied, there was a noise, and behold a shaking, and the bones came together, bone to his bone. And when I beheld, lo, the sinews and the flesh came up upon them, and the skin covered them above: but there was no breath in them. Then said he unto me, Prophesy unto the wind, prophesy, son of man, and say to the wind, Thus saith the Lord God; Come from the four winds, O breath, and breathe upon these slain, that they may live. So I prophesied as he commanded me, and the breath came into them, and they lived, and stood up upon their feet, an exceeding great army. Then he said unto me, Son of man, these bones are the whole house of Israel: behold, they say, Our bones are dried, and our hope is lost: we are cut off for our parts. Therefore prophesy and say unto them, Thus saith the Lord God; Behold, O my people, I will open your graves, and cause you to come up out of your graves, and bring you into the land of Israel (Ezek. 37:1-12).

The Nazis would have built their Reich atop ground filled with the dry bones of God's people of destiny. Adolph Hitler, Heinrich Himmler, Joseph Goebbels, Hermann Goering, Reinhard Heydrich, Martin Bormann, and the other elitist, Aryan monsters of the Third Reich, fired the engines of satanic, ideological hatred with the skeletal remains of more than six million of the house of Israel. The final solution, once and for all, would have rid the world of the despised Jew.

Instead, Hitler's ashes lie scattered in the bloody soil of German shame. The bones of all the other Nazi diabolists are strewn in ignominy — who knows where. Yet, the Jew remains, thrives, and prospers the world in every facet of life from the arts to industry, medicine, science, and beyond.

"Never Again!"

God began His chosen nation's restoration to Palestine nearly a century before the Nazi beast began its genocidal work. Migration, though a trickle at first, began about 1838. The revival of national Jewish life in that land started in earnest in 1878.

Then came the event that distinguishes it as perhaps the most important signal that Apocalypse is near, that Armageddon approaches. Jerusalem was reclaimed for the Jew in precisely the manner the prophet Isaiah had foretold more than twenty-seven hundred years earlier: "As birds flying, so will the Lord of hosts defend Jerusalem; defending also he will deliver it; and passing over he will preserve it" (Isa. 31:5).

In 1917, General Edmund Allenby, commander of occupied Palestine for the British Empire, was ordered to take Jerusalem for the Jews. He found the city in possession of the Turks. To take the city by force meant risking initiation of hostilities that might so inflame the region as to cause a massive conflict to result. Bloodshed could have raised the indignation of the whole world.

Allenby, seeking advice from his government, was told to use his own judgment. He again contacted his superiors, who told him to pray, offering no further counsel in the matter. Allenby then ordered the commander of a fleet of airplanes to fly over Jerusalem. This action so terrified the Turks that they surrendered the city without a shot being fired.

Isaiah's prophecy was thus fulfilled: "As birds flying," God "delivered" Jerusalem; the city was "defended" while aircraft "passed over."

As a result of this action, the Balfour Declaration was signed on November 2, 1917, recognizing Palestine as the rightful homeland for the Jew. The regathering began to take on new dimensions. So, too, did the ugliness of anti-Semitism.

Hatred for the Jew seemed driven by dynamics that transcended reason, reaching fever-pitch in Germany on the evenings of November 9 and 10, 1938. During these "Crystal Nights," as they have become known, Jewish homes and businesses were ravaged and destroyed, and many Jewish people were brutally assaulted.

Nazi inner-circle members haughtily termed it the "Week of Broken Glass." Hitler's plan, taken from the pages of his prison-dictated writings, "Mein Kampf," had taken root. The persecution had become full blown.

From the valley of dry bones — the crematorium/gas chamber hells of Nazi Europe — arose a God-breathed spirit that screamed then and screams still, "Never again!" The crucible of holocaust tempered a people for the rebirth prophesied almost three millennia earlier.

Modern Israel was born on May 14, 1948. The Jews have miraculously prospered. From a people near extinction in 1945, they are today the focal nation of the world. Surely, Israel is the premiere sign that God's prophetic clock approaches the midnight hour.

The Time of Jacob's Trouble

Saddam Hussein's demented obsession to become a twentieth century Nebuchadnezzar, through the elimination of Israel, was short-circuited by unseen forces greater than those of the United Nation coalition, valiant though those men and women were. Israel is in the process of being compressed and funnelled into an unalterable course. It will be a forced march which, for the last few years of human history, will cause Jewish people to wish they could trade their plight for even that suffered by their ancestors during the Holocaust of the Nazi death-camp years.

> Alas! for that day is great, so that none is like it: it is even the time of Jacob's trouble . . . (Jer. 30:7).
> For then shall be great tribulation, such as was not since the beginning of the world to this time, no, nor ever shall be (Matt. 24:21).

What will set in motion for the world in general, and for Israel in particular, a time described by Jesus himself as the worst man has ever known? There is an event that brings forth Apocalypse from the self-assured smugness of man's effort to at last establish world peace and safety. "For when they shall say, Peace and safety; then sudden destruction cometh upon them, as travail upon a woman with child; and they shall not escape" (1 Thess. 5:3).

In Daniel 9:27, the prophet Daniel speaks of the event and of the time that will begin human history's final seven years, called the time of Jacob's trouble by Jeremiah. "And he shall confirm the covenant with many for one week: and in the midst of the week he shall cause the sacrifice and the oblation to cease, and for the overspreading of abominations he shall make it desolate, even until the consummation, and that determined shall be poured upon the desolate."

To see the awesome import of this prophecy, one must understand that it relates directly to what Jesus Christ said in expounding on that most terrible time. The abomination of desolation is a future dictator whose record of atrocity will make Hitler, Stalin, Mao, and all other preceding tyrants seem hardly worthy of mention.

Jesus' words on this last and most ferocious dictator are recorded in Matthew 24:15-16. Jesus, confirming the words of Jeremiah and Daniel, is speaking to the Jews of Palestine at the end of the age.

> When ye therefore shall see the abomination of desolation, spoken of by Daniel the prophet, stand in the holy place, (whoso readeth, let him understand:) Then let them which be in Judea flee into the mountains.

Notice that immediately before the time of unprecedented terror, there is first negotiated a covenant with many. The many in this passage are the Jews — the nation Israel — returned after their dispersion. It is the Israel born in a single day — May 14, 1948.

Do we see any evidence, in the present hour, of a peace process in which Israel is involved in a major way?

Saddam Hussein, before the Persian Gulf crisis was enjoined by the United Nation coalition forces, reported a dream in which he said the Prophet Mohammed appeared to him and told him that in the event of war, he — Saddam — had his Scud missiles pointed in the wrong direction.

"Oh, great prophet," Saddam asked the figure in his dream, "which way should they be pointed?"

The prophet answered him, "You know which direction to point them."

Israel was Saddam Hussein's real target, and is the target of every anti-Israeli nation and organization in the world. Jerusalem and that tiny nation are the thorns in the side of the chaotic, incendiary, militant, Arab conglomerate. Even so, the

Palestinian homeland issue is merely a rifle scope through which to focus the hostility.

The Center of the Storm

What is the true source of the world's rage against Israel?

> And there appeared a great wonder in heaven, a woman... And she being with child cried, travailing in birth, and pained to be delivered. And there appeared another wonder in heaven; and behold a great red dragon ... and the dragon stood before the woman which was ready to be delivered, for to devour her child as soon as it was born. And she brought forth a male child, who was to rule all nations ... and her child was caught up unto God, and to his throne (Rev. 12:1-5).

Here is found the nucleus of the geopolitical storm presently gathering in the Middle East. More than a mortal storm, it is a cosmic, universal maelstrom of eternal consequence.

Lucifer, that fallen angel; Satan, that serpent called the devil — stirs the black, brewing tempest that will soon unleash his fury into man's final war. His hatred for the people through whom God chose to give fallen man His supreme love gift, His only begotten Son, Jesus Christ, in order that people can be reconciled to the Creator, grows more intense and more manifest by the hour.

The Jew, the nation Israel, is the centerpiece of the Mid-East turmoil. Why? Because the Jew, Israel, is at the center of that struggle over which man and his intellect have philosophized since antiquity but have never comprehended. The struggle is between good and evil. Many governments have tried to deal with the trouble in this region. Some seemed for a time to succeed in their efforts. But, the ancient conflict goes on, and more and more often, inflames to the point of eruption.

The wars are legendary by their very nature. Modern Israel, though surrounded on three fronts by forces thirty times greater and backed against the Mediterranean Sea, has not only survived major assaults in 1956, 1967, and 1973 — in fact, it was born in the midst of battle in 1948 — but, it has miraculously and completely routed the enemies each time while gaining additional territory.

Now, Israel faces a subtle aggression, but one much more virulent and dangerous. Diplomatic cries for peace and safety through a negotiated solution to the problem of a homeland for the Palestinian refugees are becoming demands. The "Palestinian problem," the diplomats say almost without exception, "is the key to war and peace."

The Conquering Leader

There is coming out of the soon-to-be united Europe a leader who will go "forth conquering, and to conquer" (Rev. 6:2).

"There was given unto him a mouth speaking great things . . ." (Rev. 13:5).

This mightiest leader ever will come riding the white horse of peacemaker and will confirm the covenant with many for one week. Translation: This leader from a Europe united in a configuration equivalent to the Europe of the Roman Empire days — a revived Roman Empire, a neo-Roman order of sorts — will make a covenant treaty to which Israel will be a major signatory. The pact will be for seven years, one year equaling one day of the seven day week indicated in the Scriptures.

The "conquering" by the leader at this point in time, no doubt is in the realm of diplomacy. Undoubtedly, he will offer brilliant initiatives, magnified in their allurement by a charismatic, personal charm that convinces Jew and Arab alike to trust him as a friend of all. As the guarantor of the peace not just for that region, but for a global peace upon which can be built a New World order and a new age of prosperity, he will succeed where others have failed. His promises will be sweet to the ears of a world ravenous for such lies. And lies they will be.

Globe-trotting exploits by would-be peacemakers have met with fates ranging from abject failure to moderate, though temporary, success. One recalls seeing documentary film of the well-intentioned, but fuzzy-thinking, Neville Chamberlain holding up the piece of paper Hitler duped him into believing was the megalomaniac's true desire for "peace for our time."

Henry Kissinger impressed us mightily with his seeming inexhaustible energy while pursuing an honorable peace in Vietnam. Even his brilliant efforts ultimately faded and failed. Secretary of State James A. Baker, III, of the Bush administration, eclipsed even Kissinger's air mileage as he jetted in and out of the capitals of the world in search of a formula that will defuse the time bomb that is the Middle East. He, too, has failed to secure the lasting peace for which the world hungers, although there may be temporary, superficial "progress" made.

Diplomatic Deception

There is movement in the Arab world to bring great pressure to bear on their avowed enemy, but this time they plan to use diplomatic maneuvering rather than their often failed military force and/or terrorism. These types of tactics are most likely what the world can expect from now until the nation Israel is lulled into a false sense of security.

The Scriptures plainly teach that diplomatic deception will make Israel vulnerable to attack. This prophesied end-time, caution-softening process can be sensed in a *New York Times* news service release dated July 22, 1991, by Thomas L. Friedman.

> Jordan on Sunday joined Syria, Lebanon, Egypt and Saudi Arabia in agreeing to attend a regional peace conference proposed by the United States.
>
> Israeli Prime Minister Yitzhak Shamir, however, told visiting Secretary of State James Baker that he wanted more time to consider the matter.
>
> "We are ready to attend a peace conference," King Hussein said, "and we are very happy indeed it is going to be a comprehensive one."
>
> . . . Jordan also joined Saudi Arabia and Egypt in offering to suspend the Arab economic boycott of Israel if it will suspend the building of settlements in the occupied lands.

In another press service release, it was reported that President Bush said he did not want to use a "volatile" word like "pressuring" when talking about his stance with the Israelis.

> He preferred to call it "reasoning and taking this, what I keep calling a new credibility for the United States in the Middle East, and using that to encourage what is a very reasonable and important step to peace."

Groundwork is being laid. America's well-meaning diplomacy might be the effort that makes clear the pathway for the final Fuehrer to perform his diabolical work when his time comes to step upon the world stage. This man, termed Antichrist in 1 John 2:18, is dealt with at length in later chapters of this book.

But Christians — all those who have accepted Jesus Christ as the one and only way of redemption, i.e., the means of reconciliation with God the Father — are looking not for the Antichrist. Rather, they are looking for Jesus Christ who will "descend from heaven.... Then we which are alive and remain [until His secret coming in the clouds above the earth] shall be caught up together with them [those who have died during the age since Christ's redemptive work on the cross] in the clouds, to meet the Lord in the air: and so shall we ever be with the Lord" (1 Thess. 4:16-17).

Israel is beset on all sides with demands that they submit to a peace process that will prevent their own expansion while giving the Palestinians a homeland and the world relief from the constant tensions in the region: this is the clear signal that the end has already begun!

8

Europe and the Prince That Shall Come

by David Breese

"Three days ago, no one in the world could have predicted this amazing event," so spoke James Baker, United States Secretary of State, when he referred to that remarkable set of circumstances centering around November 9, 1989.

Before the eyes of an onlooking and astonished world, the Berlin Wall was opened with the announcement that there would now be free access to West Berlin and West Germany by the citizens of the East German state. On the first day after that announcement, more than one hundred thousand came through the border crossings to participate in tearful, ecstatic reunions with relatives and loved ones in the West. They danced on the wall, broke champagne bottles, and toasted one another. While some chipped out pieces of concrete, the bands played and songs of joy were raised by citizens East and West.

In the following days, the news media carried the ever-mounting story of this amazing reversal of policy in this key nation. For forty years, East Germany had been under the dead hand of despotic communism, and now everything had changed. In subsequent days, the *L.A. Times* news service carried the story:

> Fighting for its life, the East German Communist party moved this morning to change its name and character while blaming its former leaders for betraying the nation.
>
> More than 2,700 delegates debated the future of their disgraced party in an all-night meeting that began hours after prosecutors charged former Party leader Erich Honecker and five other party officials with corruption and enriching themselves while in office.
>
> All but Honecker and one other were taken into custody; Honecker, 77, was "too ill to be questioned or jailed," the East German news agency ADN reported.
>
> Well past midnight, the emergency party congress debated about what to call the party and how to win back the confidence of a nation shocked by revelations of stealing and featherbedding by top officials.
>
> During a closed-door session later, the Communists nominated Gregor Gysi, a 41-year-old reformist lawyer who has worked for the opposition, to be party chairman, a party spokeswoman said. "He was the only candidate."

Subsequently, the press reported, "In recent days, as revelations of corruption by party leaders have filled newly liberalized newspapers, party members suddenly have found themselves targets of insults, sneers, and even physical attacks.

"'We need a complete break with Stalinism and a new form of socialism,' the new Premier Gysi said. 'Our centralized system has brought us to this crisis.'"

Still, the people were not willing to settle for cosmetic change. "When I go back to my factory with a new name, the workers will say it's still the Communist party," said Klaus Urban, a union leader. "We're not going to be able to get rid of the stench quickly."

Germany has now moved all the way to reunification and contemplates the future after what they now call "the death of communism."

The Tide of Revolution

A reunited Germany has not been looked upon with complete favor by the nations of the East or the West, in that it now poses many perplexing questions. In the West, the world remembers that Germany gave us World War I and II, with all of their unspeakably and terrible results. The former Soviet Union retains the same memories, with the addition that it saw itself nearly conquered by the efficient legions of Germany in World War II.

Nevertheless, the tide of sentiment for reunification has now come to pass, leaving the onlooking nations in a state of bewilderment as to what its possibilities might be.

The story of Czechoslovakia is amazingly similar. The press carried the story from Prague:

> Czechoslovakia's Communist rulers agreed Friday to accept a minority role in a new national government for the first time since 1948, giving the country's democracy movement its biggest victory to date.... The announcement culminated a series of Communist concessions during the past three weeks to the growing "people power" of the pro-democracy Civic Forum coalition.

But the tide of revolution rolls on in Czechoslovakia. The people have announced in many ways that they will accept nothing of Communist control for the future. Even the minority members of the government are jeered as representing a bloody, tyrannical system, which they now want to see relegated to the dustbin of history. These traumatic changes in Czechoslovakia have been viewed with equal astonishment by an attentive world.

The dramatic political changes in East Germany and Czechoslovakia are but a part of the wider changes that have affected Europe in recent years. The Czechoslovakian action was followed by similar moves by Communist parties in other

East European states to cede power to opposition movements. In Poland, the Communists surrendered the reins of government to Solidarity and took a minority position in the new government. Lech Walensa, Solidarity's intrepid leader, became president of Poland. A stunning reversal of fortune indeed!

Hungary and Bulgaria made similar changes.

The story of change continued at a blistering pace. In an editorial, the *Wichita Eagle* reported: "Baltics — Estonia, Latvia, Lithuania Are Next in Line of Freedom March." It said:

> Step by step, the Baltic republics of Estonia, Latvia, and Lithuania are moving toward their goal of independence. . . . Within hours of the Lithuanian move to create a multi-party system, the Estonian Communist Party's Central Committee acted to do almost the same thing. . . . "The Party's leading role here no longer exists anyway," said one Estonian official.

Remarkably, as if presciently sensing the inevitable dissolution of the Soviet Union, the editorial said:

> Indeed, the "leading role" of the Communist Party already has been revoked in Poland, Hungary, Czechoslovakia, and East Germany, and the Soviet reaction has been benign. For the Soviets to countenance a change of this magnitude there but not at home would be hypocritical in the extreme.
>
> The legitimacy of the Soviet government is what's really at issue here, and nowhere is this more true than in the "captured nations" of Estonia, Latvia, and Lithuania. As they go, perestroika goes — something else that shouldn't be lost on the Central Committee of the Soviet Communist Party.

The continuing stories of dramatic changes coming out of the nations of Europe leave the onlooking world reeling in amazement.

Shaking the Foundations of Communism

These developments have and continue to dynamically

influence the former Soviet Union, or the Commonwealth of Independent States, as it is now called. The beginning of the end could be seen for the USSR in stories such as this one carried in the *L.A. Times*: "Soviets May Rethink Party Primacy." From Moscow came the report:

> The Kremlin said Friday that it is willing to consider revising or even eliminating the law guaranteeing the Communist monopoly on power as part of an overall rewriting of the constitution.
>
> The legislators and activists in the Soviet Union calling for a revision of the party's role and the rise of a multi-party system on a national level also have been emboldened by the legal abolition of guaranteed Communist Party dominance in Czechoslovakia, East Germany, Hungary, and Poland.

The debate about communism and its right to rule in the Soviet Union and in Eastern Europe was then punctuated by a series of developments that had a startling effect on the Party and the people. The first was the death of Andrei Sakharov. The world was touched and startled by this event.

Sakharov, the scientist who invented the Soviet version of the hydrogen bomb, was held in high esteem in the Soviet Union. This nuclear physicist, reputed to be a Christian, began then to express his great concern about Communist tyranny. The day before his death, he had a stirring debate with Gorbachev himself at a meeting of the Communist Central Committee. This brave and defiant man predicted the death of the Soviet Union if it did not give freedom to the people. His brand of courage is rare in all the world, but it came shining through in the last speech of his life. The next day he died of a heart attack — we might even say a broken heart.

The Communist world, shaken by this event, soon heard the rumble of machine gun fire coming from Bucharest, Romania. There had ruled Nicolae Ceausescu, the most severe and brutal dictator in the entire Communist world. That rule was soon to be no more.

A few days before Christmas 1989, Ceausescu made a speech to the people in the main square at Bucharest. This speech was interrupted by jeers and catcalls as the crowd shouted, "Down with Ceausescu! Down with communism!"

Ceausescu, still under the delusion that he was in full control, ordered his troops to fire on the crowd. This they did, and hundreds died. Some soldiers, however, refused to fire on their own friends in the crowd, and these troopers were executed by Ceausescu's secret police. This was too much! The crowd, despite the danger, came surging back and demanded that Ceausescu resign.

This animalistic dictator was quickly caught in a wave of resentment. There came a speedy trial for him and his wife, which was then followed by a Christmas-day firing squad. The riddled bodies of "the Butcher of Bucharest" and his wife were photographed and shown repeatedly on television across the world. In the Romanian revolution thousands died, but communism was thrown out.

"The Antichrist is dead! What a wonderful Christmas gift we have received — the Antichrist is dead!" shouted the people. Speaking from their Christian background, the people could only use the thoughts of the Bible to express their reaction to these events.

Is the Antichrist dead? What will be the result of the breakdown of European communism? How shall we explain what has happened and is happening in the dissolving Communist world today, and what will be the outcome of these European events?

When the Romanians called their leader "the Antichrist," they reminded the world of an explanation of communism given to us by Solzhenitsyn. He said that all of the dreadful things that have come upon the Soviet Union — the murder of millions, the closing of churches, the destruction of freedom, the gulags, and a thousand other cruelties — have come because "they have forgotten God." In considering this, we remember that the Bible says:

> And every spirit that confesseth not that Jesus Christ is come in the flesh is not of God: and this is that spirit of antichrist, whereof ye have heard that it should come; and even now already is it in the world (1 John 4:3).

We must then consider the rise of Antichrist. But first, let us look through observant human eyes at the present agony of Europe.

Why the Sudden Change?

When we see the far-reaching nature of these changes, most of us understandably ask the question, "Why? What is the reason for this new permissive attitude that has effectively caused the Communist world to self-destruct?"

Some have given us the simple, facile explanation that the Communist leaders became corrupt and presumptuous, thereby losing their right to rule. Others say that Marxism itself has failed and has now become a non-viable point of view. These remarks are semi-evaluations of the situation, but they are simply half-truths.

The fact is that the leaders of the Communist world were corrupt and degenerate from the very beginning and never did have a right to rule. Marxism was not merely invalidated in these late days; it was never a valid philosophy. It is simply a collection of mumbo-jumbo about economics that has never been understood by two Communists in exactly the same way. Nevertheless, Marxism is complicated enough so that it was able to pass as a worthy object of discussion for many years. After all, Karl Marx wrote *Das Kapital* in 1863.

In history, the Communists have always presented themselves as the "proletariat," the party of the people. The nations that they brutally captured were dubbed "the People's Republic" of this and that. Indulgent academicians in the West have pandered to this nonsense for two generations, never subjecting it to the destructive criticism that it so richly deserves.

The fact is, the Communists have never come to power in any country because of the will of the people. The people were simply neutralized into political impotence while a determined elite took over the nation. This was done, albeit with difficulty, in the Soviet Union. It was done with greater ease in the captive nations because the Communist party was now backed by the merciless fire and steel of the Red Army. A minority plus bayonets carries the deciding vote against the majority every time.

Probably the best explanation for the allowances within the former Communist system, which have resulted in these widespread changes, is an explanation on a two-fold level. The first is that the Communist system was simply bankrupt. Russia, prior to the dissolution of the USSR, had a gross national product only 25 percent that of the United States, despite the fact that its population is larger than that of the United States.

For seventy years, however, the Russians promoted the fiction that the Communist system was viable and prosperous. Whatever apparent shortcomings it seemed to show were excused by the statement that "True communism has not yet come to pass because the imperialists are still with us." Under this fabrication, people were given utopian dreams rather than food, clothing, shelter, and a purpose for living.

Those who still retained their cynicism within the Communist system were simply sent to the gulag or the execution chamber. A bullet in the back of the head was the final argument the Communist bullies had in response to the objections of the people.

A second way to explain the permissiveness of the Communist governments just before their demise is that the leadership had, at least in a measure, lost its will to be as brutal as was the case in days gone by. The Chinese answer to the demonstrations at Tiananmen Square was tanks, bayonets, and thirty-six hundred bodies scattered across that bloody battleground. The consequence is that public dissent is still rather rare in China.

In Russia and the former Eastern bloc nations, however, global publicity, contacts with the West, student exchanges, and other open windows of media awareness made it impolitic for the former Soviet Union's Communist bosses to do the same. This does not imply moral superiority on the part of the former Russian Communist leaders, but it may imply that they, and their successors, have taken one small step in the direction of rejoining the human race. After all, Gorbachev seemed to know something about the Bible.

The Advantages of Perestroika

We must also remember that there are significant new advantages that came to the Eastern European and Russian states as a result of this move away from communism. What have they gained? Many things. These include:

1. *A Relaxed Defense Posture by the West*

Always prone to believing the best and the most convenient, Western leaders are now saying, "The cold war is over." They are, therefore, responding to the moves of the former Communist regimes with not only a relaxed defense posture, but with massive financial aid and other assistance to their "former enemies." The cynical Communist surely rejoices that the West has reverted to slumber instead of facing its great danger.

2. *More U.S. Aid and Investments*

The United States and other cooperating nations have now committed themselves to the investment of at least one billion dollars in Poland and Hungary alone. When this was done in days gone by, the money became an outright gift, for we never saw it again. The expectation of seeing a return on this new sizeable investment is equally remote. Still, these two nations will get one billion dollars, and we can expect that billions more will follow.

3. *Reduced American Military Forces in Europe*

The United States is now planning on a significant force reduction in Europe, perhaps by one-third. This could not be accomplished by military means on the part of the Soviet Union, but perestroika has done it.

4. *The Diversion of American Attention*

While the United States and the West are concentrating on Europe, revolutionary movements are newly active across the world. El Salvador and the Philippines have been the object of the latest bloody attempts at revolution in which the Communists are deeply involved. American preoccupation with Europe can be expected to reduce our concern over these other places. Many other revolutions, especially in Latin America, could follow.

5. *A General Power Reduction in America*

Already, the overall military budget is being greatly reduced. This grows out of the judgment now being made that the extension of American power is no longer needed in the world. This power reduction by America cannot be expected to improve the American economy. Rather, as is always the case, the money "saved" will be dissipated on other things.

These and many other benefits are now coming to the

shaky Commonwealth of Independent States. It is not impossible that Russia itself could gain a "most favored nation" status on the part of the United States. This could be worth additional billions to the Soviet Union. So, the prince of Rosh, Meshech, and Tubal, despite all his problems, is still with us.

A New Europe

The sea-change continues. There is no doubt that the most widespread movement for change, for restructuring, and for new arrangements that Europe has seen in forty years is now coming to pass. Everyone agrees that the governments of Europe, in the sense in which they relate to one another, are being reformed, recast into a new mold. Whatever may be the final outcome, Europe cannot be the same again.

Final outcomes quickly change, however. Saddam Hussein, with his invasion of Kuwait, has reminded the world of the folly of believing in permanent peace. Like a global alarm clock, the Mid-East crisis startled us out of sleep. It brought new, serious considerations to the United States, to Europe, to Russia, and to the world.

In the midst of these changes, we can be sure that the outcome in Europe, by the determination of many of its leaders, is not going to be left to mere chance. No indeed, for the nations of western Europe have decided to come together with a form of political unity that has not been known before. Political unity in Europe has always been a very elusive thing. Indeed, the largest wars of the world have started in Europe because these nations found it impossible, in the long run, to work together.

Now, however, the sentiment is different. The leaders of Europe are in effect saying, "We realize that it will not be possible for us to move again to world supremacy without unity. Therefore, we must lay aside our differences and come together as a new United States of Europe. By doing this, we will constitute a power bloc that can move to the ascendancy of world leadership."

When did all the pieces fall into place? From Strasbourg, France, came this report:

> Leaders of the twelve-nation European Community, closing ranks amid upheaval in Eastern Europe, agreed Friday to press ahead with an economic

and monetary union despite British opposition.

The decision, on the opening day of a two-day summit, means the European Economic Community will convene a special conference in December 1990, to start negotiations for the adoption of a single currency and to set up a system of central banks.

The agreement came after France and West Germany overrode objections by British Prime Minister Margaret Thatcher that radical monetary integration will rob member countries of sovereign rights to decide national economic policy.

When Margaret Thatcher, the "Iron Lady," resigned as British prime minister, her stepping aside opened the way for a speedy British integration into a United Europe.

January 1, 1993 is the announced date when this plan will in fact materialize. For months, hundreds of committees have been meeting in the nations of Europe to bring standardization to pass that will make unity possible. These committees are establishing a unified railway system, a common currency, a common political structure, free access across all borders, a common electrical voltage, and a thousand other commonalties that must be arranged for Europe to come together.

The United States of Europe could quickly become the most powerful political force in the world. With a population of 320 million, it will instantly possess unified economic strength that is larger than that of the United States. It will, therefore, have economic and commercial power second to none in the entire world.

The Europe of Hope?

Despite every difficulty, the European economic community will bring itself together to develop a powerful block of economic influence — possibly the greatest in our time.

Jacques Chirac, former conservative prime minister of France, wrote in the liberal *LeMonde* of Paris:

Despite the risk of delaying or endangering the process of integration under way among European Community nations, we must act along three lines: advance toward economic and monetary union;

strengthen measures for political coordination among the principal European states to avert the temptation of taking an "every man for himself" attitude toward relations with the East; and assemble and apply powerful means of pulling the Eastern economies out of their rut.

There remains the critical area of freedoms. A single Europe stretching from the Atlantic to the Urals should not be two-tiered where freedoms are concerned. Our "common house" cannot have wide-open doors and windows on one side, locked doors and barred windows on the other.

So, it is up to us to implement Europe-wide measures gradually to provide all citizens with the same fundamental rights. That implies putting in place a legal order consonant with the principles of freedom laid down by the Council of Europe: the freeing of all political prisoners; the closing of gulags; reform of the penal code; introduction of complete freedom of movement between the two parts of Europe by abolishing exit visas; and, finally, the symbolic destruction of the Berlin Wall.

Let us not forget that we have known the Europe of terror and conquered it; we have lived in the Europe of fear and driven it back. My confidence in the Europe of hope is, therefore, that much stronger.

"The Europe of hope," that is the note being sounded in Europe today.

We do well then to take note of the kind of language that the world is using to speak about the future. Considering the developments in Europe and related issues from across the world, there is a sense of awe, foreboding, and hope about the future.

The *Toronto Star* carried an article entitled, "Waiting for the Millennium: Where Is 'Earth, Inc.' Headed?" They said of this decade — "the last of the millennium, let alone the century — may be the toughest one yet" and described it this way:

It will be a highly complex period driven by competing forces: technology and science, plus impassioned calls for an ethical base according to which they should be monitored. Before the train of progress gets any further out of the station, it is a safe bet that mankind, at least the version of mankind dwelling in the industrialized world, will finally start examining where it is going.

So it is that the remarkable developments of our time, centering in Europe, are causing people to ask, "What of the future? How will tomorrow come together?"

Politics, Money, and Military Might

As Europe reconstituted itself into a new political entity, we can be sure the leaders of Europe intend with total conviction to become the strongest political force in the world. During the next few years, we will hear announcements, one after another, about the progressive strength and mounting capability of Europe.

The first great strength that the European leaders intend to take to themselves is commercial capability. We can expect them to bring this to pass. No thinking person must ever underestimate the brilliance of the Europeans at inventing new products, making better items, selling their wares, and then promoting them across the world. Already, Germany has become a commercial enterprise to be respected.

Soon, however, there will be added to this the organizational ability, the creativity, the salesmanship, the new ideas, and the vision for the future that will come from the English, the French, the Italians, the Spanish, the Portuguese, the Dutch, and others. The leaders of Europe can be expected to organize their inventive thinking in the world of commerce in such a way as to become catalytic. The possibilities will certainly be amazingly great.

Once Europe's commercial power is developed, they will be faced with another problem. Their newfound wealth must now be protected! Europe will immediately realize the necessity of developing a strong military establishment, an all-European army to guard their overflowing coffers. That military establishment will immediately have two great missions.

The first mission is to protect Europe itself. A revived

Europe will still face the very real danger of invasion from the east along with new military responsibilities in the Middle East.

Despite all of its inner changes, the former Soviet Union still possesses the largest military force in the world. It has more tanks, more artillery, more infantry, more airplanes, more naval vessels and submarines than anyone else on the face of the Earth. These capabilities, despite the apparent political change, still remain intact. For this reason alone, Europe must multiply its defenses rather than reduce them.

General Colin Powell, United States Chairman of the Joint Chiefs of Staff, just before the dissolution of the USSR, said, "Despite talk of disarmament, we must remember that the Soviet Union is the only nation in the world which could destroy the United States in thirty minutes." That capability has not lessened!

The second mission of a European military establishment must also be to protect the energy routes from the Middle East. A high percentage — once nearly 100 percent — of the oil that heats and energizes Europe comes from the oil-rich lands of the countries surrounding the Persian Gulf. Should these supplies be threatened, all other considerations would immediately need to be set aside in favor of guaranteeing the uninterrupted flow of Mid-East oil. Without this, homes would become cold, automobiles would be parked by the curb, and airplanes would no longer fly. The pipeline from the Middle East must always be held as a major consideration by the planners of Europe's future.

Richard Cheney, the United States Secretary of Defense, called for the reduction of the American military commitment to Europe. Our military budget will, he said, be reduced by $180 billion over the next three years. Plans are to deactivate five American fighter wings and to pull at least one hundred thousand troops out of Europe. This puts the pressure on Europe to expand its own military power.

The Europeans, being realists, must take note. Indeed, the Byzantine political leaders of Europe are not nearly as impressed by rhetoric as are the Americans. They must, therefore, expand their military capability, and they will. They can be expected to be relatively unimpressed by the sweet talk that comes from the other nations of the world. Yes, Europe could soon become the most powerful military force on the face of the earth.

How Europe Lost Its Soul

Commercial, political, and military unity may be easy to achieve, but it is difficult to sustain. The thinkers of Europe will, therefore, be expected to ask the question, "Is there some other mucilage, some other magnetism, some other great force by which we can continue to draw together the nations of Europe and even the rest of the world into our plan for the new world that we must, yes we will, create?"

Is there a magnetism that is potentially greater than commercial and political unity? Yes indeed! It is *religious* unity.

The call for some kind of common faith must inevitably grow out of the present European developments. What might that common faith be? We may answer that question readily when we remember that virtually all of Europe is a part of what has historically been called "Christian civilization." A high percentage of Europeans still hold to Roman Catholicism, and many millions are passionate in their involvement in this faith.

About 450 years ago, Northern Germany, along with England and parts of Holland, however, embraced the reformation of Martin Luther. They are Protestant, at least in name, but the form of Protestantism that is generally embraced in Northern Europe is a corruption of the reformation faith. Through the years, the form of Christianity believed on the continent and in England is mere formalism, sacerdotalism, religious practice, crosses, candles, and weather-stained buildings.

Luther's doctrine of the Bible alone, faith alone, and grace alone has been generally supplanted by a plethora of religious practices not greatly dissimilar from Roman Catholicism itself. In fact, there is already a strong call for reuniting with "the mother church" that comes from the English Anglicans and even from Northern Europe. As spiritual convictions subside, the call for organizational unity grows.

Christianity has always been the object of attempted subversion, and one of the most successful forms impacted the faith in the nineteenth and twentieth centuries. In the latter half of the last century, Europe opened itself to dreadful spiritual and cultural deterioration by allowing the Christian faith to be corrupted before its very eyes. What happened?

German rationalism and European pseudo-intellectualism ushered in religious liberalism. Julius Wellhausen presented the "Documentary Hypothesis," which really denied the inspiration of the Old Testament Scriptures. As a result, the Bible became a merely human book, devoid of divine inspiration.

The European rationalists arrogated to themselves the right to examine the Bible and pass judgments upon it, rather than allowing the Bible to examine *them*. Man became the intellectual master of his "Christian" religion, rather than Christ being the author of divine revelation and the Lord of the human condition.

What was the result? Europe, and finally most of Western civilization, lost its moorings, its spiritual foundations. European Christianity, while still meeting in buildings and lighting candles, ceased to believe in the primacy of divine revelation. Human reason became superior to the Word of God, and the will of man more desirous than the will of God. The result was that the intellectuals of Europe no longer protected themselves and the people from the evolution of Darwin, the social theories of Marx, and the deadly philosophy of Rousseau and other enemies of reason and realty.

Another strange result occurred. At the beginning of this century, Albert Einstein announced the theory of relativity. This understanding demonstrated itself to be eminently true in the realm of physics and now nuclear physics. Europe, however, by this time becoming intellectually faddist, made relativity a social philosophy. From then on, all things were relative, and final absolutes disappeared.

There are many who are willing to argue, therefore, that the two greatest wars in the history of the world grew out of European spiritual, religious, and philosophical degeneracy. The liberal poison worked, not merely to the bewilderment of individuals, but also to the destruction of the soul of Europe.

Yes, it can be said that *this is the century in which Europe lost its soul.*

Religious Magnetism

What fearful consequences will yet come upon Europe for

its rejection of biblical Christianity?

Can Europe ever regain its commanding position of influence and consequence in the world? Be very sure that this is the intention of the European political leaders, philosophers, and economists in our time. In these very days, they are thinking every moment about a sense of destiny with reference to the future. They anticipate and deliberately plan to put together a new power block that will be second to none across our present world. But they plan largely without including the true God in their ambitions.

How will they do this? It does not strain the imagination to think that there could quickly develop in Europe a composite form of theologically corrupted neo-Christianity plus New Age paganism that could be the initial magnetism to pull Europe together in a program of religious unity.

In Europe and across the world, the call for "Christian unity" is coming on very strong. Many denominations — even in America — beset by lack of attendance, financial problems, mediocre leadership, aging buildings, rusting machinery, and spiritual exhaustion are beginning to think of global religious unity as the answer, producing the dawn of a new age. Look for that call to grow, and especially listen for it to come out of the continent of Europe as the West seeks its soul again.

The Threat of War

These forms of unity — commercial, political, military, and religious — cannot, however, be expected to happen by accident. In all of history, unity has been based on two major considerations: a principle that is compelling but somewhat abstract, and a leader who is concrete and charismatic. People rarely gather or exercise great passions over mere principle or a point of doctrine. When that "ideology" or spiritual point of view is embodied in a great personal communicator, however, then presto, a catalytic conversion takes place.

We have seen this in the past, have we not? This is the way it was with Hitler in Germany, with Mussolini in Italy, and with the god-man Hirohito in Japan. Yes, this century has produced evidence, which is still frighteningly remembered, of the conversion and catalyzing of whole nations around a compelling, charismatic leader.

Can this be expected in Europe? It indeed must be the case, or the planned unity of Europe will fractionalize itself into a thousand pieces. In fact, even the present gathering of Europe is focused around individual, commanding leaders whose voices are respected. None of them, however, appears at this moment to have the ultimate charisma to gather the passions of Europe and hold them in his right hand.

What could trigger the emergence of such a leader? Many things — the paramount one being the threat of global war. Be sure that this era of "the cold war is past" and "peace is now upon us" will not continue. Christ told us this. He said, "And ye shall hear of wars and rumors of wars . . . ."

Jesus said that this would always be the case in all of history. He then expanded upon this by saying, "For nation shall rise against nation, and kingdom against kingdom." The Bible never promises that man will be able to bring peace on earth, although it indicates many peace movements will make such a promise.

The threat of war would produce great fear across Europe and the other nations of the West, including America. Such a threat often produces a degree of irrationality, whereby people accept solutions that would otherwise be rejected. They can certainly be expected to accept a solution from a great, respected world leader.

The Man With The Plan

One can easily envision such a leader presenting himself on international television as "the man with the plan." One could almost hear him say: "Dear friends of earth, brothers and sisters. Let me extend a great call to sanity. We are now presented with the possibility of nuclear holocaust, but such a thing does not have to come to pass. Why should millions die when it could be otherwise? Let us meet together under the great cause of world peace, and let us plan our tomorrows as civilized men. Yes, I have a plan whereby we can move beyond the threat of war into a millennium of peace, and yes, a new age of prosperity."

With these and many other words, a beguiling voice could easily attract the attention, the loyalty, and the cooperation of the nations of the world.

Such a person may already be a well-known religious leader, already being accepted and trusted by millions. One can easily envision the rulers of the nations responding by saying, "You be our leader! We are willing to follow you. We believe in your program for a global unity!"

We can easily see, then, how this person could be expected to say: "Thank you so much for your response! But God has called me to spiritual things. May I therefore introduce to you Mr. So-And-So, whom I consider to be one of the potentially great men of our time. He has wide vision, large comprehension, and boundless energy. He speaks many languages, and I recommend that we appoint him as chairman of the committee to plan the future and to achieve world peace and comity of nations."

Yes, a global religious leader could easily be the catalyst to install a political leader who would be instantly respected, loved, admired, and followed.

Is this a plausible scenario for the days to come? It is entirely plausible on a simple human level, but it is more than that! When we look into the Word of God and its prophecy about the future, we see that *such a development is inevitable.*

Will Europe produce a great world political leader? Yes, it will! Will this great political leader come to power with the help of a great religious leader? Yes, he will! The Bible indicates that exactly this will take place in the world as we move toward the end of the age.

Yes, observing even through human eyes, we can see the emergent inevitability of the fulfillment of the biblical picture. Considering, then, the teaching of the Word of God, let us ask, "Is the rise of Antichrist upon us?"

The Last Empire

How wonderful it is that God has given us, in His Word, the only reliable projection available to tell us of the future. We can understand the direction of our world and its ultimate outcome only by understanding the Word of God. We must take confidence in the fact that:

> We have also a more sure word of prophecy;
> whereunto ye do well to take heed, as unto a light that

shineth in a dark place, until the day dawn, and the
day star arise in your hearts (2 Pet. 1:19).

In the prophetic Word we learn that we have a dependable
source of information, and the examining of that information
produces immense profit. We do well to take heed to what the
Bible says.

What then does the Bible say about that leader who will
come to power first in Europe and then become the leader of the
entire world? The Scripture says:

And after threescore and two weeks shall Messiah be cut off, but not for himself: and the people of
the prince that shall come shall destroy the city and
the sanctuary; and the end thereof shall be with a
flood, and unto the end of the war desolations are
determined (Dan. 9:26).

Here we have a very remarkable prophecy in the Old
Testament concerning the coming of the Antichrist.

First of all, this verse reminds us of that awful event in
which the Messiah of Israel, the Saviour of the world, Jesus
Christ the King of all kings, would be cut off "but not for
himself." Here is a prophetic foretelling of the death of the
Saviour in which Christ would give His life for the sins of the
world.

Who are the people who cut off the Messiah? Who are the
people who destroyed the city and the sanctuary? Quite obviously, the answer is Rome. It was the Roman Empire that was
the master of the world in the days of the earthly ministry of
Christ. It was a Roman sword that pierced the side of Jesus
Christ, and it was a Roman soldier's arm that drove those awful
spikes through His hands and through His feet. It was a Roman
army under Titus that destroyed Jerusalem and the temple in
A.D. 70.

This prophecy in the Book of Daniel describes the activity
of a power that can only be fulfilled by the historic Roman
Empire and the Roman Empire reconstituted as the last great
empire of earth.

We must remember that only four great empires will rule
the world in the entire history of man. These four great empires

are: Babylon, Persia, Greece, and Rome. In Daniel's description, the great emphasis is on that fourth empire. The Scripture says:

> And the fourth kingdom shall be strong as iron: forasmuch as iron breaketh in pieces and subdueth all things: and as iron that breaketh all these, shall it break in pieces and bruise. And whereas thou sawest the feet and toes, part of the potters' clay, and part of iron, the kingdom shall be divided; but there shall be in it of the strength of the iron, forasmuch as thou sawest the iron mixed with miry clay. And as the toes of the feet were part of iron, and part of clay, so the kingdom shall be partly strong, and partly broken. And whereas thou sawest iron mixed with miry clay, they shall mingle themselves with the seed of men: but they shall not cleave one to another, even as iron is not mixed with clay (Dan. 2:40-43).

Here we have a perfect description of the final stage of the empire of Rome and of present-day Europe. In its earliest constitution, Rome was the great power of the world but was then divided into two great entities: the East, ruled by Constantinople; and the West, centered in Rome itself.

In its final form, the empire will be both unified and divided, divided into ten kingdoms but unified as a kingdom in and of itself under a great leader. It is that complicated political entity, the reconstituted Roman Empire, which will produce, according to the prophet Daniel, the prince that shall come.

A reconstituted Roman Empire — that means Europe. It can only mean Rome and its environs: Italy, Germany, France, Holland, Belgium, and England; all of which and more were a part of the original Roman Empire. As we see this complex coming together with breathtaking speed, we must realize that right before our eyes is developing the political base for the prince that shall come, the Antichrist. What then does the Bible say about this coming dreadful world ruler?

The Prince that Shall Come

Daniel, describing the prince that shall come, the Antichrist, gives us a real insight into his personality and power:

> And he shall speak great words against the most High, and shall wear out the saints of the most High, and think to change times and laws: and they shall be given into his hand until a time and times and the dividing of time (Dan. 7:25).

Speaking further about him, Daniel says:

> And in the latter time of their kingdom, when the transgressors are come to the full, a king of fierce countenance, and understanding dark sentences, shall stand up. And his power shall be mighty, but not by his own power: and he shall destroy wonderfully, and shall prosper, and practise, and shall destroy the holy people. And through his policy also he shall cause craft to prosper in his hand; and he shall magnify himself in his heart, and by peace shall destroy many: he shall also stand up against the Prince of princes; but he shall be broken without hand (Dan. 8:23-25).

So it is that the Antichrist will be a remarkable person, and by a *program of peace* will institute what finally will be great destruction in the world.

Who is this person who is called "the beast" (Rev. 13:4), "the man of sin" (2 Thess. 2:3), "the son of perdition" (2 Thess. 2:3)? While the Bible does not give us his name, it gives us many characteristics of this evil monster who will initially come to power in a revived Europe and ultimately, for a brief hour, rule the world. What does the Scripture say about him? Its denotations include the following:

> 1) He will come presenting a great program of peace (Dan. 8:25).
> 2) He will oppose Christ, the Prince of princes (Dan. 8:25).
> 3) He shall wear out the saints of the most High (Dan. 7:25).
> 4) He will come out of the people who cut off Messiah the Prince (Dan. 9:26).

5) He will make a covenant with the nation of Israel (Dan. 9:27).

6) He will break that covenant and persecute the Jews (Dan. 9:27).

7) He will pretend to be God Himself (2 Thess. 2:4).

8) He will occupy the rebuilt temple, the temple of God (2 Thess. 2:4).

9) He will perform the will of Satan (2 Thess. 2:9).

10) He will bring strong delusion to the whole world (2 Thess. 2:11).

11) He will be wounded to death, but he will recover (Rev. 13:14-15).

12) He will blaspheme God (Rev. 13:5-6).

13) All the world will worship him (Rev. 13:8).

14) He will be a miracle worker (Rev. 13:13-14).

15) He will set up his image that speaks like a man (Rev. 13:14-15).

16) He will cause every person to receive a mark, the mark of the beast (Rev. 13:16).

17) He will himself have a number, 666 (Rev. 13:18).

The person who has wisdom (Rev. 13:18) will note these characteristics and will possess information that will be valuable in discerning the times in which we live. These details about the Antichrist are provided in Scripture for a purpose, and we do well to carefully heed the prophetic Word and let it affect our lives. Foolish indeed is the Christian who, for whatever reason, ignores the predictions of Scripture about the last days.

The predictions of Scripture plus the developments of our times are producing a stunning impact upon our world. When we remember that Europe will be the initial power base for the Antichrist, we should be thoughtful. Remembering also that he will expand his reign to rule the world as earth's most powerful dictator, we think further. We even wonder what amazing cosmic power must be working even in our time to bring these developments so quickly to pass.

The Power Behind the Throne

We must notice from these passages that the Antichrist, when he comes, will not gain the ascendancy or the ability to rule simply by his own power. No indeed, there is a ferocious spiritual power that will give the Antichrist his capability. What is this power? Again, the Scripture describes this exactly. Speaking of the Antichrist, it says:

> And then shall that Wicked be revealed, whom the Lord shall consume with the spirit of his mouth, and shall destroy with the brightness of his coming: Even him, whose coming is after the working of Satan with all power and signs and lying wonders, And with all deceivableness of unrighteousness in them that perish; because they received not the love of the truth, that they might be saved (2 Thess. 2:8-10).

The true power behind the Antichrist is that of Satan himself. It is the devil who will finally raise up his man, his representative, who will organize the world against God.

The Scripture sounds an interesting note concerning the religious leader who will gather the religions of the world in a great ecumenical faith that will then be invoked in the service of the Antichrist. The religion of the Antichrist will ultimately be satanism. The Scripture says:

> And they [the people of the world] worshipped the dragon [the devil] which gave power unto the beast: and they worshipped the beast, saying, Who is like unto the beast? who is able to make war with him? And there was given unto him a mouth speaking great things and blasphemies . . . (Rev. 13:4-5).

So the devil produces a program of global worship in which the world falls before the Antichrist. He does use a religious leader to do this, described in Scripture:

> And I beheld another beast coming out of the earth; and he had two horns like a lamb, and he spoke like a dragon. And he exerciseth all the power of the first beast before him, and causeth the earth and them

which dwell therein to worship the first beast, whose deadly wound was healed. And he doeth great wonders, so that he maketh fire come down from heaven on the earth in the sight of men, And deceiveth them that dwell on the earth by the means of those miracles which he had power to do in the sight of the beast; saying to them that dwell on the earth, that they should make an image to the beast, which had the wound by a sword, and did live (Rev. 13:11-14).

A satanic trinity will first come to power in a revived Roman Empire and then move out to become the political and religious masters of the world. These are Satan, the Antichrist, and the false prophet.

We must also notice that the Scripture teaches that there will be a covenant between the Antichrist and the nation of Israel. This covenant (military alliance) will be broken by the Antichrist, and he will initiate a persecution of Israel that will be fearful indeed. This activity will bring to pass the last half of a period of time called "the Tribulation," this last half being "the Great Tribulation." The Scripture says:

And he shall confirm the covenant with many for one week: and in the midst of the week he shall cause the sacrifice and oblation to cease, and for the overspreading of abominations he shall make it desolate, even until the consummation, and that determined shall be poured upon the desolate (Dan. 9:27).

Notice there will be a covenant made by the Antichrist with "the many" (Israel). In response to this covenant, he may well move an army into Israel as a defense against a mighty invasion from the north when Russia moves to the south (Ezek. 38-39). Out of this notable victory, which actually will be won by the Lord, the Antichrist could well be escalated on this account to world leadership. Temporarily, he will be a great friend to the nation of Israel, but will ultimately be the bitterest enemy of God's people.

What will finally be the end of the Antichrist? The Scripture says that he will be destroyed by the return of Jesus Christ when our Lord comes at the end of the great battle of Armageddon. The Antichrist is called the one "whom the Lord shall consume with the spirit of His mouth, and He shall destroy with the brightness of His coming." When Christ comes again in power and great glory, He will depose the Antichrist, who then will be cast into the lake that burns with fire and brimstone for ever and ever.

In fact, we do well to think specifically of what will happen to the Antichrist as taught in the prophetic Word. The lesson of his tragic end is that evil will not finally triumph. The message of the Bible is that evil is temporary, but righteousness is eternal. In the last analysis, any ruler or any ordinary man is a total fool who attempts to oppose God and His program. While many make the attempt, even in our time, the life lived in opposition to God is the life of insanity. We can see this from the ultimate end of the Antichrist.

While the Antichrist will appear to be very successful for a time, that success will not continue. He will rule the world and fill himself with inexorable pride. That pride will lead him finally to make war on God himself. Does he succeed in dethroning God? No, indeed. Notice what the Bible teaches about the dreadful consequences that will come upon the man of sin:

1. He and his power will be destroyed by the brightness of the coming of Jesus Christ (2 Thess. 2:8).

2. The saints of God will share in the final defeat of the Antichrist when Jesus comes again (Rev. 19:14).

3. The Antichrist and the false prophet, his religious associate who wrought miracles and deceived the world, will be cast alive into a lake of fire burning with brimstone (Rev. 19:20).

4. He is found in that lake of fire a thousand years later, and there the beast and the false prophet will be tormented day and night for ever and ever (Rev. 20:10).

This remarkable scenario comes to us from the prophetic Word and should be the object of great attention by believers in our time.

To Rule the World

Seeing these things in the Word of God, perceptive readers of Holy Scripture should then also take notice of the circumstances in our current history. The present disturbances in Europe, along with newly formed United States of Europe, cannot be ignored. Such a historical development comes closer than anything the world has ever seen to the scenario described in the Word of God.

A revived and reconstituted Europe, in the very nature of things, must produce military power and a great political leader. It must also finally produce religious unity under a great spiritual leader as well. The conjoining of these two bases, political and religious, will make of Europe a power that will soon aspire to rule the world. All of these considerations are presented in the prophetic Word and are the near-predictable results of this present development, even to the casual, secular observer.

A friend recently called me and said, "Dave, I've just been to Germany and have visited the Berlin Wall." This was followed by a most fascinating conversation.

My correspondent said with earnest concern, "I can tell you that in Berlin today and across Germany there is being born a new, most dynamic spirit the like of which I have never seen before in my life. These people truly believe that the dawn of a new age is coming. They are confident that there will be a revived, unified Europe that will lead the world. They believe that the breakdown of the Communist system in Eastern Europe and the development of the European economic community, soon to be followed by the United States of Europe, will escalate Europe into influence such as it has never seen before. They are confident that a world economy will now develop with Europe taking the lead, and they those very words."

My correspondent then said, "I was absolutely amazed to see the utter dynamism on the part of the thinking of the people of Europe. I wanted to take the time to call you because what is reported in the press is merely a pale representation of the real scene there. The people of Germany and the balance of Europe have boundless enthusiasm and the most ambitious set of ideas for the future that I've ever seen in any culture in my entire life.

It is really something to behold."

Eyewitness reports like this are coming in from Europe by all who visit and see the amazing developments taking place. Living in times like these should cause believers everywhere to commit themselves to a new and sober reflection as to analyzing the tide of our times. We should be thinking more deeply, praying more sincerely, and laboring with the totality of our efforts for Christ to be adequate for the challenge of times like these.

What Should We Do?

There is an important final consideration that the student of the prophetic Word will never ignore. After the Bible tells us that there will be signs in the sun and in the moon and in the stars, it says that on the earth will be "distress of nations, with perplexity."

This is a reminder that the brightest secular rulers of the world will simply not know what to do or be able to handle the situation. It then follows this by saying that the very hearts of men will fail them for fear and for looking after those things that are soon to come to pass, predicting that the powers of heaven will be shaken. These are the words of Jesus in Luke 21:25-26.

After saying this, Christ then warned the world with the announcement that these events would be followed by the Son of Man coming in a cloud with power and great glory. Surely this announcement should cause every one of us to at least allow for the possibility that our generation is speeding toward the consummation of history.

Many then ask the question, "What should I do?" The answer comes from the Lord Jesus when He said, "And when these things begin to come to pass, then look up, and lift up your head; for your redemption draweth nigh."

Out of this, we have words of eternal encouragement to every person who has believed the gospel of Christ. Having believed in Jesus, His person, and His death upon the cross, one becomes a Christian and the inheritor of everlasting life. The developments of our time should cause every believer to look forward with greater anticipation than ever to his translation from this world to the world that is to come. He should look up for a redemption that draws nigh.

These events should have a second result. For everyone who has not yet believed in Jesus Christ as their personal Saviour, the Bible warns them that there is terror, judgment, and condemnation to come. The amazing unfolding of the events of these times should cause each person who is not a Christian to face the fact that they are lost without Christ.

Each person, then, who is not a Christian does well to ask the question, "What shall I do?" The answer is very clear in the Word of God. In order to be a Christian the Bible says to "believe on the Lord Jesus Christ, and thou shalt be saved . . ." (Acts 16:31). It announces very clearly that "He that believeth on the Son hath everlasting life: and he that believeth not the Son shall not see life; but the wrath of God abideth on him" (John 3:36). The eternal destiny of your life depends on whether you do or do not believe in Jesus Christ.

Looking at the events of our day, at the Middle East, at Europe, at the United States, at our beleaguered world, we are forced to agree that the biblical picture of the future is true. The earnest recommendation that we have for all, then, is to be sure that you have received redemption in Jesus Christ.

The Bible promises you "that whosoever believeth in him should not perish, but have everlasting life" (John 3:16). Make this the day you believe the gospel! The gospel is the marvelous announcement that "Christ died for our sins according to the scriptures; And that he was buried, and that he rose again the third day according to the scriptures" (1 Cor. 15:3-4). Believing this opens the door to life eternal!

Salvation, then, is a most urgent call. The events of our time add to that urgency. "Now is the accepted time, today is the day of salvation."

9

The New World Order in Prophecy

by Robert Lindsted

President Bush made his first speech concerning the Gulf War at the National Religious Broadcasters Convention in Washington, DC. To an audience of about three or four thousand, the president presented his stand on the war, and then went on to say, "You know what is going to solve all of our problems? There is something new called the New World order."

He went on to say, "When this comes in, it's going to bring peace like we have never seen. We are going to be able to lay down all of our weapons. The New World order is the solution to all of our problems."

Most of the several thousand religious broadcasters stood and applauded the president. Only a dozen or so people remained seated. Stunned, they wondered, as I did, "Can this really be happening?"

Many who heard that speech did not realize the significance of the president words. But those of us who have studied biblical prophecy knew George Bush was articulating, for the first time in a public forum, what we knew would come to pass some day.

The New World order will indeed bring the world together under one government, but it will create more problems than it will solve. In fact, in the end this New World order will neatly give its power to the Antichrist exactly as the Bible predicted hundreds of years ago.

What is an antichrist? It is one who will pretend to be everything for which Christ stands, but he will be the exact opposite. So, he is anti-christ because he is really opposed to Christ. He will pretend he is the Christ, hoping to win the affection of people.

The Bible says there will come a time when there will be one world government with one economic system under the control of one man. Scripture says there will be a revived Roman Empire that will rule for a short time. Then, people will give their allegiance to this Antichrist for the rest of time.

These predictions were given to the prophet Daniel some twenty-four or twenty-five hundred years ago; and to the apostle John some nineteen hundred years ago. Bible prophecy is different from the predictions found at the grocery tabloid counter — whose predictions were made last week with most of them never coming true. The Bible's predictions were made hundreds of years ago, and every one of them is coming true; not some, but all of them!

The Royal Nightmare

One night, about twenty-five hundred years ago, King Nebuchadnezzar had a nightmare. After tossing and turning, he sat up in bed and said, "I have just had this royal dream, and I know it is important because if I dreamed it, it *has* to be important. Nothing but important things go through my mind."

He called for all the royal wise men and demanded they tell him the royal interpretation of his royal dream.

"If you will tell us the royal dream, Your Highness, we will make up the royal lie; we mean the royal interpretation," they replied.

The king interrupted them. "As a matter of fact, I've been meaning to talk to you about that. I tell you my dreams, and you guys make up these interpretations that never come true. If you are so smart, you figure out what I dreamed and then the meaning of it, too!"

"Oh, no!" they quickly reminded him. "That's not in our royal contract."

The king responded, "I tell you what. If you can't figure out the dream and give me its interpretation, I am going to cut off your heads." (This threat was extended to the prophet Daniel, too.)

Now, Daniel was a Hebrew, who, as a teenager had been taken from his home in Jerusalem and transported some eight or nine hundred miles away by the conquering Babylonians. When he was brought to this foreign kingdom, they tried to change his name, his language, and his diet.

He said, "Wait a minute! You will have to excuse me, but you see, I'm a Jewish boy. There are certain things a Jewish boy doesn't eat and drink. If you don't mind, I'll have my own food, and I will eat that instead."

"Oh, Daniel," the king urged, "when in Babylon, do as the Babylonians do." But Daniel refused that generous invitation.

Since Daniel was not afraid to take a stand, God blessed him. God is still looking for young people who will take a stand. If they do, He will bless them. God delights in blessing people.

When Daniel heard about the execution notice, he went to King Nebuchadnezzar and said, "Would it be okay, before you chop our heads off, if I pray to my God?"

The king answered, "Sure, you can pray."

Daniel had more freedom to pray in a foreign kingdom than we do in our public schools today! Isn't that pathetic? But, it is true. I don't know if you believe in prayer or not, but I believe my God hears and answers prayer.

I remember a story about a young man who was going to study medicine. He went to a university where there was a noted chemistry teacher who hated Christians. Every year, the professor would ask if there were any Christians in the class. If someone was brave enough to admit to being a Christian, he would have them stand up. "You pray to your God that as I drop this beaker, it will not break when it hits the floor," he would say. Of course, everyone would laugh, and no one would stand up and pray.

One semester, a young Christian man who was studying to be a doctor found himself in the atheist's chemistry class. A few days into the semester, the professor came in and asked, "Is there anyone here who is a Christian?" The young man raised his hand, and the professor told him to stand up.

When asked if he believed in prayer, the student responded, "Yes, Sir."

The professor said, "Well then, I want you to pray to your God that when I drop this beaker, it won't break."

As everyone else in class began to laugh and snicker, the young man bowed his head and prayed out loud. When he was through, the professor dropped the beaker. Because this atheist was so nervous about having had someone pray in his class, when he dropped the beaker, it fell, hit his toe, and then rolled onto the floor without breaking. The professor was laughed right out of his classroom.

You see, I believe in a God to whom you can pray, and so did this young man.

The Head of Gold

Daniel prayed, and God told him the king's dream and its interpretation! The next day, Daniel went back into the king's presence and said, "Listen, King. I think I know what you saw in your vision. You saw a huge image with its top made of gold."

Amazed, the king admitted that was his dream. "How did you know?" he asked.

Daniel replied that his God had revealed the dream to him and went on to tell the king the rest of the dream.

"After the head of gold, there was a chest and arms of silver. The belly and thighs were made of bronze with legs of iron. Finally, there were feet, but they were part iron and part clay. They were extensions of the iron legs, but clay had been mingled in with the iron."

The king said in astonishment, "That is exactly what I saw!"

Daniel continued with the dream. "You then saw a stone that looked as if it came out of the mountain, but it was not cut with hands. As it came, it rolled toward the image and crushed it. In fact, it ground the image into powder. The stone then began to grow until it filled the entire earth."

The bewildered king then said, "That's exactly what I saw!

But, what does it mean?"

Daniel said, "All right, here is the interpretation, and it is a sure one. If my God could show me the dream, then His interpretation of it is sure."

He then said, "Thou, O King, art the head of gold."

Nebuchadnezzar liked this interpretation. Frankly, I don't think he heard another word Daniel said. I believe he thought, *Wow! I am the head of gold . . . that's me. That's me, all right, way up there on the top!*

What did he do? He built a golden image to himself and placed it in the plain of Shinar. As everyone came from all over the world, they would bow down to the golden image of him. Yes, he liked that interpretation.

Daniel, however, told him, "God said you are not going to be the king forever. You are going to be replaced by another country that is inferior to you. It will be the silver. After it will come another, even more inferior nation, and it will take over the world. It will be the bronze. Then, there will be another part with two legs of iron that will be yet another kingdom. Finally, at the end of time, there will be ten toes. They are part iron and part clay; and they are going to be an extension of those iron legs, even though they will be another kingdom. However, this kingdom will only rule a little while. A stone will come and crush all of it. This stone will begin a kingdom of which there will be no end."

This stone is none other than the kingdom of God. Remember, when Christ begins to rule and reign, He will rule forever.

The Ram and the Goat

Let's look at Daniel's prophesies concerning the two world empires that were to follow King Nebuchadnezzar's Babylonian Empire:

> And after thee shall arise another kingdom inferior to thee, and another third kingdom of brass, which shall bear rule over all the earth (Daniel 2:39).

These kingdoms have come into reality, exactly as the Bible said. In the Book of Daniel, not one time, but four times, God described every world power, in order, and called them by name.

In order to understand their significance, look at what Daniel 8:3-8 says:

> Then I lifted up mine eyes, and saw, and, behold, there stood before the river a ram which had two horns: and the two horns were high; but one was higher than the other, and the higher came up last. I saw the ram pushing westward, and northward, and southward; so that no beasts might stand before him, neither was there any that could deliver out of his hand; but he did according to his will, and became great. And as I was considering, behold, an he goat came from the west on the face of the whole earth, and touched not the ground: and the goat had a notable horn between his eyes. And he came to the ram that had two horns, which I had seen standing before the river, and ran unto him in the fury of his power. And I saw him come close unto the ram, and he was moved with choler against him, and smote the ram, and brake his two horns: and there was no power in the ram to stand before him, but he cast him down to the ground, and stamped upon him: and there was none that could deliver the ram out of his hand. Therefore the he goat waxed very great: and when he was strong, the great horn was broken; and for it came up four notable ones toward the four winds of heaven.

After the head of gold, which was Nebuchadnezzar's Babylon, the kingdom of the Medes and the Persians became the next world power. The two arms represent the two parts of their kingdom.

In verse 20 Daniel writes, "The ram which thou sawest having two horns are the kings of Media and Persia." Like a lopsided ram with one horn bigger than the other, the Persian Empire would come up last and be the dominant power. Just as Daniel predicted that is exactly what happened.

The third kingdom, represented in this vision as the mean he-goat with one horn, beat up the ram with two horns, and the he-goat began to rule the world. This is the Grecian Empire seen as the belly and thighs of bronze in the king's dream. Then, when the he-goat was in his prime — in his great fury — the big horn broke, and four horns popped out of his head. The kingdom represented by the he-goat was that of Alexander the Great, the dominant king of Greece who died in his prime. His four generals took power after him.

Look at verse 21: "And the rough goat is the king of Grecia: and the great horn that is between his eyes is the first king." Isn't that pretty simple? That is Alexander the Great.

Alexander the Great conquered the world when he was barely thirty years old and then became frustrated because there was nothing else to conquer. Instead, he went around the world putting on marching exhibitions. He caught a marsh fever and died a fool's death while putting on a parade. His generals came home to his infant son to say, "Your daddy's dead, now you rule the world."

The son asked, "What do I do with the world?" It is recorded that the four generals of Alexander the Great killed his son and divided the kingdom among themselves.

Consider what the Bible said 175 years before Alexander the Great was ever born! Verses 21 and 22 state:

> . . . and the great horn that is between his eyes is the first king. Now that being broken, whereas four stood up for it, four kingdoms shall stand up out of the nation, but not in his power.

These verses refer to Alexander the Great, and the last verse tells us that his son would not rule after him. Isn't the Bible clear?

The head of gold is Babylon; the arms and chest of silver are the Medes and the Persians; and the belly and thighs of bronze are none other than Alexander the Great.

These empires are recorded in yet another manner. Daniel described them as three animals: the first one like a lion with eagle's wings (Babylon); next, a bear with three ribs in his mouth (the Medeo-Persians — this is a matter of recorded history); and third, a leopard with four wings that depict the swiftness of Alexander the Great's world conquest.

The Fourth Kingdom

What about the fourth kingdom? In the interpretation of

the king's dream, Daniel wrote:

> And the fourth kingdom shall be strong as iron: forasmuch as iron breaketh in pieces and subdueth all things: and as iron that breaketh all these, shall it break in pieces and bruise. And whereas thou sawest the feet and toes, part of potters' clay, and part of iron, the kingdom shall be divided; but there shall be in it of the strength of the iron, forasmuch as thou sawest the iron mixed with miry clay. And as the toes of the feet were part of iron, and part of clay, so the kingdom shall be partly strong, and partly broken. And whereas thou sawest iron mixed with miry clay, they shall mingle themselves with the seed of men: but they shall not cleave one to another, even as iron is not mixed with clay. And in the days of these kings shall the God of heaven set up a kingdom, which shall never be destroyed: and the kingdom shall not be left to other people, but it shall break in pieces and consume all these kingdoms, and it shall stand for ever. Forasmuch as thou sawest that the stone was cut out of the mountain without hands, and that it brake in pieces the iron, the brass, the clay, the silver, and the gold; the great God hath made known to the king what shall come to pass hereafter: and the dream is certain, and the interpretation thereof sure (Dan. 2:40-45).

What kingdom do the legs of iron represent? The Roman Empire with its two capitals: Rome and Constantinople.

How do we know? Revelation 17:10 tells us that seven kings will rule the world. The first two were Assyria and Egypt. Then Daniel comes in chronologically with Babylon as number three. The fourth and fifth kingdoms were the Medes and the Persians followed by Alexander the Great.

In verses 10-13 we find:

> And there are seven kings: five are fallen, and one is, and the other is not yet come; and when he cometh, he must continue a short space. And the beast that was, and is not, even he is the eighth, and

is of the seven, and goeth into perdition. And the ten horns which thou sawest are ten kings, which have received no kingdom as yet; but receive power as kings one hour with the beast. These have one mind, and shall give their power and strength unto the beast.

The Bible says, ". . . five are fallen, one is . . . ." Who would be in power when Revelation was written at about A.D. 95 or A.D.96? — Rome. This passage states there are seven kings; five are fallen, one is right now, and the other will come later.

The last kingdom will be an extension of the iron legs that Daniel wrote about. It will be a revived Roman Empire. It will be part iron and part clay, a mixture of religion and politics. In Daniel 7:7-8, we read:

> After this I saw in the night visions, and behold a fourth beast, dreadful and terrible, and strong exceedingly; and it had great iron teeth: it devoured and brake in pieces, and stamped the residue with the feet of it: and it was diverse from all the beasts that were before it; and it had ten horns. I considered the horns, and, behold, there came up among them another little horn, before whom there were three of the first horns plucked up by the roots: and, behold, in this horn were eyes like the eyes of man, and a mouth speaking great things.

In verse 7, Daniel said he saw a beast so terrible, it was like nothing he had ever seen before. This dreadful, ugly beast was so strong that it had great iron teeth (like the iron legs). It broke all the other kingdoms.

Ten horns then came up representing the ten kings — in other words, an extension of those legs would be the feet, part of iron and part of clay.

The Revived Roman Empire

The Bible states what has and is going to happen. There will be Babylon; the Medes and the Persians; Greece and Alexander the Great; the Roman Empire; and then an extension of one — a revived Roman Empire with ten horns or ten kings.

Once this last kingdom comes to power, it will rule for one hour, and then will give its power to the beast. He will rule and make war against the Lamb.

An article in the *Wichita Eagle* stated, ". . . Since the fall of the Roman Empire, there has been the dream of a unified Europe. We are . . . seeing a brand new Roman Empire reconstructed." Even news reporters call the unified Europe the new Roman empire.

On December 31, 1992 the European Economic Community took power, and on January 1, 1993, its policies went into effect.

Until recently, the European community was considered to be only a political coalition. Now, it has gone from an economic dream to a political reality.

The *Kansas City Star* recently ran an article, "Is Euro-man Kinda' Like Superman?" It goes on to state that most of western Europe will be combined into one, big, powerful, economic unit that will be the envy of the world.

Will it work, will it dominate America? Will America be second class? The answer is yes. The European community is on the verge of becoming the dominant power of the world. It is a revived Roman Empire.

Northwest Magazine, sponsored by an airline, carried an article declaring that America will take a second seat to the revived Roman Empire.

After the Persian Gulf crisis, I flew back from Israel and landed in Greece. I was handed a card stating that any person who is a citizen of any one of the twelve Common Market nations does not have to fill out any legal papers when going from one country to another in Europe. However, any person who is not from one of the Common Market nations would have to fill out all of the papers.

Forbes Magazine wrote: "There will only be one Europe. It will be a super power."

Will there be one currency or many?

This magazine answers: "Ultimately, the move to a single currency is about symbolism and power. There will be only one economy, and it will not only be a united Europe, but it will probably be a united world."

In the business section of the previously quoted European

newspaper, there is a very interesting second section depicting what Europeans describe as a historical moment — "Making History, A Unique Moment As World Leaders Gather in London." Why? To launch the first test for the Euro-bank and the new Euro-dollar. It's already here; it's already been issued; and now, it's on its way.

The New World Order

How close are we to the New World order?

An article in the *Atlantic Journal* begins by announcing a New World order — a world quite different from the one we have known — with a United Nations that performs as envisioned by its founders. It goes on to say that following the Persian Gulf crisis, the New World order is emerging as our only hope for peace around the world.

This is it. Utopia. It is finally here, bringing the nations of the world under one government. If we have one government, we will have no wars, they say. This deceptive promise of heaven on earth is winning great popularity.

Howard Wilkins, an ambassador to one of the Common Market nations said, "We will not recognize the world because of the change militarily and politically in Europe. Once it is united, it will be as big or bigger than the United States in terms of its marketing power."

He is right. Soon we may not recognize the world. The truthful observer must agree that America is in decay. A new superstar on the scene — a united Europe — a revived Roman Empire exactly as the Bible said.

The Common Market says to the industrialized nations, "Hey, the United States is in decline. If you want to look at the future, you'd better align with the Common Market — the seat of world power."

Presently, there are twelve countries in the Common Market with several others who want in. Do you know what is so interesting about that? The Bible states that when the Antichrist comes to power, he will pull three nations out. Then he will put himself in power, allowing only ten nations to remain. Now, if he is going to pull out three and leave ten, that means he will have begun with thirteen.

In a special edition of the *Jerusalem Post*, which featured the twelve stars of the Common Market nations, guess which nation the *Post* was recommending for number thirteen? The Israeli Star of David! Entering Europe's charmed circle seems to be Israel's goal.

The Lady and the Tower of Babel

The cover of the book, *Europe Is Rising,* pictures the tower of Babel, a symbol commonly used by the Common Market, and includes these words: "Europe, many tongues, one voice."

In the background, a modern crane leans against the ancient tower. In addition, the twelve stars of the Common Market are inverted, converting them into the sign of Satan. Just coincidence?

Canadian television aired a two-hour special called "Europe Unbounded" in which a United Europe was predicted to rule the world while the United States and Canada would be left powerless. During the program some of the symbols of the United Europe were shown, including the tower of Babel and the image of a woman.

Why are these two symbols important? According to the Bible, the last world political system will be composed part of iron and part of clay. What do these two parts represent?

Revelation 17 says that in the last days there will be a prostitute, a harlot, and she will commit fornication. She (religion) will sell herself to the kings of the world. In other words, religion and politics will join together. Why? To bring all men under one single government and one single religion.

What will be the foundation of this world religion? The New Age movement — the fastest growing religion in America today. In fact, it has already infiltrated churches, businesses, the media, sports, and even our schools. Children can learn how to visualize and have out-of-the body experiences; they can be hypnotized, but they cannot pray to the God of all creation.

The present unity movement, under the guise of the New Age movement, is none other than the plan of the Antichrist and Satan. To understand how the world could be fooled into believing the lies of this Satanic religion, we need to go back to the tower of Babel, where the New Age had its beginning.

In Genesis, Chapter 11, we read of an unnamed people building a great city on the plain of Shinar. To the narrator of this parable, peering across time and desert from his Nomadic traditions, these folks were awesomely clever. Since they all spoke one common language, nothing was impossible for them.

The plan of these ingenious people was to erect a huge tower whose top would reach to heaven. It would be an altar to their own intellect called Babel, or Gate of God. Their idea was to build a tower to God, to reach up and touch Him, so they, too, would become gods. The religion of Nimrod and Babel taught that we are all gods.

An advertisement that appeared in the *Wall Street Journal* concerned the ancient Tower of Babel and was presented as a parable.

The ad states:

> Babel or Gate to God, the God himself came down. Walked the streets of their cities, saw their project under construction. The arrogant race angered him. He passed his hand over the city, cursed it, now where there had been one language, suddenly there were hundreds. Confusion reigned. Nothing was possible.

The ad said the lesson taught by this ancient parable is uncannily applicable for us in the twentieth century. They are saying, "Listen, people, we have got to get together."

Get it? If we can come together — if we can all have one common language, one common government, one common religion — nothing will be impossible for us.

Revelation 17 said in the last days there will be a harlot, a prostitute, who will sit on a beast; and she will ride across all the world. She will represent a religion that will bring everyone together. The harlot (the end-time religious system) will sit on the beast (the Antichrist and his end-time dictatorship), and she will ride around the world collecting all peoples into one.

The Bible says that the harlot, the woman, will ride a beast.

I used to think this parading harlot was just an accident until I ran across the front cover of the June, 1975, edition of *European Official Magazine*. Even then, it showed a Roman goddess riding on a beast as one of the official symbols of the Common Market. Accident? Not at all.

One of the first stamps put out by the Common Market — a collective stamp used for the entire Common Market — showed the god of Europe riding on the back of a bull (god), begging to be worshipped. This is an exact picture of Revelation 17.

The Bible says that when Europe finally gets to the position where it has all the power — economically, politically, and religiously — it will have but a short time to live. The New World order will rule only one hour and will give its power, strength, and might to the beast.

The Antichrist

Telemarketing Magazine ran an article addressing the future of Europe. Is Europe actually going to unite and work together in a unified form? The article states, "I think it remains to be seen, but if it is going to work, a united Europe will need a leader. Yes, only one overall leader to function effectively. If they are going to work, they will have to have one man who will head up the entire thing."

George Will, of the *Shreveport Journal* writes, "Europe Moving Toward A Bureaucratic State." You know what? He is right.

When I was in Washington, DC in early 1991, I saw a long line of limousines snaking down the street in front of one of the city's plush hotels. I asked a chauffeur who the dignitary was. "Ah", he said, "it is the president of Europe."

The president of Europe? I didn't know they had one. I discovered that he is not really as much of a potentate as his title implies or as he plans to be. But there is a president of Europe who is appointed, not elected, to bring about a political unity in Europe and around the world. He has fifteen thousand employees to help him.

As I passed through Europe last year, I picked up a copy of a European newspaper. The front page read, "The New Mr. Europe." It stated that he will take over the presidency in January, 1993, at what (in theory) will be the dawn of a new Europe. It will be a time when Europe will dominate and control the world.

Before all these events fully takes place, the trumpet is going to sound, and all true believers are going to be taken out of this world. How do I know? Because the Bible says that is exactly what is going to happen.

I really believe we are living near the end of time. If we are the people who are going to see the last political system, then the system cannot take over and rule until the Church is gone. We may see this last empire beginning to form, but it will not fully be in place until after the rapture of the Church.

That's why we as Christians must be different from any other people who have ever lived before. Jesus could come today to take every born-again person home to heaven.

When the Antichrist makes his appearance, he will speak great, swelling words of promise. I believe there will be people, maybe even someone reading this book who will attend that first unholy Sunday.

You and others may say after that great disappearing of the true Church, "Something is going on, and I have to find out what it is." The great orator, the Antichrist, will have magnificent, thrilling explanations for the disappearance of the millions of true Christians.

This tremendous, worldwide religious movement will bring all people into a single religion, and some into one government with one economy exactly as prophesied in God's Word.

The apostle John saw two beasts. The first beast came out of the sea, that is, out of the Gentile world powers. "I . . . saw a beast rise up out of the sea, having seven heads and ten horns, and upon his horns ten crowns, and upon his heads the name of blasphemy" (Rev. 13:1).

The one who appears is the Antichrist. He will come up out of the kingdoms of the Gentiles.

The False Prophet

Just as there is a true Trinity; there is a false trinity. There is God, the Father; God, the Son; and God, the Holy Spirit. Satan's trinity puts him in the place of God; the Antichrist in the place of Jesus Christ; and an anti-prophet (or anti-spirit) in the place of the Holy Spirit.

In Revelation 13, we are introduced to this false prophet. It appears to me that he comes up out of the land of Israel because in verse 11 we find: "And I beheld another beast coming up out of the earth; and he had two horns like a lamb, and he spake as a dragon." Revelation says the land, or the earth, represents the land of Palestine.

What will be the purpose of the false prophet? Verse 12 explains, "And he exerciseth all the power of the first beast before him, and causeth the earth and them which dwell therein to worship the first beast, whose deadly wound was healed."

The first beast mocks death and resurrection. Notice, I said "mocks" because Satan does not have the power of resurrection. He is going to fake death and fake resurrection because he realizes that in order to be the Messiah, he *must* have a death with a resurrection. Therefore, he must fake it. The false prophet will give testimony to him saying, "Hey, look! He has died, and now he is resurrected!"

Verse 14 states: "And deceiveth them that dwell on the earth by the means of those miracles which he had power to do in the sight of the beast; saying to them that dwell on the earth, that they should make an image to the beast, which had the wound by a sword, and did live."

Men will be deceived by miracles. The false prophet will be a great orator. He will do miracles. He will speak great, lying wonders. He will fake death and resurrection. "And he had power to give life unto the image of the beast, that the image of the beast should both speak, and cause that as many as would not worship the image of the beast should be killed" (vs. 15).

Revelation 17:1 says:

> And there came one of the seven angels which had the seven vials, and talked with me, saying unto me, Come hither; I will shew unto thee the judgment of the great whore that sitteth upon many waters.

You may ask, "What are those waters?" Let us now consider Revelation 17:15: "And he saith unto me, The waters which thou sawest, where the whore sitteth, are peoples, and multitudes, and nations, and tongues." In other words, it is a worldwide, false religious system "With whom the kings of the earth have committed fornication, and the inhabitants of the earth have been made drunk with the wine of her fornication" (vs. 2).

Verse 3 states: "So he carried me away in the spirit into the wilderness: and I saw a woman sit upon a scarlet coloured beast, full of names of blasphemy, having seven heads and ten horns." Notice the similarity between the seven heads and ten horns — the symbols of religion and government.

The Mark

At that point and time, according to Daniel 7, the Antichrist will speak great and powerful things. He will do miracles. People will begin to say, "Well, I guess this has got to be the Messiah." He will change the laws. He will change the times and the seasons. Everything will be different.

In Daniel we read how life will be under the Antichrist:

> And the ten horns out of this kingdom are ten kings that shall arise: and another shall rise after them; and he shall be diverse from the first, and he shall subdue three kings. And he shall speak great words against the most High, and shall wear out the saints of the most High, and think to change times and laws: and they shall be given into his hand until a time and times and the dividing of time. But the judgment shall sit, and they shall take away his dominion, to consume and to destroy it unto the end (Dan. 7:24-26).

Revelation 13:16-18 also explains:

> And he causeth all, both small and great, rich and poor, free and bond, to receive the mark in their right hand, or in their foreheads; And that no man might buy or sell, save he that had the mark, or the name of the beast, or the number of his name. Here is wisdom. Let him that hath understanding count the number of the beast: for it is the number of a man; and his number is Six hundred threescore and six [or 666].

He will say, "Listen, if you are going to go to school, if you are going to buy food, if you are going to have a job, then you have to accept my mark."

I read an article written by a man who owns a company that designs small, electronic devices — miniscule silicone chips. When a dog or cat is taken to the veterinarian for a vaccination, a chip is placed in the animal's back with a wand; thus allowing authorities to be able to prove exactly who the pet's owner is. This is done to cattle in Canada, also.

Incredibly, leading companies are now considering how soon these same chips can be implanted into people who perform various job functions. Cosmetically, the chip is concealed beneath the skin and is not noticeable. However, it does not escape the scanners that register all movement of those who go in and out of those areas being monitored. What a great way to "brand" people.

You know what? If you don't take the mark of the Antichrist, (whether it is a chip or not, I don't know), you will not be able to buy or sell. You will not be able to hold a job or buy food at the grocery store. The Antichrist will require that everyone commit to him.

I believe there is a coming mark but only after the rapture of the Church.

Right on Schedule

When Christ returns, He will defeat the Antichrist and his cohorts.

Revelation 17:14 makes that clear:

> These shall make war with the Lamb, and the Lamb shall overcome them: for he is Lord of lords, and King of kings: and they that are with him are called, and chosen, and faithful.

Is the lamb a pretty good fighter? Not usually. This Lamb, however, is going to fight the beast, and the Lamb is going to win. I believe the lamb is none other than the Lamb of God, the person of Calvary, Jesus Christ. You see, history has recorded it.

Reading on in Daniel 7:13-14, we find these words:

> I saw in the night visions, and, behold, one like the Son of man came with the clouds of heaven, and came to the Ancient of days, and they brought him near before him. And there was given him dominion and glory, and a kingdom, that all people, nations, and languages, should serve him: his dominion is an everlasting dominion, which shall not pass away, and his kingdom that which shall not be destroyed.

Yes, friend, everything is right on schedule. Didn't the Bible say that Israel would be back in the land? Iraq would be destroyed once, twice, then devastated the last time? Is Germany united? Is Israel not reborn? Is Europe reconfiguring into a New Order, the Roman Empire reviving?

My dear friend, I believe we are living in the last days. No other generation who ever lived on planet earth has seen as much as you and I have seen. Subsequently, no other people who have ever lived are as accountable as we are.

You and I are responsible for deciding whether we will spend eternity in heaven with Jesus Christ who died and rose again to save us, or whether we will spend all eternity in hell with Satan and his demonic fallen angels, for whom hell was created in order that sin can ultimately be purged and God's creation reconciled to himself.

Jesus is the Prince of Life. Satan is the cannibal of death. You decide. Jesus is the truth and the life. Satan is the father of lies and the master of death. You decide.

Where Will You Spend Eternity?

The story is told of a man who once had a stray dog show up on his porch. For a day or two, he tolerated the dog, then he decided he had to get rid of the critter. But, the dog was faithful, and it followed him everywhere, no matter where he went what he did. Frustrated by this faithful, old dog, the man said, "I have got to get rid of this dog."

He didn't have the heart to shoot the dog, so he loaded him into a simple row boat along with a big brick and rope. When he reached the middle of the lake, he called the faithful dog over to him, tied the rope around its neck, and the other end around the brick. Then he threw dog, brick, and rope into the lake. But the brick was not heavy enough to pull the dog all the way under!

Still being faithful, the old dog swam around and around and around the boat trying to get back to his master, all the while hauling the brick around with him. Now frustrated, the man felt he had to drown the dog somehow. He took an oar and began to hit this dog on the head, trying to poke it under the water. In the course of doing this, the man fell overboard into the lake, and he could not swim.

Seeing the man thrashing in the water himself, the dog came over, grabbed him by the collar, and began to swim toward the shore towing the brick, rope, and the man. Finally, when the dog could swim no longer, the man put his feet down, only to find that he could now walk up on the bank. He looked back to find the brick had finally taken its toll on the dog — he had drowned.

When I heard this story, it made me think about a tale even more pathetic. I think an old man who would drown a dog is a pretty cruel man. But, I will tell you what is more cruel — for a person not to receive Christ!

Jesus came to earth and did nothing but good. But some

people don't want Him; they do everything they can to get rid of Him and keep Him out of their lives. They don't realize that the gospel is a story of love and faithfulness: "For God so loved the world that He gave His only begotten Son" (John 3:16). He sent His Son to die for you.

I don't know your heart's condition, but I do know that Jesus paid an incredible price to save you. He gave His life, and He did it willingly.

If you have never received Christ as your personal Saviour, then you need to make that decision today.

Jesus allows you the option to say, "No, I don't want to be saved." He died for you; He arose again. The gospel is available, but He lets you say no — the choice is yours.

Do you know what keeps a person from coming to Christ once they know they need Him? It is something called pride. Jesus himself said, "No man comes to the Father [God] but by me." To be saved, simply admit to God that you are a sinner.

Dear friend, Christ came to this wretched, strife-torn, sinful world to save sinners. To qualify for the gospel of Jesus Christ, you have to be a sinner. And, you are a sinner whether you admit it or not. But, if you'll admit it, if you come to Christ who loves you so much He died for you, He will save you in an instant.

Instead of going through eternity in hell, where you and I deserve to go, you will live eternally in heaven, where God has a place reserved for you. Because of the sacrifice the Lord Jesus Christ made for you and me on that cruel Roman cross nearly two thousand years ago, you can live forever. Accept Him today. He is the only way.

10

Israel — The Heart of Prophecy

by David Allen Lewis

We are living in the close of the church age and the "times of the Gentiles," as outlined in Luke, Romans, and the Book of Revelation.

Jesus predicted:

> And they shall fall by the edge of the sword, and shall be led away captive into all nations: and Jerusalem shall be trodden down of the Gentiles, until the times of the Gentiles be fulfilled (Luke 21:24).

Listen, Gentiles, it's about over for you. Born-again Christians, however, are not Gentiles (heathen). Paul spoke to believers as having formerly been Gentiles. He wrote to the Corinthian church: "Ye know that ye were Gentiles carried away unto these dumb idols . . ." (1 Cor. 12:2). "Wherefore remember, that ye being in time past Gentiles in the flesh . . ." (Eph. 2:11).

Although my ancestry is British and French (no Jewish ancestors), I am no longer a Gentile. But neither am I an alien to the commonwealth of Israel. It is important for us to know our identity in God. That, however, should not cause us to overlook

His continuing plan for national Israel. The existence of the Church, the spiritual Zion, does not negate the existence of the original Zion — Israel. My identity with God is established in Christ as noted by the apostle Paul:

> Wherefore remember, that ye being in time past Gentiles in the flesh, who are called Uncircumcision by that which is called the Circumcision in the flesh made by hands; That at that time ye were without Christ, being aliens from the commonwealth of Israel and strangers from the covenants of promise, having no hope, and without God in the world: But now in Christ Jesus ye who sometimes were far off are made nigh by the blood of Christ (Eph. 2:11-13).

Paul's brilliant exposition to the Roman church includes a definite statement about natural Israel's future. Note the use of the name Jacob referring to Israel in verse 26. Never in the entire Bible is the name Jacob used to refer in fact or type to the Church. It always, without exception, refers to natural Israel.

> For I would not, brethren, that ye should be ignorant of this mystery, lest ye should be wise in your own conceits; that blindness in part is happened to Israel, until the fulness of the Gentiles be come in. And so all Israel shall be saved: as it is written, There shall [future] come out of Zion the Deliverer, and shall [future] turn away ungodliness from Jacob: For this is my covenant unto them, when I shall [future] take away their sins (Rom. 11:25-27).

The Israel that is to be saved cannot be the Church. The Church is comprised of people who are already saved. The Israel in view here is an Israel that will be saved at a future time when Zechariah's prophecies are fulfilled (Zech. 3:9; 12:10; etc.).

A Matter of Interpretation

I frequently hear the wearying, worn-out statement, "I don't know about all this prophecy business. There are so many points of view. It's all a matter of interpretation." Exactly! It is a matter of interpretation. Either you believe the Word of God literally, or you explain it away. It is as simple as that, and there is no need for further complication.

Even symbols have a literal meaning, which are defined in the Word of God. No external evidence should be used to interpret biblical symbols. The moment you go outside the Scripture to interpret its symbols you introduce an anarchy of interpretation. Every person becomes a law unto himself or herself. Then you can make the Bible say whatever you want it to say, according to your own preconceived notions.

Israel, Duty or Dilemma?

Winston Theodore Pike's book, *Israel Our Duty — Our Dilemma,* is in fact a vicious attack on Israel. Although filled with distortions, misappropriation of Scripture, and scurrilous slander against the Jews, Pike nevertheless professes a compassion for the Jews. That is hard to fathom in the light of Pike's suggestion that the best thing for the Jews would be for Israel to cease to exist!

It is no wonder Pike cannot define our duty to Israel, and why he finds himself in such a dilemma.

Our duty to Israel is clearly declared in Isaiah's prophecy:

Comfort ye, comfort ye my people, saith your God. Speak ye comfortably to Jerusalem . . . (Isa. 40:1-2).

Who is to speak comfort to Jerusalem? It is not the Jews speaking comfort to themselves. What is in view here is a new people of God whose existence was in Isaiah's future. Those mandated to comfort Jerusalem are the born-again members of the Church, the body of Christ. We clearly see and know our duty, and it is no dilemma.

Days of Prophetic Fulfillment

The very existence of Israel is proof that we are living in the final period of this age of grace, the church age.

Get Israel in place in the prophetic plan of God, and you can see the whole thing. Get Israel misaligned, and prophecy becomes incomprehensible.

Behold, the days come, saith the Lord, that the plowman shall overtake the reaper, and the treader of grapes him that soweth seed; and the mountains shall drop sweet wine, and all the hills shall melt. And I will bring again the captivity of my people of Israel, and they shall build the waste cities, and inhabit them; and they shall plant vineyards, and drink the wine thereof; they shall also make gardens, and eat the fruit of them. And I will plant them upon their land, and they shall no more be pulled up out of their land which I have given them, saith the Lord thy God (Amos 9:13-15).

God means what He says, and His Word has been fulfilled in most remarkable fashion, beginning with the miracle of the rebirth of the nation of Israel on May 14, 1948 (Ezek. 36, 37). There is coming a golden Messianic age when all of the visions of the prophets will be fulfilled. We know the church of redeemed persons, adopted into the commonwealth of Israel, will share in the glory of that age and in the complete fulfillment of the hopes and dreams of the ages that are now only fulfilled in a fragmentary way in Israel and in the Church. In the meantime we have God's mandate for the present age in which we live. We are to comfort and bless Israel.

In 1961 Rev. Louis Hauff wrote:

> The Scriptures show that the eyes of the nations will be upon the nation of Israel in the last days. We are aware that Israel is today the center of attention of the world. All nations are aware of the existence of the nation of Israel and are concerned about what happens there. Each one is taking sides either for or against Israel. This could lead to a world conflict.
>
> In July 1958, a time of crisis occurred when Russian communists infiltrated Syria and supplied arms to the Syrians. Suddenly the United States fleet landed Marines in Lebanon, and Great Britain flew paratroopers into Jordan. The stage seemed set for a great battle. The battle of Armageddon seemed very close.
>
> Look at a map of Palestine and you will see that Armageddon (Har Megiddo, Mount Megiddo and the Plain of Esdraelon) was surrounded by the United

States to the northwest, Russia to the northeast, Great Britain to the east, Israel to the south, and Egypt to the southwest. Happily, the alert soon ended, but we were able to see how quickly the nations of the world could assemble at Armageddon in a great last conflict.

After the Lord fights for and delivers Israel, there will come a spiritual awakening to the people. The prophet Zechariah stated: "And it shall come to pass in that day, that I will seek to destroy all the nations that come against Jerusalem. And I will pour upon the house of David, and upon the inhabitants of Jerusalem, the spirit of grace and of supplications: and they shall look upon me whom they have pierced, and they shall mourn for him, as one mourneth for his only son, and shall be in bitterness for him, as one that is in bitterness for his firstborn . . . . In that day there shall be a fountain opened to the house of David and to the inhabitants of Jerusalem for sin and for uncleanness." (See Zech. 12:9-10; 13:1.)[1]

Although written over 25 years ago, this book is still up to date because Pastor Hauff relied on the Word of God for his insight into Israel's place in prophecy.

Is Israel in God's Plan?

The Holocaust is an event so horrible that millions have blinded their eyes to its reality. In a sense they have forgotten that it ever happened. Would you be surprised to discover that some people in your city could not even define the term Holocaust or the Hebrew word Shoah?

Some, having faced the horror of history, choose to deny it ever happened. They write learned books disdainfully proclaiming that the whole thing is a hoax perpetrated by the Jewish people themselves. St. Paul rightly says that Satan, the god of this world, is capable of blinding the minds of them that believe not. (As in 2 Cor. 4:4.)

In his compelling dialogue on Christian-Jewish relations in the Epistle to the Romans, Chapters 9-11, St. Paul makes some observations that are vital to the Church. First of all, the passage clearly establishes that God still has a plan for national Israel.

Perhaps my knowledge is limited, but so far as I know the only church body that gives recognition to this fact in its creed is the Pentecostal denomination, the Assemblies of God. Surely there are other churches that have such a statement in their creed. If you know of one, please inform us as we are anxious to expand our research in this area. On the other hand, since Evangelicals tend to base all their beliefs on sound interpretation of the Scripture, historically, an acceptance of Israel in God's plan has been common in our circles.

Raising the Question

Our faith does not rest on individual denominational or church creeds but on the revealed truth recorded in the sixty-six books of the Bible. Further, when I speak of a plan for national Israel, I am not referring to individual salvation. Individual salvation is personal, to be worked out in the light of God's Word between the person and God. The Evangelical view is clearly and universally established that the Mosaic (salvation) covenant is fulfilled in the New Covenant of Calvary. On the other hand, the Orthodox (and some other) Jewish people hold that the Mosaic covenant is still in force.

All agree that the Mosaic was always a conditional covenant. Is God still in covenant agreement with the people of Israel? Are there covenants other than the Mosaic to be considered? A major question that confronts the Church is this: Can God be in covenant with more than one group at the same time?

Multiple Covenants

The word covenant implies a contract or an agreement. It can be conditional, requiring the participation of two parties, or it can be unilateral, proceeding directly from God as a sovereign act of His will. In the case of the unilateral covenant, no condition or action is required on the part of the second (human) party.

To clarify, the conditional covenant always has God saying to mankind, "If you will do certain things, then you can expect Me to do certain things in response."

On the other hand, a unilateral (unconditional) covenant always depicts the sovereign determination of God, which He simply announces to mankind, letting man know what God plans to do — regardless of what we do or do not do.

God can be, and certainly is, in covenant with more than one group of humans at the same time. This is evident from a study of the Noetic covenant. After the Flood, God put His rainbow in the clouds signifying that He would never again judge humanity by a watery destruction. This covenant was totally unilateral in nature. This covenant with the whole human race was not and is not conditional.

The Abrahamic Covenant

The covenant God made with Abraham was a unilateral covenant. Once Abraham obeyed God on one point, to leave the land of Ur of the Chaldees, God entered into and revealed a marvelous and everlasting covenant to the father of the Hebrew people. This is revealed in the twelfth and fifteenth chapters of Genesis. God evidently wanted us to know that the covenant was unilateral, for it is stated in Genesis 15 that He put Abraham into a deep sleep as He entered into and established the covenant. Abraham had nothing to do with the covenant, except for the fact that he was there and was the original recipient of the covenant.

Christians believe that the Mosaic covenant has been fulfilled, but the Abrahamic covenant, which includes determinations concerning the nationhood and land ownership of the Israelite people is inviolable and unconditional. It is not dependent on what any human person or group does or does not do. It is based entirely on the integrity of God and His ability to bring His determinations to pass.

In short, God has declared that the natural seed of Abraham, the nation of Israel, will never go out of existence. Further, He has decreed that the tiny bit of land known as Israel (1/2 of 1 percent of the land mass of the Middle East) is in perpetuity to be the property of the seed of Abraham, Isaac, and Jacob for all of time. The Scripture says that the Arabs have a right to exist there in the midst of their brethren, for they, too, are descendants of Abraham, though not of Jacob.

Caution, Boast Not!

In the light of this Abrahamic covenant, Paul cautions the converted Gentiles of Rome not to boast against the natural branches (Jewish people) that have grown out of the root of Abraham. We former Gentiles are wild branches grafted into the natural tree of Israel. The Wycliff Bible Commentary correctly establishes that Abraham is the root of us all. Note that Paul says, "Remember that you do not support the root, but the root supports you."

While Israel can easily explain her existence without the Church, the Church cannot explain her existence without Israel. Jesus was Jewish, as were His disciples and followers. The only Bible Jesus and His followers had was the the First Testament. The entire body of Christian Scripture was penned by Jewish authors, with the possible exception of Luke and Acts.

At the very first, the Church was entirely Jewish in its membership. Paul is blunt in informing the Romans that the olive tree into which we Gentiles have been grafted is the property of Israel. What else could be derived from these words: "For if thou [Gentile converts] wert cut out of the olive tree which is wild by nature, and wert graffed contrary to nature into a good olive tree: how much more shall these [Jews], which be the natural branches, be graffed into *their own olive tree?*" (Rom. 11:24).

The early Church in its primitive days was never thought of by the Jewish people, in or out of the Church, as anything more or less than a Jewish sect. Gentile converts were thought, in the early years of the Church, to be proselytes to the Jewish faith and nation. It was not until after the Bar Kochba revolt in the year 135 that the Jewish and Gentile elements in the Church finally separated and went their own ways. The way the Gentile branch of the Church followed tragically led directly to the Holocaust. Can this be true?

The Dark Side of Church History

The sad saga of early Church history records the animosity that arose in the Gentile church against the Jewish believers and the Jews in general. As time went on, the Church became more and more anti-Semitic.

This situation reached a zenith when Constantine granted the edicts of toleration. Christianity was not made the state religion by Constantine, and Constantine never was a convert to Christianity (he submitted to baptism by sprinkling upon his deathbed, thus adding "Christ" to his list of pagan Roman deities, not an uncommon practice in the pagan world of multiple gods). Nevertheless, under the edicts of toleration, Christianity was popularized, and tens of thousands of unconverted pagans were baptized into the church because it was the popular social or politically expedient thing to do.

Malcom Hay, Fr. John T. Pawlikowski, Fr. Edward Flannery, and other Roman Catholic authors, along with many modern Protestant writers such as Roy and Alice Eckardt, Reinhold Niebuhr, Franklin Littel, Michael Brown, Isaac Rottenberg, and David Rausch have extensively documented the historic anti-Semitic bias of the Church.

Harsh Words From Early Church Fathers

Consider the harsh words of Saint Ambrose, who said that the Jewish synagogue was "a house of impiety, a receptacle of folly, which God himself has condemned." It is no wonder that his followers then went out and set fire to the local synagogue.

Saint Gregory of Nyssa spoke with eloquence, saying that the Jews are "Slayers of the Lord, murderers of the prophets . . . advocates of the devil, brook of vipers . . . men whose minds are in darkness . . . haters of righteousness."

Saint John Chrysostom must have had some good qualities, for Cardinal Newman wrote of him, "A bright and cheerful gentle soul, a sensitive heart, a temperament open to emotion and impulse; and all this elevated, refined, transformed by the touch of heaven — such was St. John Chrysostom." A Protestant theologian wrote, "Chrysostom was one of the most eloquent of the preachers who, ever since apostolic times, have brought to men the divine tidings of truth and love."

It must have been difficult for the Jewish people of his time to see his good points for in his homilies against the Jews, St. John Chrysostom said, "The synagogue is worse than a brothel . . . the temple of demons . . . and the cavern of devils . . . . I hate the synagogue . . . I hate the Jews for the same reason."

Even the Great Reformer

Martin Luther, beloved among Protestants and Evangelicals, made strong anti-Semitic statements late in his life. "Verily a hopeless, wicked, venomous, and devilish thing is the existence of these Jews, who for fourteen hundred years have been, and still are, our pest, torment, and misfortune. They are just devils and nothing more."

Luther accused the Jews in terms that today we would consider vulgar:

> When Judas hanged himself and his bowels gushed forth, and, as happens in such cases, his bladder also burst, the Jews were ready to catch the Judas-water and other precious things, and then they gorged and swilled on the merd among themselves, and were thereby endowed with such a keenness of sight that they can perceive glosses in the Scriptures such as neither Matthew nor Isaiah himself ... would be able to detect; or perhaps they looked into the loin of their God "Shed" and found these things written in that smokehole . . . . The devil has eased himself and emptied his belly again — that is a real halidom for Jews and would-be Jews, to kiss, batten on, swill and adore; and then the devil, with his angelic snout, devours what exudes from the oral and anal apertures of the Jews; this is indeed his favorite dish, on which he battens like a sow behind the hedge.

Regarding Luther, Malcom Hay comments, "His doctrine provided many suitable texts for Hitler's program of extermination. Today various hate groups reprint Luther's pamphlet, *The Jews and Their Lies*, to support their vengeful attacks on the Jews.

Haman in the Church

In 1558 the Protestant preacher Ehrhardt wrote, "We ought not to suffer Jews to live amongst us, nor to eat and drink with them." Following the precedent of Saint Ambrose he also recommended that "their synagogues should be set on fire."

Our beloved church became a Haman to the Jews, bringing on the dark ages, the horrors of the inquisition, the bloody crusades, and ultimately producing the climate in which a Hitler could succeed with his diabolical plot. Hitler — who was a church member until the day he died.

Can we be offended at the Jewish scholar, who indicts

Christianity as the prime cause of anti-Semitism for the past eighteen hundred years?

It might be convenient if we could ignore the dark side of our heritage, but, if we ever hope to improve conditions in the world, it would be more practical to face up to history, ourselves, and our society.

Theological Anti-Semitism Today

What a perverse joke it is when present day replacement theologians accuse their premillennial brethren of being socially irresponsible in the face of the drastic, crisis needs of our world, and yet they themselves are provoking an evil hatred for the nation of Israel through their tired, old, worn-out anti-Semitic theology. How have they managed to resurrect these ancient errors and breathe such new vigor into them until they are now sweeping like an "ill wind that bodes no good" throughout the ranks of the Church? The two major anti-Semitic Christian doctrines are replacement and the theology of contempt.

What is being preached in certain quarters today is exactly what both the Protestant and Roman Catholic teachers were promoting in pre-Nazi Germany. We had better be alert to these alarming facts. Don't ever say, "It cannot happen here."

I hear from some of my brethren that God no longer has any use for natural Israel. The Church has taken the place of Israel in God's economy. That is called the *Doctrine of Replacement*.

Then there is the *Doctrine of Contempt*. Simply stated it claims that since the Jews killed Christ they are worthy of any punishment that falls upon them. The Holocaust? Good enough for them.

In the light of this strange, unbiblical philosophy how should one view the killing of Christian martyrs under the old Roman Empire and more recently under the Communists? Good enough for them? You cannot have it both ways.

Germany Then —America Today?

Dr. Roland Pritiken, a retired Air Force general, recently sent me an interesting list of comparisons between pre-Nazi Germany and conditions in America today. There is indeed cause for concern. The church in pre-Nazi Germany was preaching the twin doctrines of Christian anti-Semitism. They are the doctrine of replacement and the doctrine of contempt.

The theology of replacement contends that the Church has replaced Israel and that God no longer has any purpose for Israel. Contempt declares that the Jews crucified Jesus, therefore they are under a curse and whatever happens, including the Holocaust, is good enough for them.

While both of these errors have been refuted, nevertheless Hitler's henchmen were able to quote both Roman and Protestant theologians in justifying their heinous acts against the Jewish people. Thus, in a Christian nation, out of a perverted Christianity, came the Holocaust, costing the lives of six million Jews and millions of other casualties throughout the world.

Can Evangelicals Boast?

My Evangelical brethren cannot boast that our colleagues performed any better in the Nazi era. The late Dr. Oswald Smith, pastor of the great People's Church in Toronto, Ontario, Canada, came back from Germany with a glowing report in the mid-1930s. He spoke of over fourteen thousand Evangelical pastors who felt that Hitler was the answer to Germany's problems, and that probably the new Nazi movement would bring spiritual revival to Germany. Later Dr. Smith realized the awfulness of what was happening in Germany and recanted, but it was too late.

We still have time to speak out and prevent another holocaust in our times, but the handwriting is on the wall. If we are silent, history will repeat itself. The Holocaust is not mere history, it is potential.

Where is the Church of Today Heading?

Is the Church in America different from the Church in pre-Holocaust Germany? I hope that it is, but I have some deep concerns. Perhaps the fourteen thousand Evangelical pastors that Dr. Smith spoke of were not actively anti-Semitic. Perhaps they were simply unconcerned.

We have heard some strange things in recent times from modern churchmen. After Israel was savagely attacked by Syria and Egypt on the Day of Atonement, October 1973, Father

Daniel Berrigan accused Israel of behaving like a "criminal" and "racist state." Then Henry Pit van Deusan, former president of the Union Theological Seminary, likened the Jewish nation to Nazi Germany. To this, Methodist theologian Roy Eckardt commented, "Whenever Israel is assailed, certain suppressed, macabre elements in the Christian soul are stirred to sympathy with the assailants."

Have We Learned Anything From the Holocaust?

We wonder if the Christian world has drawn any lessons at all from the Holocaust. We should have because the greatest events of mankind's history will include the creation of earth, the fall of man, God's provision of redemption through Jesus, the destruction of Jerusalem in A.D. 70, the reformation, two world wars, the Holocaust, the re-establishment of the nation of Israel, and the second coming of Christ.

Being an Evangelical, however, I should not presume to speak for the older churches. My colleagues in the National Christian Leadership Conference for Israel, Dr. William Harter, Presbyterian; Dr. Franklin Littel, United Methodist; Father Edward Flannery, Roman Catholic; Reverend Isaac Rottenberg of the Reformed Church, and a host of others have documented the anti-Semitic and anti-Israel bias that has been consistently manifested by the National and the World Council of Churches.

I have heard a Roman Catholic nun, the great and compassionate scholar Sister Rose Thering, professor at Seton Hall University, lament the Vatican's refusal to recognize the state of Israel. Concluding, therefore, that there are strong voices in the old-line churches calling for repentance in that quarter, I will speak primarily to my own Evangelical brothers and sisters.

Danger In Our Own Churches!

In the past we Evangelicals have prided ourselves in using the Bible as our mandate for action. Some of us have boasted confidently of the strong support for Israel and resistance against anti-Semitism that exists in our ranks. We still have great strength in such areas, but a certain erosion of these values is in progress. New waves of anti-Semitism are sweeping through our own churches. Strange new anti-Semitic doctrines are being promoted, and whenever there is anti-Semitism, Holocaust is potential, not merely historic.

Kingdom Now, Dominion, Theonomy, and Reconstruction are labels attached to vigorous Evangelical movements that not only differ from us in eschatological interpretations but also have an agenda for political takeover, for establishing a world theocracy before the return of Christ, to abolish democracy, do away with pluralism, and put the Jews in their place. Of course, before the Dominionists can capture the world, they must first conquer the church.

It must be recognized that not all in the above mentioned theological camps are anti-Semitic, but in the most part they are, at least by our common definition of anti-Semitism. Surely to teach people that God has no more use for the Jews or the nation of Israel is not in the best interest of the Jews, hence it is against the Jews and Israel. Is that not theological anti-Semitism? Theological or philosophical anti-Semitism always precedes active programs and persecutions of the Jews.

To achieve the goal of world domination, a number of secretive, and, in some cases, hidden networks exist among the Charismatics and Evangelicals. There are also open conferences and conventions designed to effect major theological changes in our churches. "Their" leadership is encouraged to stay put in our ranks and work for control within. Newly appointed Charismatic apostles and prophets exert a self-aggrandizing authority to which some of my own brethren are willing to bow. The thirst for political power in the ecclesiastical world is wondrous to behold.

Who Will Dominate the Pentecostals?

Pentecostals and Charismatics represent a particularly vocal and aggressive branch of Evangelicalism. Their local churches are growing. A major percentage of the world's "super churches" with membership of five thousand to five hundred thousand fall into this category. They have more radio and TV time than any other segment of the church. The strength and influence of the Pentecostals and Charismatic must not be overlooked.

Who will be the Pope of the Pentecostals? With control of 176 million denominational Pentecostals and 156 million

Charismatics at stake, that is a foremost question! Which apostle will your pastor be asked to bow to? How will they overcome existing church governments and capture the clergy in classical Pentecostal churches? Will the cry, "Unity at any cost" be the nemesis of those stubborn people who insist on believing that Israel and the Jewish people are still significant to the plan and purposes of God? Are you even aware of what is going on?

Could the silencing of my voice and that of my colleagues open the door for a future holocaust? Does anyone even care? Even though a time of wrath is inevitable (i.e. the Great Tribulation), woe to those by whom it comes. Blessed are those who do the will of God and resist the darkness of error regardless of personal cost. Remember, "faith without works is dead."

The existence of the anti-Semitic Christian doctrines I speak of are further evidenced by an outpouring of attractive books and literature promoting theological anti-Semitism and thus potential hatred for the Jewish people.

Some Good News

For some years it looked like the anti-Semites in the Church were winning. We felt like we were on the run. They attacked and accused us in their papers and books. But now the tide is turning. Even in the ranks of the Charismatics there is an awakening to sound biblical doctrine in relation to Israel.

Christians United for Israel, The National Christian Leadership Conference for Israel, The International Christian Embassy of Jerusalem, the new Evangelical Christian Zionist Congress of America, Iowans for Israel, Bridges for Peace, Friends of Israel, and a host of others are making a difference simply by refusing to be silenced. But we must not let our successes go to our heads. The moment we let up, our opponents will advance again. I have seen some of their expansionist plans, and it is awesome. But we have plans, too, and we believe God for His constant aid and guidance.

Neo-Nazis Abound

We continually see articles about Neo-Nazi activity in the daily news. Recently a group of five radicals from Texas were apprehended in Washington, DC. The FBI reported that their possessions included an M-16 grenade launcher, machine guns, rifles, shotguns, handguns, and silencers, along with a Nazi flag.

Law enforcement officials here in our area tell us that these Aryan groups are now common all over America. Our formerly quiet, rurally oriented area is a hotbed of Neo-Nazi activity. Our Evangelical colleagues are properly shocked at these media revelations. Even more shocking is the discovery that many of the Nazi groups claim to be fundamentalist Christians.

It is not enough to speak out against Aryan radicals in our culture. Never mind the fact that right here in Southern Missouri we are surrounded by the skinheads; The Order; The Covenant, the Sword, and the Arm of the Lord; Pentecostal Nazis; and that the Ku Klux Klan has moved its international headquarters to within 70 miles of my front door. We expect Jew hatred from the Nazis. The most serious problem is when anti-Semitism invades the churches.

The Deeper Problem

It is of even greater concern that the biblical position on Israel has been eroded, and even though we have seen an encouraging reversal of these trends, we still have a long way to go. A lot of theologically anti-Semitic literature is available right in your local religious bookstores. We hear the concepts of replacement and contempt on our local religious radio stations. It is preached in local churches.

Rousas John Rushdoony, creator of the Chalcedon Foundation and grandfather of the Dominionist movement, says that Christians who are supportive of Israel and the Jewish people are heretical.

Rushdoony wrote in his book, *Thy Kingdom Come*, "Premillennial and amillennial interpretations are tainted with the background of Manichaean heresy. A further heresy clouds premillennial interpretations of Scripture — their exaltation of racism into a divine principle. Every attempt to bring the Jew back into prophecy as a Jew is to give race and works (for racial descent is a human work) a priority over grace and Christ's work, and is nothing more or less than paganism. It is significant that premillennialism is almost invariable associated with Arminianism, i.e. the introduction of race into prophetic perspectives is accompanied by, and part and parcel of, the introductions of works into the order of salvation. This is the essence, after all, of the Phariseeism which crucified Christ and which masqueraded, as it still does, as the epitome of godliness. There can be no compromise with this vicious heresy."

The Holocaust Is More Than Just History

We normally speak of the Holocaust as an historic phenomenon. But if we allow these ideas to advance in our churches, if we are silent, as so many were silent in Germany, it could happen here. It could happen again. The Holocaust must never be viewed only as history. It is potential.

The TV cameras were running in the Yad Vashem Holocaust Memorial in Jerusalem where we were involved in the production of a Christian documentary on the Holocaust. The lights were on, and the videotape rolling.

Suddenly, out of the shadows stepped an elderly Jewish man who called out, "Mister, I was there. It really happened." Rolling up his sleeve, he thrust forth his arm, revealing a tattooed number on his wrist. "Look, look, I was there. Don't let them tell you it never happened."

His embarrassed wife pulled at his coattails until he backed away from the lighted area. We watched his retreating figure fading back into the darkness. We hear his plaintive final cry, "Mister, listen to me. Mister — it could happen again."

Prayer

Almighty God, we confess our sins and the sins of the Church. As the ancient prophets of Israel sometimes confessed the sins of their nation — sins of which they had no personal guilt — so we confess the sins of our church and our nation. We have not pleased You when we have participated in slander against the Jewish people. Forgive us for remaining silent when we should have spoken out against evil hatred of Your people Israel. Forgive us for being intimidated in the face of anti-Semitism.

Having confessed our sin, we pray that You will give us the resolve and courage to act upon our faith. Anoint us by thy Holy Spirit to receive Your truth. Let our belief be our mandate to action. May we never again be silent when anti-Semitism raises its ugly head in our midst. Strengthen us in this determination. In the name of the Lord Jesus Christ. Amen.

Yehuda's Story

I feel that God sent him to me for many strange reasons. Yehuda came to the hotel to listen to one of our lecturers. After the meeting we spent several hours talking of many things.

Everyone in Jerusalem has a story to tell. The air is full of parables. Mystery and intrigue permeate the atmosphere. The story Yehuda told me is like a parable. Though dark may be the night imposed on humanity by man's brutality to his fellow man, nevertheless there is a wheel of justice that turns full circle in the passage of time.

Yehuda came to us during the feast of Purim. That is the time when the Jewish people celebrate the victory of Mordechai and Esther over Haman, the Hitler of his day. Haman built a gallows on which to hang the Jews, but God turned the situation about, and Haman hung on his own gallows.

Yehuda told of an ex-Nazi Luftwaffe officer who engaged in conversation with him some time ago. The Nazi was loud, arrogant, and boastful. "You Jews," he argued, "are always stirring up the stink of the past. Why can't you leave the past alone?"

Yehuda inquired of him, "I suppose, sir, that you would admit Hitler started the Second World War?"

"You see," said the Nazi, "that's exactly what I mean, always digging up old history. Why can't you forget it and live for today?"

"Well," said Yehuda, "I guess you could further admit that Hitler was responsible not only for the death of 6 million of my people, the Jews, but also for 50 million other casualties in World War II?"

"Yes, yes, of course — we all admit that Hitler was a devil. We Germans made a mistake about him, but what good does it do to remember it now?"

Yehuda continued, "I must tell you, sir, that the Nazis did a 'good' job on my family. All my family — mother, father, brothers, sisters — were killed in your death camps. All, that is, but me and one uncle."

"You have a sick mind," the Nazi shouted. "I know you

have experienced personal tragedy, but you need to forget it. Leave the past in the past. Furthermore, I have had enough of this conversation."

"Not quite enough. I have one more thing to tell you. Something you do not know. You admit that Hitler started the Second World War, but what you do not know is that one Jew, my uncle, ended it!"

"What insanity is this? Surely you Jews are mad, but you especially! I have never heard such nonsense. And who might this uncle of yours be?"

"My uncle was Robert Oppenheimer," said Yehuda as his eyes pierced into the soul of the unrepentant Nazi.

The Nazi literally shook like a leaf in the summer breeze. Unable to say another word, he turned and walked away. You see, he recognized the name Robert Oppenheimer as the man who was chiefly responsible for the atomic bomb.

There is a wheel of justice that turns full circle with the passing of the years of time.

Haman hangs on his own gallows. Hitler burns the Jews in the gas furnaces and then burns himself in his own bunker in Berlin. They that curse Israel are cursed by the Almighty.

Robert Oppenheimer, a physicist, was a professor at the University of California and the California Institute of Technology. He directed atomic energy research and the manufacture of the atom bomb during the Second World War. From 1947 until 1966, he was director of the Institute for Advanced Study at Princeton University. Oppenheimer served as chairman of the general advisory committee of the U.S. Atomic Energy Commission until 1954.

After seeing the horrible effects of the atomic bomb, he refused to work on the hydrogen bomb. He was accused of being a security risk and was suspended from the A.E.C. in 1954. Allegations against him were never proven. It is well known that this man was responsible for guiding the research and production of the atom bomb, which so dramatically brought the Second World War to its conclusion, with victory falling into the hands of the free world.

Was Hitler a Christian?

Adolph Hitler, perpetrator of the worst horrors ever visited upon the world, was not a Christian, not in the light of our definition of the word Christian. However, it is apparent that not everyone defines the word Christian in the same way.

Ask the average American if he is a Christian, and about 77 percent will respond in the affirmative. You will hear: "I belong to the Presbyterian church — of course I am a Christian." And, "Yes, my dad was a Methodist preacher." Or, "My Uncle Del is a missionary in Zimbabwe." Someone will say, "Sure, I was born right here in Christian America." But all of that has nothing to do with the question of being born again, being a member of the true united Church of Jesus Christ consisting of those, and only of those, who have been redeemed.

But, Hitler was a church member until the day he died, and in the view of most of the people in this world, a church member is a Christian. It is understandable that Jewish people view the Holocaust, perpetrated by "Christian" Hitler in Christian Germany, land of the Reformation, as a Christian phenomenon.

One Who Protested

American clergyman Arno C. Gaebelein, an outstanding Evangelical-fundamentalist writer and preacher of the early part of this century, was alert to the threat of Nazism. Long before Hitler's worst side had been seen, he was warning the world of the dangers inherent in Nazism. This is pointed out by Herman Voss and David Rausch in their book, *Protestantism — Its Modern Meaning*. In 1930 Gaebelein described Hitler as being "an outspoken enemy of the Jews . . . one of the most fanatical anti-Semites of Europe." Voss and Rausch describe Gaebelein's thought in some detail:

> An avid reader with contacts around the world, including Germany and Russia, Gaebelein underscored the growing power of fascism in Europe in the 1920s, and in *Our Hope* (August 1932) remarked: "Especially threatening is it in Germany. Adolf Hitler, the clever fascist leader who is winning out in Germany and holds the power in his hands, is a rabid anti-Semite. When Hitler became chancellor in 1933, Gaebelein saw this as a serious setback for the Ger-

man people, and he detailed Nazi boycotts of Jewish department stores, and limitation of Jewish rights. To Gaebelein, fascism meant the political conditions of the entire world are breaking up." It appeared as though the Great Tribulation was near.

And yet Gaebelein had no patience with those who tried to pinpoint or date prophetic events or who would try to guess who the Antichrist might be. His philosophy was well illustrated when he wrote in *Our Hope* (November 1933): "The editor has no use for day-and-year-setters, nor has he any use for figuring out the duration of the times of the Gentiles, nor has he any sympathy with men who prophesy that Mussolini, Hitler, Feisal, or any other person is the Antichrist. It is a morbid condition which seems to suit certain minds."

Gaebelein continued to write about atrocities against the Jewish people and the rise of German Teutonic paganism. An article on the Nazis in February 1936 was entitled *The Devil Marches On In Germany*. When Adolf Hitler used the 1936 Olympic Games as a great propaganda play and tried to hide the persecution of the Jewish people from journalists, tourists, and government officials, Gaebelein was appalled that even David Lloyd George (1863-1945), the British statesman, was misled.[2]

Wrong Assumptions

Many Evangelicals assume that the Evangelical church in Germany would have despised Hitler and rejected his leadership. This is not the case, however. There were few who stood up against him. I have personally met Evangelical preachers who were once in the Nazi party in Germany. Since their conversion to Jesus Christ, some have repudiated Nazism and Hitler's actions. However, some are still defensive of Hitler and the Nazi regime.

One preacher criticized me for mentioning the Holocaust. "Let the past be in the past," he said. "Don't keep digging it up. Besides, Hitler was not all bad. He was against the Communists. He built the autobahn (superhighway) and promoted the Volkswagen. He loved little children. He was kind to animals, and besides, he made the trains run on time." It is impossible to treat such words with anything but the utter disgust of which they are worthy.

Suppose someone would say to you, "Yes, I know Joe Smith raped and killed my wife, murdered the rest of my family, and was the mass murderer of twenty-seven other people. But he wasn't all bad, after all he ran a nice ice cream parlor, and he was a faithful church member and always gave to the Red Cross Foundation."

One could only say, "How disgusting! You have a sick mind."

Fooled by Hitler

The sorry fact is that the German church leaders in general, including the Evangelicals, did nothing to resist Hitler. In fact, many favored him.

Voss and Rausch cite the late Oswald J. Smith, pastor of the great Evangelical People's Church of Toronto, Ontario, Canada, in this regard. Evidently, Oswald Smith was completely fooled by Hitler, although later on, his eyes were opened and he repented, reversing all his previously held opinions. Oswald Smith was a good man who simply misunderstood the situation in Germany.

Yet, Smith's article, "My Visit to Germany," shows how effective Adolf Hitler was in his Olympic campaign and in his brainwashing of good, decent Protestants. The forty-six-year-old Smith was taken in by the fervent testimony of "true Christians" he visited in Germany during the Olympic Games. "What," you ask, "is the real attitude of the German people toward Hitler?" Smith wrote, "There is but one answer. They love him . . . every true Christian is for Hitler . . . ."

They also impressed upon Smith that "the Bolsheviks were prepared to take over the country," and "Hitler has saved Germany." Smith listened "spellbound" to the contented, happy Protestants, joyously writing that "all girls are trained to be mothers," use of makeup and lipstick had been eliminated, and mass immorality was being eradicated.

"Before Hitler's days, spiritism flourished," Smith rejoiced. "Now occultism of every description is banned." In addition, Smith was more than thrilled that Russellism (Jehovah's Witnesses) was banned as dangerous to the nation.

He suggested that the "United States and Canada could learn a valuable lesson in this regard." In actuality, both Smith and the German Protestants were to learn that when one person's religious freedom is violated, all religious freedom is on the chopping block.

Smith was so completely deceived by the propaganda that he referred to the "spiritual awakening that is coming to the German people." The Cathedral in Berlin was full, with a minister who "preaches the old-fashioned gospel. He spares no one. And none interferes with him. He deals openly with sin and salvation." The "true Christian" Protestants of Germany had convinced Smith that they were on the brink of religious revival. "France I do not trust. France is Red, immoral and godless," Smith concluded. "Germany is Protestant. It was from Germany that Luther came."[3]

Spiritual Treachery

Gerald Winrod, who died in 1957, quoted Smith extensively, and published his articles in his *Defender Magazine*. (*Defender* has since been taken over and retitled by a pro-Israel Pentecostalist, Hart Armstrong). Actually Winrod had been a defender of the Jews in the1920s, but by 1935 he was justifying Hitler and had turned against the Jews. Gaebelein was to identify Winrod as a "secret follower of Hitler."

It is startling to discover that Winrod, a strong biblical Zionist could turn about-face and persecute the Jews through his writings. Yet, we see the same thing happening today in certain Evangelical and Charismatic camps. May God deliver us from this spiritual treachery. May God deliver us from this spiritual insanity.

Currently, Rev. Gordon Winrod, a fundamentalist, is carrying on his father's tradition of Christian anti-Semitism. His anti-Semitic literature is published under the auspices of a church he pastors in Gainesville, Missouri. Gerald Winrod was a great believer in the spurious *Protocols of the Learned Elders of Zion*, and he distributed copies widely. The Protocols purport to be an outline of a Jew-Zionist plot to rule the world.

American Evangelical leaders like Arno Gaebelein, Harry Ironside, Keith Brooks, and many other Evangelicals signed Dr. Donald Gray Barnhouse's petition denouncing the Protocols as an anti-Semitic forgery. Pastor Barnhouse, a Presbyterian minister wrote one of the greatest commentaries on the Book of Revelation. Barnhouse was a premillinnarian and ardent supporter of Israel.[4] At the same time, most German Evangelicals were silent, or even supportive of Hitler.

Good and Bad News

It is encouraging to discover that many American Evangelicals did actually denounce Hitler. Voss and Rausch state:

> During Hitler's "final solution" to the Jewish problem, Fundamentalist-Evangelicals believed that the Jewish people were being exterminated by the millions, while more liberal Christians, and periodicals such as *The Christian Century*, were labeling the reports of atrocity "propaganda." Gaebelein's *Our Hope* magazine gave factual reports of atrocities against the Jewish people during the 1930s and 1940s. The Fundamentalist-Evangelical world view lent itself very well to such convictions, even when they seemed beyond the realm of belief and left the premillennialists in shock. [5]

The good news is that there are many Evangelicals and Pentecostals who are in tune with biblical truth in relation to Israel and the Jewish people. How I thank God for those who refuse to be intimidated, who rise above the general apathy that attends this subject. One might smugly take comfort in the fact that many American Evangelicals did resist Hitler from afar, while condemning our German colleagues. It is easy to be self-congratulatory when surrounded by our agreeing brethren.

Looking at the current American Evangelical scene, however, in certain quarters, we see a shift away from biblical literalism. It reminds one of the kind of reversal made by Gerald Winrod on the Israel/Jewish issue.

I am distressed to see certain pastors and leaders who once took a strong biblical stance on God's promises to national Israel who are today hobnobbing with the Kingdom Now and the Dominion crowd. Some have openly embraced anti-Israel doctrine. The silence of others, formerly so outspoken, is significant. If Charismatic brethren are going to fellowship with our Kingdom Now brethren, they should take every opportunity to correct them on their unscriptural attitude toward Israel.

Strange Unity

Many have been silenced for the sake of "unity." But what kind of unity is it that calls for silence on major issues? What kind of unity is it that denies us the right to speak out on vital issues? What kind of unity is it when a few brethren with strange new doctrines, set the agenda for us all? What kind of unity is it that causes Kingdom Now friends to accuse those of us who are friends of Israel of being satanic, inspired by the devil, deceived, and guilty of preaching heresy?

I am told that I should either change my views concerning Israel, or if I cannot do that, then I should be silent for the sake of unity. What unity is this?

Some time ago I attended a leadership conference. We were told that Israel and prophecy are low on the agenda of priorities in the Church of today, so we should keep silent on the subjects. Is this unity or spiritual blackmail and brainwashing?

My view is that, regardless of disagreements, I am united with all born-again believers. We have one head, even Jesus Christ (1 Cor.12). We certainly need a more visible manifestation of that unity, but the neo-modernist Evangelicals and Pentecostals are not promoting that concept of unity.

Unity we have, but truth is elusive and must be pursued with vigor. Regardless of what you may hear or think to the contrary, the devil's principle end-time tactic is not to cause division but to promote deception. Indeed, division is deplorable, and Satan will use it, but deception is worse and can hinder the kingdom of God and, in the extreme, can even damn souls.

Neo-Kingdomists and Dominionists

Some of the Neo-Kingdomists (Kingdom Now) and the Dominionists are promoting the same anti-Semitic theology that the churchmen of Hitler's day were preaching. Hitler's henchmen actually quoted pastors and church leaders in justifying their horrible persecution of the Jews. Not all people in the Kingdom Now and Dominion movements are doctrinal anti-Semitics, but most of them are.

Let a major depression hit the world. Let really hard times

come to this country. Let another Hitler arise, this time in our midst. Some of the modernistic Evangelicals I have described will be the first to follow him. They may not light the gas furnaces at Auschwitz, but, like their fellow German churchmen of the Nazi era, they will provide the fuel.

Pastor, I urge you to get involved in this important issue facing the Church today. Speak out and repudiate false teaching now, before it is too late.

Evangelicals ought to know that we have a vested interest in being protective of our Jewish friends. It is a fact that the same anti-God forces that have eternally wanted to destroy the Jews also want to destroy us. I appeal to my Kingdom Now and Dominionist brethren to rethink their theology and return to a biblical standard.

Only One Man

Only one man in the whole history of the world was given the privilege of choosing his birth place, his race, and his mother. That one man was Jesus who chose to be born in Bethlehem to a Jewish mama. He chose to be of the tribe of Judah, from which the word Jew is derived. He lived the life of an observant, orthodox Jew. He never had the privilege of attending a church service. He never saw a Sunday school. He worshiped, prayed, taught, preached, and healed the sick in the Jewish Temple on Mount Moriah, which He reverently referred to as His Father's house. He was a Jew when He died on the cross at the hands of the Romans, and when He rose up from the dead He was a Jew.

The one who makes intercession for you at the right hand of the Father is the Jew, Jesus. Our divine Lord retains His humanity (1 Tim. 2:5). That one mediator between God and man, the MAN Christ Jesus is still a Jew in heaven. When He comes back He will still be a Jew. He will be a Jew for all eternity, for He is the "Lion of the tribe of Judah" (Rev. 5:5).

Listen, anti-Semite, Jew hater, the Jew is coming back, and He is angry with you. I would not want to be in your shoes for anything.

Zion Calls

Theodore Herzl did not invent Zionism when he held the

first Zionist Congress in the Stadt Cassino Music Hall in Basel, Switzerland in 1897. He simply jumped on a bandwagon that had been rolling through the corridors of history for thousands of years since the time of Abraham. The Almighty Jehovah is the inventor of Zion and Zionism. Listen to the joyous proclamation of the prophets:

> O Zion, that bringest good tidings, get thee up into the high mountain; O Jerusalem, that bringest good tidings, lift up thy voice with strength; lift it up, be not afraid; say unto the cities of Judah, Behold your God! (Isa. 40:9).
> Sing and rejoice, O daughter of Zion: for, lo, I come, and I will dwell in the midst of thee, saith the Lord (Zech. 2:10).
> Thus saith the Lord; I am returned unto Zion, and will dwell in the midst of Jerusalem: and Jerusalem shall be called a city of truth; and the mountain of the Lord of hosts the holy mountain (Zech. 8:3).
> And I will bring them, and they shall dwell in the midst of Jerusalem: and they shall be my people, and I will be their God, in truth and in righteousness (Zech. 8:8).

Lord, haste the day of the reign of Israel's Messiah who will bring peace on earth, with goodwill toward all people.

[1]Louis Hauff, *Israel in Prophecy* (Springfield, MO: Gospel Publishing House, 1961, 1974) pp. 22, 23.
[2]David A. Rausch and Carl Hermann Voss, *Protestantism — Its Modern Meaning* (Fortress Press), p. 150.
[3]Ibid., p. 151.
[4]Ibid., pp. 152-153.
[5]Ibid., p. 153.

11

Will God Destroy Russia?

by Tim LaHaye

The unbelievable upheaval in the Soviet Union that has already toppled that government has caused many to ask, "Will God still destroy Russia on the mountains of Israel the way the prophet Ezekiel described in Ezekiel Chapters 38 and 39?"

Since that prophecy has never been fulfilled, you can be sure that as long as there is a God in heaven who always keeps His Word, it will come to pass some day. The fact that the Arab "hordes," even after the war in the Persian Gulf of 1991, are still allies of Russia indicates it *may* be sooner than most people think.

If, as biblical prophecy predicts, Russia is going to lead an attack on Israel and be destroyed by God in the process, that nation had better get with it or they will no longer be a world power. At the rate they are collapsing internally, Russia will be a fifth-rate nation by the twenty-first century.

To help you put all these events in perspective, read Ezekiel 38 and 39 before proceeding with this chapter.

Why Single Out Russia?

Next to His Son, human beings are dearest to the heart of God. He seems to love them even more than He does the angels, for He sent His only begotten Son to die for human beings. Only mankind can sin against God yet be forgiven and granted eternal life through belief in His Son.

In two chapters of the Book of Ezekiel, however, God establishes that He is *against* the nation of Russia. That is most unusual because history shows that God is *for* mankind. There must be some compelling reason why God, who loves us so much that He gave His Son for us, would turn so aggressively against an entire nation.

The key, I believe, is the satanic presence that indwelt many of the Russian leaders for so many years. In several Old Testament prophecies, God's proclamation of judgment went far beyond the immediate kingdom to the spirit of Satan that controlled the rulers.

The power of government to oppress billions of people was never lost on Satan. Early in human history he learned to give special attention to world leaders — as he will to the Antichrist world dictator during the Tribulation period. For if Satan controls the dictator, king, or leader of a country, he can ultimately tyrannize that country.

In Daniel's day the supreme example was Nebuchadnezzar. Satan exercised dominion over both king and country; thus God opposed both the nation of Babylon, because of its unrighteous ways, and the spirit of Satan, which indwelt the king.

So it has been with Russia since 1917. God not only abhors the philosophy of the former Soviet system but the source of power behind it, Satan himself. Consider these prophecies from a loving God who declares He is *against* Russia, her leader, her capital city, and one of her major provinces.

> And the word of the Lord came unto me, saying, Son of man, set thy face against Gog, the land of Magog, the chief prince of Meshech and Tubal, and prophesy against him, And say, Thus saith the Lord God; Behold, I am against thee, O Gog, the chief prince of Meshech and Tubal (Ezek. 38:1-3).

Therefore, thou son of man, prophesy against Gog, and say, Thus saith the Lord God; Behold, I am against thee, O Gog, the chief prince of Meshech and Tubal: And I will turn thee back, and leave but the sixth part of thee, and will cause thee to come up from the north parts, and will bring thee upon the mountains of Israel: And I will smite thy bow out of thy left hand, and will cause thine arrows to fall out of thy right hand (Ezek. 39:1-3).

God not only opposes Russia but vividly describes her coming destruction, vowing, "I will give you as food to all kinds of carrion birds and to the wild animals" (Ezek. 39:4;NIV). This is similar to our Lord's prediction concerning the armies of the Antichrist. (See Matt. 24:28 and Rev. 19:17-21.) Such graphic prophecies are reserved not just for Stalin-like dictators who brutalize their subjects but the satanic spirit that indwells them. This judgment is really aimed at the satanic power within "Gog," the chief ruler of the Russians.

God Against Gog

Ever since the Bolshevik Revolution, Satan has ostensibly made his anti-human headquarters the city of Moscow and his personal dwelling such leaders as Lenin, Stalin, Khrushchev, Brezhnev, Andropov, and for six and one-half years, Gorbachev, who was more subtle than all of them. Under satanic influence, they incited communism's anti-human governmental systems to enslave upward of 1.5 billion people and thus incurred the wrath of God for three reasons:

1. They propagated an atheistic religion.

The most heinous sin in God's eyes is to deceive people by teaching a religion other than the gospel of Christ.

Our Lord revealed the attitude of God in every deed. He always had time for repentant sinners and showered mercy upon them. He reserved His severest strictures not for adulterers, tax collectors, or other sinners but for the religious leaders of His day. Why? They had deceived people about God.

The doctrine of atheism is such an integral part of communism that wherever the philosophy has gone — either in a totalitarian takeover of a country or in the infiltration of the universities of the free world — its teachers have always taught materialism and atheism, the fundamental doctrines of Karl Marx and his disciples. They have appealed to the masses with their philosophy of economic socialism because it attracts votes.

An irony of history is that the precepts of communism have never worked successfully. Never has communism raised the standard of living in any country. In addition, every country that has voted Communists into power in a free election has always voted them out of power at the first opportunity. Witness the dissolution of the USSR.

Since its inception, communism has consistently fostered a rejection of God, supplanting Him with a belief in "man's potential, not God's." It is safe to say that no other philosophy of life has created more skeptics, agnostics, and unbelievers, and it would never have had the worldwide impact it has had without the power of the former Soviet Union behind it.

Communism has been effective in polluting the minds of young people in the Western world because it is so close to secular humanism. This philosophy of life, to one degree or another, is held by most of those who occupy chairs of philosophy, law, or education in the major universities and other educational institutions of the West. As I have explained in my four books on secular humanism, not all secular humanists are Communists, but all Communists are secular humanists.[1] Therefore, it would be easy for Communists to infiltrate educational institutions in any country, even in the free world.

Posing as secular humanists, these Marxist professors teach their anti-God, anti-morality, anti-free enterprise, and anti-Christianity philosophy. Many Communists have used this subterfuge to earn their living at taxpayers' expense in our educational institutions, spending their entire lifetimes polluting the faith of as many of the thirteen million college students in America as they can. Despite recent events, they continue to pursue the same ends throughout the rest of the Western world.

I debated one secular humanist who has been a philosophy professor in a major educational institution on the West Coast for forty years. He proudly testified that he had changed the faith of many of his students who came from "fundamentalist Christian homes." I do not know whether the man is a Communist, but it really doesn't matter. The shocking effects on his students are the same whether he is or isn't.

The great tragedy in all of this is that young people do not become unbelievers because of lack of evidence. God has supplied overwhelming testimony in the Bible regarding His existence, His supernaturalness, and the supernaturalness of Jesus Christ. I have had the joy of leading many people to Christ after they have thoroughly investigated the logical reasons for accepting the bodily resurrection of Jesus as historical fact.

Why, then, in the face of persuasive evidence, do so many young people become unbelievers in our secular institutions? It is simply that the evidence is not taught in those institutions. Consequently, young people become atheists or agnostics after examining only one side of the issue — the infidel's side.

Most college professors believe that their anti-God position is the only one entitled to exposure in the halls of academia. When one contemplates the infiltrated universities of the Western world, and the many other places that Communists and humanist sympathizers have penetrated with their educational missionary work, it is probably safe to say that Russia has damned as many souls intellectually as she has destroyed physically. No wonder God says, "I am against you, O Gog."

2. Russia has violated more biblical principles than any other nation.

The former Soviet Union continually taught people to act as she did. It is one thing to blatantly teach atheism; it is another to infuse a lifestyle that is diametrically opposed to the purposes of God.

The Bible makes it clear that happiness is the result of obeying God's principles (Luke 11:28). We are seeing this vividly illustrated in the social and family scene in the United States today. The Christian families who practice biblical principles enjoy harmony and love in an openly anti-Christian culture. By contrast, those who follow the philosophy of secular humanism and communism — man as the center of all things, and self-indulgence, self-actualization, and self-realization as his primary purpose — seriously compound their difficulties.

It is one of the long-standing tactics of Communists to

pollute the morals of a nation they have targeted for takeover. They successfully assaulted the morals of Great Britain before and during World War II, then came to Canada and America to duplicate the process during the past three decades.

For example, who has advocated "free love," "permissive sex," "abortion on demand," "homosexual rights," "the free distribution of pornography," and "the removal of laws against non-prescriptive drugs and marijuana?" It has not been parents, church leaders, construction workers, or family-oriented people. These radical social activities have been consistently advocated from the halls of our prestigious universities and colleges, where secular humanist and Communist teachings are welcomed with open arms.

If Jesus were on earth today, He would say of the Communists what He said of the Pharisees in Matthew 23:15-16;NIV: "You travel over land and sea to win a single convert, and when he becomes one, you make him twice as much a son of hell as you are. Woe to you, blind guides . . . !"

God is against Russia because of its soul-damning philosophy of atheism.

3. Russia has persecuted the Jews.

Everyone knows that Karl Marx was a Jew, and most people realize that both Lenin and Stalin were partially Jewish. But, many do not realize that the majority of the leading fifty men who seized control of Russia in the Bolshevik Revolution were also Jews.

Since then, however, there has been a systematic purge of Jewish leadership within the Communist party in Russia, primarily instigated by Stalin. He authorized the extermination of many Jewish leaders in the party as well as ordinary Jewish citizens.

We cannot identify with certainty the reasons for this deep-rooted antagonism between Communist leaders and the Jews. It could be nationalism — that is, Russian Communists do not trust non-Russians. Consequently, they might have used the Jews to foment revolution early in the century then have them systematically removed from positions of power. But quite possibly the Communists felt intimidated by the intellectual gifts of their Jewish comrades.

Not content just to silence Jewish opposition in Russia, the

Communists were unwilling to permit the large Jewish population of the nation to emigrate to Israel until forced to do so by the refusal of our government to grant them "Most Favored Nation" trading status. Even when they have begrudgingly permitted them to emigrate, it has been accomplished by difficulty and disagreement.

God made it very clear in His Word that He would bless the nations that are good to the Jews and curse those that persecute them. In all history there has never been a case where a nation that has mistreated the Jews has conquered a nation that was benevolent to them. As we will see later, America's policy of defending Israel is probably our greatest line of national defense. By contrast, Russia's policy of persecution will prove to be her death knell.

The Coming Destruction of Russia

The recent coup in the former Soviet Union may provide welcome change within the new Commonwealth of Independent States. It appears now that the days of the Soviet empire are over. But be sure of this, whether it be Boris Yeltsin or some other "former" Communist, Russia will come out of all the present turmoil in charge. Why is that? She already has control of the thirty thousand missiles and the military capability of the country. A new and more ruthless Gorbachev or Yeltsin could emerge and consolidate the empire and still maintain good relations with the Arab allies.

No rational person takes pleasure in the destruction of an entire nation, not even when that destruction is an act of judgment by a righteous, sovereign God. However, we must recognize that 2,500 years ago the Hebrew prophets, under inspiration of the Holy Spirit, made such a prediction, and world conditions seem to indicate that the coming destruction cannot be far off. Russia is unquestionably the nation identified in the prophecies of Ezekiel 38 and 39.

It is not sufficient just to say that Bible scholars for several hundred years have interpreted Ezekiel 38 and 39 as referring to Russia. We must be more explicit than that, for the proper identity of "Gog" and "Magog" is essential to the interpretation of this passage. Therefore, I suggest three reasons that confirm the identity of that nation, which is also predicted to invade Israel in the last days.

1. Russia's Philosophy

We have already seen in the Bible that God is against "Magog" (the country) and "Gog" (the chief prince of the country). Why would a loving God who has always been *for* mankind be against this nation? Because the nation is against *Him*.

As the preceding section showed, "Magog" exhibits her antagonism toward God by opposing humanity, the special object of God's love; defying God's Word; and above all, antagonizing His people, the nation of Israel. Philosophically and religiously, the nation of Russia qualifies in every way. It is anti-God, anti-human, anti-Bible, and anti-Israel. But there is another reason for recognizing "Magog" as Russia.

2. Russia's Geographical Location

Another significant reason for identifying Russia as Magog is her geographical location. The Bible usually describes geography in relation to Israel. For example, "south" means south of Israel; "north" signifies north of Israel.

The only likely exception would come in this instance, in that Ezekiel was in Babylon when he spoke the prophecy. A case could be made that he may have meant "north of Babylon" when he said, "You will come from your place in the far north" (38:15;NIV), or, "I will bring you from the far north and send you against the mountains of Israel" (39:2;NIV).

The following map shows that it doesn't matter whether one starts in Israel or Babylon; north in either case leads to the broad expanse of the former Soviet Union. Unquestionably, the invading forces that will march against the nation Israel, recalled from the nations of the world and established in her own land, come from none other than Russia.

3. The Study of Etymology

Etymology is the study of linguistic changes and the history of words. We will investigate the etymology of the names of nations. As we will see, "Magog" is an ancient name for the nation now known as Russia. "Gog" merely means "the chief prince of Magog," or more literally, the chief prince of Meshech and Tubal (38:2-3; 39:1).

Genesis 10 helps to establish the identity of these people. Magog was the second son of Japheth who, according to

Josephus, the great Jewish historian, settled north of the Black Sea. Tubal and Meshech were the fifth and sixth sons of Japheth, and their descendants settled south of the Black Sea. It is believed that these people intermarried and became known as Magog, the dominant tribe.

The name "Moscow" derives from the tribal name "Meshech," and "Tobolsk," the name of the principal state, from "Tubal." The noun "Gog" is from the original tribal name "Magog," which gradually became "Rosh," then "Russ," and today is known as "Russia."

In *The Late Great Planet Earth*, Hal Lindsey offers a helpful discussion on the identity of these nations.

Dead Men Do Tell Tales!

It is necessary on the next few pages to establish some documentation from ancient history. Some people find this subject "a little dull," to say the least. If this is your case, you may wish to skim over the high points. For others, it will prove to be rewarding to check carefully the grounds upon which the historical case is built.

Herodotus, the fifth century B.C. Greek philosopher, is quoted as mentioning Meshech and Tubal. He identified them with a people named the Samaritans and Muschovites who lived at that time in the ancient province of Pontus in northern Asia Minor.

Josephus, a Jewish historian of the first century, says that the people of his day known as the Moschevi and Thobelites were founded by Meshech and Tubal, respectively. He said, "... Magog is called the Scythians by the Greeks." He continued by saying that these people lived in the northern regions above the Caucasus Mountains.

Pliny, a noted Roman writer of early Christian times, said, "Hierapolis, taken by the Scythians, was afterward called Magog." In this he shows that the dreaded barbaric people called the Scythians were identified with their ancient tribal name. Any good history book of ancient times traces the Scythians to be a principal part of the people who make up modern Russia.

Wilhelm Gesenius, a great Hebrew scholar of the early nineteenth century, discusses these words in his unsurpassed Hebrew Lexicon. "Meshech," he says, "was founder of the Moschi, a barbarous people, who dwelt in the Moschian mountains."

This scholar went on to say that the Greek name, "Moschi," derived from the Hebrew name Meshech is the source of the name for *the city of Moscow*. In discussing Tubal he said, "Tubal is the son of Rapheth, founder of the Tibereni, a people dwelling on the Black Sea to the west of the Moschi."

Gesenius concludes by saying that these people undoubtedly make up the modern Russian people.

Rosh is Russia

There is one more name to consider in this line of evidence. It is the Hebrew word, "Rosh," translated "chief" in Ezekiel 38:2-3 of the King James and Revised Standard Versions. The word literally means in Hebrew the "top" or "head" of something. According to most scholars, this word is used in the sense of a proper name, not as a descriptive noun qualifying the word "prince."

The German scholar, Dr. Keil, says, after a careful grammatical analysis, that it should be translated as a proper name, i.e., Rosh. He says, "The Byzantine and Arabic writers frequently mention a people called Ros and Rus, dwelling in the country of Taurus, and reckoned among the Scythian tribes."

Dr. Gesenius in his Hebrew Lexicon says, ". . . Rosh was a designation for the tribes then north of the Taurus Mountains, dwelling in the neighborhood of the Volga."

He concluded that in this name and tribe we have the first historical trace of the Russ or Russian nation.[2]

In 1857, Rev. F. E. Pitts delivered two sermons on prophecy before a joint session of the houses of the United States Congress. His was one of the most respected prophetic voices of his day. Sixty years before the Communist conquest of Russia, he had the boldness to warn the United States government of the coming day when Russia would be a dominant world power. Obviously he had insight, unpopular in his day, derived from Ezekiel 38 and 39.

Pitts had access to prophetic literature that is no longer available — literature showing that more than a hundred years ago it was popular to identify "Rosh" as Russia.

The Sons of Japheth

The very name of the ancient patriarchs of the Russian dominions determine their location and nationality. "Gog" signifies a prince, or head, of many countries. Magog, Gomer, Meshech, and Tubal are four of the seven sons of Japheth. (See Gen. 10 and 1 Chron. 1.) These patriarchs, according to Calmet, Brown, Bochart, and others, settled within the bounds of what is now the Russian dominions.

"Magog," says Josephus, "founded the Magogue, whom the Greeks call Sythee." The Scyth form almost one-fourth of the Russian population. They extended from Hungary, Transylvania, and Wallachia, on the west, to the River Dan on the east. The Russian territory of this people embraces a large portion both of Europe and Asia.

Meshech, the sixth son of Japheth, settled in the northeastern portion of Asia Minor. His posterity extended from the shores of the Euxine [Black] Sea along to the south of the Caucasus. He was the father of the Rossi and Moschi, who dispersed their colonies over a vast portion of Russian territory. And their names are preserved in the names of Russians and Muscovites to this day. The Septuagint version of the Old

Testament renders the term "Meshech" by the words "Mosch" and "Rosch;" while "Moscovy" is a common name for Russia, and the city of Moscow is one of her principal cities.

Tubal, or Tobal, the fifth son of Japheth, settled beyond the Caspian and Black Seas in the eastern possessions of Russia, embracing a very large portion of these dominions. The name of this patriarch is still preserved in the river Tobal, which waters an immense tract of Russian territory; and the city of Tobalski in Russia is still a monument to this son of Japheth.

All these facts make it certain that, as Magog, Meshech, and Tubal compose the present possessions of Russia, the sovereignty of that empire is the chief prince addressed in the prophetic message.

Destined for Greatness

We must look to Russia, then, as the colossal giant of reconstructed monarchy, embodying the show of autocracy in the last grand organization — embracing all the principles foreshadowed in the metallic symbol of the vision "whose brightness was excellent, and the form thereof terrible." In fact, the emperor of all the Russians still bears the royal cognomen of the golden-headed monarchs of ancient Babylon.

Who is the present emperor of Russia? Alexander the Czar. And who are found among the monarchs of Assyria? Nobonazar, Nebuchadnezzar, and Belshazzar. These were not accidental terminations of their respective names but were doubtless terms of Assyrian royalty. So also the Roman Caesars, which scarcely vary from the true pronunciation of the czars. We behold in Russia the original trunk of autocracy.

In the time of Catharine, she arose in august magnitude and entered into the European state system about the time of the rise of our great country. We see rising on the one hand and on the other, the two great powers that represent, respectively, their opposing principles of government that will come in collision in the last dreadful fray.[3]

In the light of the evidence that is available, we are not surprised that students of prophecy foresaw Russia's role as a world power years ago — long before her country showed any signs of greatness. Bishop Lowth of England wrote in 1710, "Rosh, taken as a proper name, in Ezekiel signifies the inhabitants of Scythia, from whom the modern Russians derive their name."[4]

It should be remembered that most of these quotations were written many years before the Bolshevik Revolution and the rise of Russia to power. Bible scholars anticipated Russia becoming a dominant power in the end time while she was literally a nonentity as a nation. Early in this century, she was still a second-rate influence in the affairs of nations; in 1905 little Japan defeated Russia in the Russo-Japanese War.

Why Will Russia Attack Israel?

During the past sixty years, Russian diplomats and foreign policy strategists have proved that they are much smarter than their Western counterparts. Every time our diplomats engage them in conference, we lose land, friends, people, or rights.

What would make a superpower like Russia, at the end time, abandon the path of diplomacy and attack the little nation of Israel? There are four possible reasons.

1. Russia's Long-Standing Hatred of the Jews

It is clear from history that the Jews cannot be intimidated by the Russians or anyone else. We can be certain that the Russians are not pleased with Israel's four military victories since 1949.

It is highly possible that the Russians will finally decide that they cannot defeat the Israelis through their Arab allies without personally engaging them on the field of combat. This decision could be the one that summons them to march against Israel.

2. Plunder, Spoil, and Wealth

In Ezekiel 38:12-13;NIV we read,

> I will plunder and loot and turn my hand against the resettled ruins and the people gathered from the nations, rich in livestock and goods, living at the center of the land. Sheba and Dedan and the merchants of Tarshish and all her villages will say to you, "Have you come to plunder? Have you gathered your hordes to loot, to carry off silver and gold, to take away livestock and goods and to seize much plunder?"

These verses seem to suggest two important possibilities. One is that the economic conditions of Israel are destined to improve and those of the former Soviet Union deteriorate. We have already seen that, as a result of the peace treaties made between the Jews and the Arabs, Israel will experience a time of phenomenal material blessing, making her an object of greed on the part of those who will again inevitably be the Russian dictators.

As we see from daily news accounts, the future is not so bright for Russia. One way in which God has manifested His displeasure with Russia as a nation during the past six decades, lies in her total economic failure under communism. The Crimea was known under the czars as "the breadbasket of the world." The wheat harvested there was bountiful and more than sufficient for the needs of the Russian people; large quantities were exported to other nations of Europe.

Since the Russian Revolution, however, the severe weather of the Soviet Union has worsened, producing some of the harshest winters on record. Russia has become notorious for poor wheat crops — partly because of the weather and partly because of the lack of motivation among the Russian workers under communism.

Reports from Russia that scientists have desperately tried to manipulate the weather are probably fraudulent; if they are true, they give evidence that the scientific endeavors have not worked or have even made the situation worse.

Economic judgment from God is destined to continue, bringing the need to purchase increasing quantities of foreign grain. Again, daily news accounts tell of their plight. It appears critical.

3. God's Sovereign Will

The primary reason Russia will invade Israel is that God has decreed it. Ezekiel 38:3-4,8;NIV declares:

> This is what the Sovereign Lord says . . . I will turn you around, put hooks in your jaws and bring you out with your whole army — your horses, your horsemen fully armed, and a great horde with large and small shields, all of them brandishing their swords.

After many days you will be called to arms. In future years you will invade a land that has recovered from war, whose people were gathered from many nations to the mountains of Israel, which had long been desolate. They had been brought out from the nations, and now all of them live in safety.

Ezekiel 39:2;NIV adds: "I will turn you around and drag you along. I will bring you from the far north and send you against the mountains of Israel."

Why? "This is what the Sovereign Lord says: On that day thoughts will come into your mind and you will devise an evil scheme" (Ezek. 38:10;NIV).

The attack on Israel is conceived and mobilized by almighty God. This implies that God will stir the Russians' greedy plan, fulfilling Ezekiel 38:4;NIV: "I will ... put hooks in your jaws and bring you out ...."

In studying these two chapters of Ezekiel, I sense that God will pour out His wrath upon Russia not only to demonstrate His power but also to heap judgment on those who have persecuted human beings, especially Israel.

When will this happen? The prophetic scenario is plain: at a time when Russia does not have Israel as her *primary* target. Russia's major objective has admittedly been world conquest. One way in which the Communists were consistent for the last seventy-four years was in their implacable movement toward that primary objective.

God has proclaimed that He raises up whom He will and puts down whom He will. (See Ezek. 21:26 and Dan. 4:24-25.) Even at the end time, when Russia reigns as a superpower, God will still be in control for He is able to "put hooks in her jaw" and lead her to obey His will.

4. A Matter of Safety

We have said that Israel is the third most powerful nation in the world, particularly if we limit that assessment to nations within a thousand miles of her homeland. Apart from world conquest, what was the chief objective of the former Soviet Union? To conquer the United States of America. Who is to say that quest was lost in the recent changes — or if it was, that it won't be returned in a short time?

At present, no one really knows whether the United States

military forces are more powerful than Russia's or whether our government leaders will have the moral courage and national will to oppose Russia when these climactic events occur. Many knowledgeable people believe that the mood in this country is so anti-war as to be anti-self-defense. Our nation may prefer to capitulate even to Communist domination rather than to fight.

My point, however, is that no one — not even the Russians — really knows whether they would be victorious in a first-strike attack against the United States, particularly after the incredibly accurate, pinpoint bombing and the use of "smart weapons" during the attack on Saddam Hussein, who was using Soviet-built equipment. Therefore, before attacking the United States, they would surely attempt to nullify military assistance from any other source on earth.

The government of Israel is pragmatic enough to know that if Russia attacks the United States, Israel herself would be the next target. Therefore, the Commonwealth of Independent States' military leadership, headed by Russia, may theorize that an invasion of Israel must precede a frontal assault on the leader of the Western world. Consequently, an invasion of Israel may be just one more step in the fulfillment of their objective of world conquest.

Russia's Allies in the Attack on Israel

The only war that Russia has ever fought alone, they lost — against Afghanistan. We can be certain that the Russians will not invade Israel alone. The prophet Ezekiel stipulates that they will bring "many nations with you .... hordes gathered about you..." (Ezek. 38:6-7;NIV). But, he also notes that Russia will be in command (38:7).

1. Persia, or Iran

Russia's confederates, as disclosed in Ezekiel 38:5-6, are among her current friends. Those not in her orbit of friends at present are being cultivated either secretly or openly. Hal Lindsey offers interesting suggestions as to the identity of Russia's allies.

All authorities agree on who Persia is today. It is modern Iran. This is significant because it is being wooed to join the United Arab Republic in its hostility against Israel. The Russians are at this moment seeking to gain footholds in Iran by various overtures of aid.[5]

Secret information coming out of Iran indicates the government is shaky and could easily be toppled replacing it with a ruler favorable to Russia and the eventual leaders. It would not be surprising to see Russia invade Iran if it seemed necessary to achieve her ends, particularly now that Iran is weakened militarily and economically through her long war with Iraq.

Lindsey continues,

> In order to mount the large-scale invasion predicted by Ezekiel, Russia would need Iran as an ally. It would be much more difficult to move a large land army across the Caucasus Mountains that border Turkey, than the Elburz Mountains that border Iran. Iran's general terrain is also much easier to cross than Turkey's. Transportation, however, will be needed through both countries.

2. Ethiopia or Cush (Black African Nations)

Ethiopia is a translation of the Hebrew word, "Cush." Cush was the first son of Ham, one of the sons of Noah. Moses mentions "the land of Cush" as originally being adjacent to an area near the Tigris and Euphrates rivers (Gen. 2:13).

After examining many authorities on the subject, the writer discovered once again why Dr. Gesenius is recognized as one of the great scholars of history. Gesenius summarized all of the evidence as follows: (1) The Cushites were black men. (2) They migrated first to the Arabian peninsula and then across the Red Sea to the area south of Egypt. (3) All the black people of Africa are descended from Cush.

Cush is translated "Ethiopia" twenty-one times in the King James Version, which is somewhat misleading. It is certain that the ancient Ethiopians (modern Abyssinia) are made up of Cushites, but they do not represent all of them, according to history.

The sobering conclusion is this: many of the African nations will be united and allied with the Russians in the invasion of Israel. This is in accord with Daniel's graphic description of this invasion (Dan. 11:36-45).

The Russian force is called "the King of the North" and the sphere of power that the African (Cush) will be a part of is called "the King of the South."

One of the most active areas for the Communist "gospel" is in Africa. As we see further developments in this area in the future, we realize that many African nations will become converted to communism.

3. Libya or Put (Arabic African Nations)

Libya is the translation of the original Hebrew word, "Put." We have the same problem pinpointing these people as with Cush. Put was the third son of Ham (Gen. 10:6). The descendants of Put migrated to the land west of Egypt and became the source of the North African Arab nations, such as Libya, Algeria, Tunisia, and Morocco. The first settlement of Put was called Libya by the ancient historians, Josephus and Pliny. The Greek translation of the Hebrew Old Testament, called the Septuagint, translates Put as Libya in about 165 B.C.

The conclusion is that Russia's ally, Put, certainly included more than what is now called Libya. Once again, there are current events to show the beginning of this alliance. The territory of Northern Africa is becoming solidly pro-Soviet. Algeria appears to be already Communist and allied with Russia.

As we watch this area in the next few years, we will see indications that it is destined to join the southern sphere of power that will attack Israel along with the "King of the North."

4. Gomer and All Its Hordes (Iron Curtain Countries)

Gomer was the eldest son of Japheth and the father of Ashkenaz, Riphath, and Togarmah. These people make up an extremely important part of the future Russian invasion force.

Dr. Young, citing the best of the most recent archaeological finds, says of Gomer and his hordes, "They settled on the north of the Black Sea, and then spread themselves southward and westward to the extremities of Europe."

Gesenius speaks of part of Gomer's "hordes" as being Ashkenaz ". . . the proper name of a region and a nation in northern Asia, sprung from the Cimmerians who are the ancient people of Gomer. The modern Jews understand it to be Germany, and call that country by this Hebrew name . . . ."

Josephus called the sons of Ashkenaz, "the Rheginians," and a map of the ancient Roman Empire places them in the area of modern Poland, Czechoslovakia, and East Germany to the banks of the Danube River. The modern Jewish Talmud confirms the same geographical picture.

The conclusion is that Gomer and its hordes are a part of the vast area of modern Eastern Europe that was totally behind the Iron Curtain. This includes East Germany and the Slovak countries.

5. Togarmah and All Its Hordes (Southern Russia and the Cossacks)

In Ezekiel 38:6;Amp. "the house of Togarmah . . . and all his hordes" are specifically pointed out as being from "the uttermost parts of the north and all his hordes." Dr. Bauman traces evidence of some of the sons of Togarmah to the Turkoman tribes in central Asia. This would explain the statement, "of the north quarters, and all his bands."

The conclusion is that Togarmah is part of modern Southern Russia and is probably the origin of the Cossacks and other people of the Eastern part of Russia. It is interesting to note that the Cossacks have always loved horses and have been recognized as producing the finest army of cavalry in the world. Today, they are reported to have several divisions of cavalry.

It is believed by some military men that cavalry will actually be used in the invasion of the Middle East just as Ezekiel and other prophets literally predicted. During the Korean War, the Red Chinese proved that in rugged mountainous terrain, horses are still the fastest means of moving a large attacking force into battle zones.

Isn't it a coincidence that such terrain stands between Russia and Israel?

6. Many People Are With You

Ezekiel indicates that he hasn't given a complete list of allies. Enough is given, however, to make this writer amazed by the number of people and nations that will be involved.

Ezekiel, prophetically addressing the Russian ruler, commands him to "be prepared; yes, prepare yourself, you and all your companies that are assembled about you, and you be a guard and commander for them" (Ezek. 38:7;Amp.).

In other words, the Russian ruler is to equip his confederates with arms and to assume command. If you have doubts about all that has been said in this chapter, isn't it a bit unnerving to note that almost all of the countries predicted as part of this great army are already armed with weapons created and manufactured in Russia or her satellite nations?

What's Your Name, Gog?

We have seen that Russia will arm and equip a vast confederacy. This powerful group of allies will lead an attack on restored Israel. Russia and her confederates, however, will be destroyed completely by an act that Israel will acknowledge as being from their God. This act will bring many in Israel to believe in their true Messiah (Ezek. 38:16).[6]

Additional insight is found in the address delivered by the Rev. F. E. Pitts before the U.S. Congress more than 135 years ago.

> "Gomer, and all his bands; the house of Togarmah of the north quarters, and all his bands: and many people with thee" (Ezek. 38:6).
>
> "Gomer," another son of Japheth, settled farther down westward in Europe; and has left his name entailed in Hungary, in a city and country both known to this day as the city and country of Gomer.
>
> "Togarmah," the son of Gomer, according to Cicero and Strabo not only peopled a large portion of Western Europe but sent settlements into Turcomania and Scythia in Russia.
>
> Russia, then, according to the Scriptures, is the headship or leading power around which the multitudinous armies of allied monarchy shall be gathered together.
>
> "Persia, Ethiopia, and Libya with them; all of them with shield and helmet" (Ezek. 38:5).
>
> Persia here represents the swarming hosts from the Asiatic possessions; Ethiopia, Libya, and the armies of Africa.
>
> "Thou shalt ascend and come like a storm, thou shalt be like a cloud to cover the land, thou, and all thy bands, and many people with thee" (Ezek. 38:9). The invasion is here announced by an armament

such as the world never saw. For the millions that are to assemble under Gog or Russia embrace nearly all of Europe, as well as a large portion of Asia and Africa. This army is drafted from three continents to invade a fourth. It rises dismal as a cloud, and dreadful as a storm.[7]

From all this we learn that a dominant leader, called Gog, described as the "chief prince of Rosh," is going to arise and lead Russia into a vast northeastern confederation of nations including Iran, Ethiopia, and other African nations, Germany, Armenia, possibly Turkey, conceivably some orientals, and whoever else can be included with the statement, "And many peoples with thee." This group of nations, headed by Russia, will advance against Israel in the last days.

The Russian Invasion of Israel

Some 2,500 years ago the Hebrew prophet Ezekiel described in considerable detail the circumstances under which God-rejecting Russia and her hordes of anti-Semitic nations would attempt to invade the little nation of Israel.

> I will turn you around, put hooks in your jaws and bring you out with your whole army — your horses, your horsemen fully armed, and a great horde with large and small shields, all of them brandishing their swords.
>
> After many days you will be called to arms. In future years you will invade a land that has recovered from war, whose people were gathered from many nations to the mountains of Israel, which had long been desolate. They had been brought out from the nations, and now all of them live in safety. You and all your troops and the many nations with you will go up, advancing like a storm; you will be like a cloud covering the land.
>
> You will come from your place in the far north, you and many nations with you, all of them riding on horses, a great horde, a mighty army. You will advance against my people Israel like a cloud that covers the land. In days to come, O Gog, I will bring

you against my land, so that the nations may know me when I show myself holy through you before their eyes (Ezek. 38:4, 8-9, 15-16;NIV).

There are two legitimate ways to interpret the kind of weapons used in this prophecy — literally and symbolically. Bible-believing scholars can be found on either side.

A literal interpretation of the passage suggests that modern methods of warfare may someday become obsolete, and man will return to primitive weapons. That is not as far-fetched as it may appear at first. For years, electronic scientists have reportedly been working on heat-ray devices that would have the capacity from many miles distant to render metallic surfaces so hot they could not be touched.

If such an invention were produced by the West, Russia could not invade Israel with tanks, bazookas, and modern weaponry. They would have to resort to horses. Metal weapons would be replaced with wooden; these would not be wooden swords and spears as used in ancient days, but implements fashioned with enormous strength out of basic wood materials seasoned with resin, or lignostone, or other chemically treated woods that already are used industrially and have an amazingly long burn life.

If, on the other hand, the passage is to be taken symbolically, the prophet Ezekiel is merely describing implements of war in terms meaningful to his contemporary audience. We must always remember that the Bible was written to specific people at a specific time and must therefore be meaningful to them. If the prophet 2,500 years ago had addressed himself to tanks, half-tracks, aircraft carriers, and airplanes, no one would have understood what he meant.

Regardless which approach we take in interpreting this passage of Scripture, Russia will mount a massive military attack on Israel, and only God will be Israel's defense. God's supernatural intervention will save her.

"The Hordes" Who Join Russia in This Invasion

Russia almost never does anything alone. We have already seen that when they pursue a goal unilaterally, as in Afghanistan, they get bogged down in an endless war. That is usually not Russia's style. Instead, she prefers to supply the military technology and money to her satraps, such as the Palestine Liberation Organization, Cuba, Syria, or Egypt. Consequently, when Russia comes down to invade Israel, she will use Middle East hatred of the Jews to her advantage and inveigle these nations to help her in the fighting.

This will probably be the most massive invasion army assembled in the history of the world — all in opposition to Israel, a nation of less than four million people. For the first time since World War II, Israel's friends will betray her.

Two Confederations of Nations

I am convinced, for two reasons, that the invasion described by Ezekiel is not the Battle of Armageddon — warfare between Jesus Christ and the nations — described in Revelation 16.

First, at this time there will be two leagues of nations: the northeastern confederation that invades with Russia, and the western confederation that has befriended Israel in the past.

Second, in Ezekiel's account only a certain number from the armies of the world will march against the Jews. In the Battle of Armageddon, armies will come from all the countries of the world against Christ — not Israel. Yet, while this warfare will not be the real Battle of Armageddon, to the participants it will seem like it.

1. The Northeastern Confederation

We have already identified some of the nations that will join Russia. Actually, five countries will constitute the northeastern confederation:

1. Russia, the instigator and leader;
2. Persia (Iran), if the former Soviets can somehow repair the breach between Iraq and Iran, Iraq may also be included;
3. Ethiopia (Cush), which could involve Libya and representatives from many other African nations;
4. Gomer (Germany) "and its hordes," now that Germany has been unified, this is even more plausible;
5. Togarmah "and its hordes" — Armenia, which may well involve Turkey and other nations or peoples remaining from the Turkish Empire. Some diplomatic efforts are needed

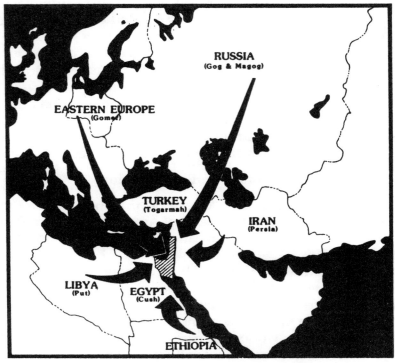

here, but remember, those allies have a common religion.

2. The Western Confederation

The western confederation of nations also appears in Ezekiel's prophecy.

> Sheba and Dedan and the merchants of Tarshish and all her villages will say to you, "Have you come to plunder? Have you gathered your hordes to loot, to carry off silver and gold, to take away livestock and goods and to seize much plunder?" (Ezek. 38:13;NIV).

Who are these nations that greet force with diplomacy? There is little doubt that the western confederation comprises the democracies of the West, principally the United States, Great Britain, and Canada. "Sheba and Dedan and the merchants of Tarshish" were the seafaring Phoenicians, many of whom migrated to Europe, particularly the British Isles and

Spain. These countries, the colonizers of the seventeenth and eighteenth centuries, provide the only vigorous anti-Communist spirit in the world today.

The American Standard Version renders "Tarshish and her villages" in verse 13 as "Tarshish and her young lions [or strong lions]." For this reason, many Bible scholars identify America, Canada, Australia, and other western democracies as the "cubs" of Great Britain and Spain, the colonizers of the West. Certainly, that is historically valid. Therefore, this probably does identify the nations of the prophecy. If the invasion were to take place in the decade of the nineties, the western democracies would qualify.

It stands to reason that Russia does not take the entire world with her against Israel. At a time when two confederations of nations exist — basically still Communist versus anti-Communist — Israel is allied with the anti-Communists, as it is today.

Unfortunately for Israel, instead of meeting the gathering invasion horde with force, the western democracies will confront it with diplomacy. This historically represents the weak response of the democracies in both the world wars and in almost every conflict since. Instead of sending help at the moment when Israel needs the support of her allies, they will send a diplomatic note (perhaps through the United Nations) that essentially inquires of Russia and her hordes, "What are you going to do in little Israel — loot and carry away silver and gold, take away livestock and goods, and seize many riches?"

This may be the most breathtaking, dramatic moment in the history of modern Israel. Until this time, Israel could depend at least on the United States of America.

I well recall an incident that occurred as I jogged along a Mediterranean beach during one of my trips to Israel. A young English-speaking college student — an Israeli — began to jog with me, and we started a conversation. As we discussed Israel's victory in the Six-Day War, I asked if it ever occurred to him that Russia might someday invade Israel herself instead of sending the Arab nations.

Pointing through the evening fog that was settling on the waters of the Mediterranean Sea (where the U.S. Seventh Fleet sailed in military splendor), he responded, "Oh, we're not worried about that; we know America would come to our rescue!" He was right for it was our Patriot Missiles that saved Israel from Saddam Hussein's Scud Missiles in the Persian Gulf War.

According to Ezekiel's prophecy, the day will come when Israel's friends will not always come to her aid. When Russia's invasion forces rattle their spears, the western democracies, including America, will use the impotent instrument of diplomacy instead of the one power that all terrorists, murderers, dictators, and lawless individuals or nations understand: force.

In the history of the world, no nation except Switzerland has ever enjoyed peace through weakness, and her peace was only an accommodation by the militaristic nations of the world wars to maintain free access to the exchange of money. All other nations have found that peace comes exclusively through strength.

The use of diplomacy, at this strategic time in prophetic history, would indicate that the Western democracies will continue to dissipate their strength and military might while Russia builds her power base, probably through unfair trading policies that permit Russia to rape the technology of the West.

Nevertheless, when she finds herself confronted by her enemies and betrayed by her allies, the little nation of Israel, who has not set her heart toward God since returning to the Promised Land, will turn to Him in desperation — and in that moment find Him a ready deliverer.

How God Delivers Israel

The scenario that develops at this point in our prophetic story is exciting. Confronted by overwhelming forces from Russia and forsaken by her friends, Israel will turn to God, and He will do for modern Israel what He did for ancient Israel. As the God over all forces, He will deliver Israel from the hands of the oppressor. As certain as it is that Russia and her Middle East hordes will come down against Israel, so certain is it that God will destroy the invading forces and deliver Israel supernaturally.

The prophet does not leave us in doubt as to the methods that God will use in this destruction. It is noteworthy that this is not the first time they will have been used by the Almighty, for all of them have precedence in the Old Testament.

1. A Mighty Earthquake

In my zeal and fiery wrath I declare that at that

time there shall be a great earthquake in the land of Israel. The fish of the sea, the birds of the air, the beasts of the field, every creature that moves along the ground, and all the people on the face of the earth will tremble at my presence. The mountains will be overturned, the cliffs will crumble and every wall will fall to the ground (Ezek. 38:19-20;NIV).

Evidently, God permits the Russians and their hordes to begin an airborne invasion while the infantry launches a ground assault. But at a strategic moment, He generates a powerful and destructive earthquake that causes people to "tremble" at His presence. This catastrophe will manifest the power of a supernatural God.

Earthquakes were, of course, used by God in ancient days; Amos 1:1 and Zechariah 14:5 recount the terrible earthquake that rocked the land of Palestine in the days of Uzziah, king of Judah. It was no doubt a special intervention of God that caused that earthquake.

Jesus predicted that earthquakes would be one of the signs of His return and the end of the age (Matt. 24:7-8). The record shows that we have experienced an alarming increase in earthquakes during the past fifty years. One seismologist has stated that in each of the past five decades, the number and severity of earthquakes have surpassed the preceding decade.

We should also remember that the Book of Revelation predicts that during the first quarter of the Tribulation, a mighty earthquake will create havoc throughout the entire world (Rev. 6:12-17). Another earthquake in the middle of the Tribulation will rock the city of Jerusalem (Rev. 11:13), and still another at the end of the Tribulation could well be the mightiest earthquake ever to shake the earth (Rev.16:17-21). Consequently, it is not unlike God to use His power to create earthquakes in defense of Israel when Russia's armies come against her.

2. The Sword of the Lord

I will summon a sword against Gog on all my mountains, declares the Sovereign Lord. Every man's sword will be against his brother (Ezek. 38:21;NIV).

Nothing shakes man from his independence and false sense of security like an earthquake, particularly one having the magnitude that God will provide for Israel's deliverance. And because Israel is no match for the invading hordes of military personnel about to devour her, the Lord will confuse her enemies, and they will do battle with each other. If they are using tanks, they will train them on each other. If they are using airplanes, they will dogfight against their own planes. Or if, as already indicated, they have reverted to more primitive weapons of warfare, Israel's enemies will skirmish among themselves rather than against their originally intended foe.

One precedent for such an incredible event appears in Judges 7:8-22, where the story is told of a large army becoming so confused that the soldiers attacked each other and fled in fright from a mere three hundred Israelites.

3. Plague and bloodshed

> I will execute judgment upon him with plague
> and bloodshed . . . (Ezek. 38:22;NIV).

History shows that plagues have often accompanied the wanton killing of human beings in battle. Human carnage, blood, and the remains of a battlefield breed disease. But in the case of Russia's invasion of Israel, the plague seems to be something uniquely manipulated by God to further destroy the effectiveness of the enemy.

The next judgment to befall the invaders is a plague-like pestilence that causes much bloodshed. Pestilence associated with the aftermath of war is similar to that foretold by our Lord in Matthew 24. Those who survive the earthquake and the hand-to-hand combat will certainly perish in the plague.

4. Floods

> . . . I will pour down torrents of rain, hailstones
> and burning sulfur on him and on his troops and on
> the many nations with him (Ezek. 38:22;NIV).

The portion of the invading force that is left after the earthquake, the fighting, and the plague will be destroyed by hailstones and burning sulfur.

For those who interpret this verse literally, there are Old Testament precedents both in the destruction God reigned down on Sodom and Gomorrah and in some of the battles of Israel. For example, Joshua 10:11;NIV, states that when Joshua's armies fought against the Amorites that "the Lord hurled large hailstones down on them from the sky, and more of them died from the hailstones than were killed by the swords of the Israelites."

This final stage in God's judgment on the invaders could create not only a muddy terrain that would bog down any military advance but also flooding conditions that would imperil human life.

5. Burning sulfur

The use of burning sulfur as a means of judgment recalls the destruction of Sodom and Gomorrah, with both earthquake and fire and brimstone — that is, burning sulfur.

The troops who survive the other four judgments will die as a result of the falling, burning sulfur. No wonder God says in Ezekiel 39:4; NIV, "On the mountains of Israel you will fall, you and all your troops and the nations with you . . . ."

These five judgments of God will result in the annihilation of the armies of Gog and his allies. This will undoubtedly be the greatest holocaust fulfilled in a single day in the history of the world. But, there is more.

God Destroys the Spies "In the Isles"

> You will fall in the open field, for I have spoken, declares the Sovereign Lord. I will send fire on Magog and on those who live in safety in the coastlands, and they will know that I am the Lord (Ezek. 39:5-6;NIV).

As a special demonstration to the world of God's omnipotence, Ezekiel gives an unusual prophecy. God will not only destroy the entire army of Magog but also consume with fire those who "live in safety in the coastlands." The word "coastlands" is understood by Bible scholars to mean "the nations;" some older translations render it "in the isles."

Who would qualify as those who live in nations not involved in the conflict? They could be individuals who live in safety or security on islands, or this could refer to uninvolved coastland nations.

The verse probably refers to the many Communist spies and sympathizers who live in the western democracies — who regularly take advantage of their freedom by pursuing subversion for the cause of Moscow and the Kremlin. Such spies or Communist infiltrators occupy many key positions throughout America — in the bureaucracy, universities and colleges, and the media — and subvert the minds of our citizens.

These people who have spent much of their adult life betraying the country that gives them freedom and safety will suddenly be consumed by fire. The United States will not have to reactivate the House Un-American Activities Committees to administer justice. Rather, the God who knows "the thoughts and intents of the heart" will judge these traitors by fire.

We can only imagine the number of vacancies that will occur in one day in the federal and state governments and in the three thousand universities and colleges of America. In all likelihood, this same judgment will create similar vacancies in Canada, Australia, and the British Isles. At the United Nations, divine fire judgment will suddenly fall and reveal the identity of those who really are Communist spies or sympathizers. Such an event will create electrifying headlines.

The World in Chaos — Time for the Antichrist

Can you imagine the chaos into which the world's nations will be plunged the day after God destroys not only the invading armies of Russia but also the Communist spies in the Western world? On the one hand, the skeptical attitude of the secular humanists toward the existence of God will suddenly be confronted with irrefutable evidence of a supernatural God. There will be absolutely no other explanation for these events. In addition, many trusted leaders in key positions of influence will have been destroyed by fire because they were traitors to their country.

Probably the greatest result of this chaos will be that Western democratic leaders who survive will become the dominant leaders of the world. The threat of worldwide communism will have been destroyed in a single day, leaving Israel and the Western confederation of nations in a world-dominating position.

We cannot be certain what will occur politically immediately after this awesome event. But I believe that the rising tide of interest in world government under the guise of the New World order will suddenly find little opposition. Communism will have been removed as a world threat — in reality rather than merely in rhetoric as with the supposed changes that have taken place in the former former Soviet Union. The humanistic politicians of the world will naturally assume, therefore, that a one-world government — within either the United Nations or its replacement — should provide the solution to this planet's ills.

All this will prepare the way for the Antichrist to consolidate the nations in preparation for the day when he signs a covenant with Israel and ushers in the Great Tribulation period spoken of so frequently by our Lord and the Hebrew prophets.

Of this we can be certain: all the world will momentarily stand in awe of the supernatural God in heaven who, after more than 1900 years of silence, has spoken in terms that even the most unbelieving can understand. And the time of that coming destruction may not be too far off.

It is my prayer that during the rapid organization of the New World order government, millions of people who have been hood-winked by secular humanism, rationalism, skepticism, and the New Age religions will suddenly realize there is indeed a God in heaven and call upon Him in simple faith.

[1]*The Battle for the Mind* (1980); *The Battle for the Public Schools* (1982); *The Battle for the Public Schools* (1983); *The Hidden Censors* (1984), all published by Fleming H. Revell, Old Tappan, N.J.

[2]Hal Lindsey with C. C. Carlson, *The Late Great Planet Earth* (Grand Rapids: Zondervan, 1970, 1977), 52-54. Used by permission.

[3]F. E. Pitts, *The U.S.A. in Prophecy* (Baltimore: J. W. Bull, 1862).

[4]John Cumming, *The Destiny of Nations* (London: Hurst & Blackette, 1864).

[5]Lindsey with Carlson, *The Late Great Planet Earth*, p.56.

[6]Lindsey with Carlson, *The Late Great Planet Earth*.

[7]F. E. Pitts, *The U.S.A. in Prophecy* (Baltimore: J. W. Bull, 1862).

12

The Rapture

by David Breese

A stunning event is quickly approaching for our world!
That event will be thrilling beyond measure to every
Christian. It will be dismaying and most frightening, however,
to each person in the world who has not believed the gospel and
has not become, thereby, a possessor of eternal life.

We have come to call that event "the rapture of the
Church." It is that coming awesome moment that enables us to
promise that there is a generation of Christians who will not
die. Rather, they will be caught up while yet in their living
physical bodies, taken suddenly from this world to meet face to
face with the Lord Jesus Christ. They will meet Him in the air
and then be personally escorted by Christ, the Maker of the
universe, into heaven and the presence of God.

The fact that the Bible describes in the clearest terms the
utter reality of this event cannot be denied by clever detractors
or contradicted by coy pretenders to faith. Rather, this promised event of the catching away of Christians is the right and
proper source of great anticipation on the part of genuine
believers across the world of our time.

The Hope of the Christian

The subject of the rapture of the Church was introduced to

believers in the New Testament era in a most interesting fashion as the answer to a critical doctrinal question. How did that question arise?

In the early days of the Church, the believers had a general knowledge about the coming of the Lord, the end of the world, and the consummation of history. They paid no attention to any theory that argued the world has been here forever and would, in like fashion, go on interminably.

The disciples one day asked Christ, "Tell us, when shall these things be? and what shall be the sign of thy coming, and of the end of the world?" (Matt. 24:3).

With this question, the disciples revealed that they wisely did not believe the various views of the uniformity and eternity of nature — false doctrine that was floating in that time and continues today. The disciples were very conscious that existence on earth, and even the existence of earth itself, was a finite and passing thing. Their knowledge that the world would come to an end is obvious from their question. Our Lord himself instructed us that this view is true.

Christ's response to the disciples' questions compose what we know today as the Olivet Discourse, two full chapters in Matthew's Gospel account. The general view of the consummation of things, however, becomes more refined in the epistles of the New Testament.

In the letters of the New Testament writers to the early churches, we see the emergence of a people who are given a very special destiny by the Lord. These people came to be called "Christians," believers in Jesus Christ who constitute a mysterious entity in our world called "the Church." Of this the apostle Paul speaks when he says that, following Christ's crucifixion, His burial, and His resurrection, our Lord has taken His seat at the right hand of the Father,

> Far above all principality, and power, and might, and dominion, and every name that is named, not only in this world, but also in that which is to come: And hath put all things under his feet, and gave him to be the head over all things to the church, Which is his body, the fulness of him that filleth all in all (Eph.1:21-23).

Out of the wounded side of Jesus Christ, God created a totally marvelous entity, which is called in Scripture the body of Christ. The existence of the body of Christ, however, was unknown and unforeseen by the prophets in Old Testament days. It was a "mystery, which from the beginning of the world hath been hid in God, who created all things by Jesus Christ: To the intent that now unto the principalities and powers in heavenly places might be known by the church the manifold wisdom of God" (Eph. 3:9-10).

Christians are, therefore, instructed that they live in a very special age in which God is taking out of the world a people for His name and forming them together into a mysterious and beautiful living entity in the world, the body of Christ himself. One of the less-realized, but most wonderful, aspects of Christianity is that to be a Christian is to be in indissoluble union with God through Christ.

The Believer's Destiny

The New Testament Christians were then instructed that they were inheritors of a stupendous eternal destiny. Speaking to them, the apostle Paul said, "He that spared not his own Son, but delivered him up for us all, how shall he not with him also freely give us all things?" (Rom. 8:32).

So, wonder of wonders, the Christians are to inherit not merely the world, which is the case with Israel, but they are inheritors of the universe. "All things" are in the process of being given to them by the Lord, the totality of which will one day be their inheritance. Expanding on this, the apostle Paul said to the Corinthians,

> . . . For all things are yours; Whether Paul, or Apollos, or Cephas, or the world, or life, or death, or things present, or things to come; all are yours; And ye are Christ's; and Christ is God's (1 Cor. 3:21-23).

This awesome destiny of the believer needs to be better understood by Christians today. One of the greatest motivations for the believer to live a splendid Christian life is a sense of the eternal destiny that is his. Every one of us should be lifted up from ordinary circumstances by reading that the Bible says,

> For unto the angels hath he not put in subjection the world to come, whereof we speak. But one in a certain place testified, saying, What is man, that thou art mindful of him? or the son of man, that thou visitest him? Thou madest him a little lower than the angels; thou crownedst him with glory and honour, and didst set him over the works of thy hands: Thou hast put all things in subjection under his feet. For in that he put all in subjection under him, he left nothing that is not put under him . . . (Heb. 2:5-8).

What then is God doing today in the light of the bright destiny that He has prepared for us? The answer is that He is bringing many sons into glory (Heb. 2:10). All of the events of life are, therefore, calculated by God to produce maturity in His sons in preparation for the rulership of eternity.

What wonder must have progressively taken over the minds of the members of the New Testament body of Christ as they thought of their destiny. Living as ordinary, lowly individuals in Corinth, Athens, Rome, or the provinces of Galatia, they are now offered a greater hope beyond this life. Some of them were wicked sinners, prostitutes, whoremongers, thieves, and even tax collectors. Out of their degenerate pasts, the believers crossed over the bridge of faith in Jesus Christ to become heirs of God.

Coming from nothing, from a life of sin, they were overwhelmed with the teaching that, as a gift from God, they possessed eternal life and along with it, the never-to-fade riches of the universe. They were even promised by Jesus Christ that they would never die. Had not He said,

> I am the resurrection, and the life: he that believeth in me, though he were dead, yet shall he live: And whosoever liveth and believeth in me shall never die. Believest thou this? (John 11:25-26).

Their understanding of future glory was expanded by reading from the apostle Paul about the work of Jesus Christ,

> Who hath saved us, and called us with an holy calling, not according to our works, but according to his own purpose and grace, which was given us in

Christ Jesus before the world began, But now is made manifest by the appearing of our Saviour Jesus Christ, who hath abolished death, and hath brought life and immortality to light through the gospel (2 Tim. 1:9-10).

Receiving letters like this and listening to the face-to-face teaching of the apostle Paul, these early Christians pursued with joy and astonishment the truth of the resurrection of Christ and, therefore, of their own personal resurrection.

What About Those Who Have Died?

Five years, ten years, twenty years had gone by, and Christ had not come. Believers were burying their brothers and sisters as the inevitable ending of life took place for one Christian after another. Those first Christian funerals must have been most moving occasions. But they also produced a series of questions in the minds of the believers still alive.

These Christians, knowing that their departed loved ones were present with the Lord, wondered how they would share in the coming of Christ. They were certainly also concerned about when these departed loved ones would be resurrected from the dead. The bodies were in the grave, and their spirits were with Christ.

Jesus was coming again; therefore, the believers asked, "How does the coming of Christ for His church relate to those Christians who have gone before? How do those who have already died in Christ share in the moment of His return with those who are yet alive? Is there a special resurrection for the Christian?"

These were understandable concerns and, to be sure, concerns that remain today among untutored believers.

The New Testament Christians corresponded with the apostle Paul, asking him about those who had died and how they will share in the return of Christ. We can rejoice in this because we have Paul's answer to the questions about death and resurrection that were raised by the early Christians.

A Special Resurrection

In the letter of the apostle Paul to the saints of Thessalonica, given by divine revelation, he revealed that wonderful truth of the special resurrection of believing Christians:

> But I would not have you to be ignorant, breth-
> ren, concerning them which are asleep, that ye sorrow
> not, even as others who have no hope. For if we believe
> that Jesus died and rose again, even so them also who
> sleep in Jesus will God bring with him. For this we say
> unto you by the word of the Lord, that we which are
> alive and remain unto the coming of the Lord shall not
> prevent them which are asleep. For the Lord himself
> shall descend from heaven with a shout, with the
> voice of the archangel, and with the trump of God: and
> the dead in Christ shall rise first: Then we who are
> alive and remain shall be caught up together with
> them in the clouds, to meet the Lord in the air: and so
> shall we ever be with the Lord. Wherefore comfort one
> another with these words (1 Thess. 4:13-18).

This passage presents the truth of the rapture of the
Church. What lessons can we learn from Paul's writing? They
certainly include the following:

1) Spiritual ignorance is not complimented in the Word of
God. By paying attention to the sure word of prophecy that
God has given us in His Word, we can become knowledgeable,
rather than ignorant Christians.

2) Christians who have died are with the Lord, and they
will be brought by Christ to the Rapture. Many Christians are
concerned about the location and state of mind of departed
loved ones even today. The Scriptures reassure us that they are
"safe in the arms of Jesus" and are tenderly cared for by Him.

3) Christ will descend from heaven to meet believers in the
air. Notice that the Lord Jesus does not return the entire
distance to this world but, rather, awaits that rendezvous in the
air and will catch us up to that point of greeting and reunion.
We can, therefore, suggest that this moment of tender reunion
will not be observed by the people of earth. Indeed, even their
observation would profane so holy an occasion.

4) The Rapture will be the occasion of the resurrection of
believers. One of the cardinal doctrines of the Christian faith is
that of the resurrection of the body. This resurrection for
believers will be on the identical occasion of the Rapture, at

which time the bodies of Christians, glorified, will be reunited with their spirits which have been in the presence of Jesus Christ.

5) The Rapture will reunite believers with loved ones who have died in Christ. First, we will have the opportunity to greet one another, and together we will then be taken into the presence of Jesus Christ and into the presence of God.

6) This event will unite believers with Christ, never again to be separated. One of the great promises of the Rapture is that we will be present with the Lord, no longer to walk by faith but, rather, by sight. What an awesome occasion that will be, as John discovered when he met the Lord on the occasion of the writing of the Book of the Revelation (Rev. 1:9-18).

By so writing, Paul gave us the classic passage in the New Testament that tells us in no uncertain terms that there is a generation of Christians who will not die. Rather, they will be caught up into the presence of Christ along with resurrected believers whom Christ will bring with Him when He comes for that last set of living Christians who will be alive when Christ comes for His church.

The Mystery Revealed

We must note that the doctrine of the catching up of the Church was a mystery, which in this passage was made known to people who already knew the general outline of the prophetic future. This is clear because Paul says that,

> But of the times and the seasons, brethren, you have no need that I write unto you. For yourselves know perfectly that the day of the Lord so cometh as a thief in the night (1 Thess. 5:1-2).

This same message, that of the hitherto unannounced rapture of the Church, is also emphasized by the apostle Paul when he wrote to the Corinthians. He said,

> Behold, I shew you a mystery; We shall not all sleep, but we shall all be changed, In a moment, in the twinkling of an eye, at the last trump: for the trumpet shall sound, and the dead shall be raised incorruptible, and we shall be changed (1 Cor. 15:51-52).

As we have noticed, the general message of the coming of the Lord was no mystery; the Thessalonians knew this perfectly well. The mystery was that the Church, in the form of the last generation of living Christians, was to be instantly transported and transformed without experiencing physical death itself.

By this, it then becomes clear in Scripture that God has produced a special entity in the world, the body of Christ, and for that Body, He has a special destiny. That destiny is to inherit all things and to participate in the rulership of the universe one day.

What a joy this truth became to the members of the early Church. We know that the first Christians were called upon to live for Christ in the midst of adverse circumstances. Sometimes, they were the object of severe persecution, even martyrdom. Because of the blessed hope which they now understood, they could receive the Word in much affliction, continuing to rejoice despite their circumstances.

From their example, the lesson is clear that one derives joy not from present cooperating circumstances but from the promise of the prophetic Word. The believing Christian knows that the fleeting joys and the temporary adversities of this world are to be accounted as little by comparison to the joy that awaits us when we step into the presence of Christ. The apostle Paul says this most strongly:

> For which cause we faint not; but though our outward man may perish, yet the inward man is renewed day by day. For our light affliction, which is but for a moment, worketh for us a far more exceeding and eternal weight of glory; While we look not at the things which are seen: but at the things which are not seen: for the things which are seen are temporal; but the things which are not seen are eternal (2 Cor. 4:16-18).

The best of this life is not then to be compared with the joys of the future. This life is not final reality, it is the prelude to that reality. The worst circumstances imaginable in this world are but light affliction that lasts but for a moment. Reality, fullness of joy, comes to us from God when we pass from this life into the life to come.

The Body of Christ

We learn, therefore, from the Word of God, that the Lord has produced a special period of time, which is the Church Age. During that period of time, there is being fashioned by God himself that wonderful entity, the body of Christ.

When the body of Christ is complete, of which each believer is a member, we will be caught up into heaven to be with Christ. The bodies of those who have gone before will be resurrected, and a living generation of Christians will be caught up without dying to meet with those who have gone before to be taken by Christ into heaven.

There is an exact moment when this completion of the body of Christ will happen. That moment, at this present time known only to God, will bring the translation of the body of Christ into heaven. All believers at that moment will move from the Church militant to the Church triumphant.

In eternity, the believers will realize their true destiny: to be the inheritors and the co-rulers of the universe with Jesus Christ. It is no small thing to be a Christian! Believing in Jesus Christ is not merely the emotion of a moment, it is to be eternally joined with God himself and literally a partaker of the divine nature. It is to have the hope of eternal life, which God, who cannot lie, promised before the world began.

The proper attitude, therefore, of the believer is to brightly anticipate the joys of heaven. The proper sentiment is also to allow for the possibility that, "Perhaps today, perhaps this very hour, I will be caught up into the presence of Christ and so to be with Him forever."

Let us remember, then, that there is not one but two possible ways in which the believer will go to heaven. One of them is via physical death. Concerning this, we ought not to be afraid because, in fact, the Christian does not die. Christ has abolished death and promised that when we believe in Him, we will never die. The Christian, even in "dying," does not even lose consciousness but discovers the marvelous truth that absent from the body is present with the Lord.

The other possibility for going to heaven is the Rapture, the catching up of the Church into the presence of Christ. So thrilling is this prospect that we ought to learn more about this event in which many of us may well participate. Happily then, though there are many related questions concerning the Rapture, we can discover the answer by looking into the blessed pages of the Word of God.

What Is the Tribulation?

We have learned that the Rapture is the method by which Christ will take that last generation of believing Christians home to be with himself. There is little disagreement by those who pay the proper, studious respect to the Word of God that the Bible teaches the physical transport of believers from the earth to heaven. That is a fact which is presented undeniably and without apology in the Scriptures.

The questions which then arise have to do with the timing of the Rapture. People ask, "When?"

The Rapture event is the object of much discussion with reference to the timing, relative to a special era in history called "the Tribulation." Therefore, the question often takes the form of "Will Christians go through the Tribulation?" and "Will Christ come for His own before the Tribulation?" and other related concerns.

To discover the answers to these questions, we must think concerning the basic question, "What is the Tribulation?" A proper understanding of the days of the Tribulation can go a long way toward answering the question of the timing of the Rapture relative to the Tribulation.

What then is "the Tribulation" so commonly spoken of in Scripture?

The 69th Week

The first and most basic answer to that question is that the Tribulation is the seventieth week of the prophecy of Daniel. One of the most consolidated histories of the world, of the divine intention, is found in that prophecy.

> Seventy weeks are determined upon thy people and upon thy holy city, to finish the transgression, and to make an end of sins, and to make reconciliation for iniquity, and to bring in everlasting righteousness, and to seal up the vision and prophecy, and to anoint the most Holy (Dan. 9:24).

Here we have the goals that God is determined to fulfill in that seventy-week period of time that will bring us to the consummation of history.

Daniel's prophecy says that a most notable and tragic event will take place at the end of the sixty-ninth week, namely that Messiah shall be cut off. So the somber prediction of the death of the Messiah of Israel, Jesus Christ, is presented to us by the prophet Daniel. So stunning is this event, so awesome a proof of the rebellion and sin of the people of God that the crucifixion of the Son of God stops the clock of prophecy.

On the occasion of the death of Christ, the veil of the temple was rent in twain, split from top to bottom, and the program of God for His people, the Jews, came to an abrupt halt. The unspeakably sad result is pictured in most moving fashion in Matthew's Gospel, presenting us the words of Christ.

> Oh Jerusalem, Jerusalem, thou that killest the prophets, and stonest them who are sent unto thee, how often would I have gathered thy children together, even as a hen gathereth her chickens under her wings, and ye would not! Behold, your house is left unto you desolate. For I say unto you, Ye shall not see me henceforth, till ye shall say, Blessed is he that cometh in the name of the Lord (Matt.23:37-39).

Here we have Christ stating in advance the results of the rejection of their Messiah by the Chosen People of God. Their house would be left unto them desolate!

So it is that the house of Israel has been left desolate now for nearly 2,000 years. The children of Israel have been scattered across the world and have been subject to calumny, persecution, and rejection in nearly every nation of the world. This period of time has been the era of Israel being cut off from the true vine and the Church grafted in.

During the Church Age, therefore, God has had no specific program with the nation of Israel. Rather, in this day of grace, He has been calling both Jew and Gentile to faith in Jesus Christ as the Saviour of the world. All who so believe in this day are members of the body of Christ.

But God has not entirely forsaken His people. He has one last cycle of discipline for Israel. That period of discipline will come during Daniel's seventieth week, the week of the Tribulation.

The Time of Jacob's Trouble

The Tribulation is, therefore, the time of Jacob's trouble. Jeremiah says, "Alas! for that day is great, so that none is like it: it is even the time of Jacob's trouble; but he shall be saved out of it" (Jer. 30:7).

Israel is held responsible by the Lord, along with the Gentiles, for the crucifixion of Christ. This is the reason for the awesome silence of Jehovah in relating to His people during the two millennia that have transpired since the death of Christ. Clearly, however, the Word of God declares that God has not finally and completely cast away His people.

Indeed, the Scripture speaks of the casting away of Israel and announced that that produced the reconciling of the world. The Scripture then speaks of the receiving of Israel, which will be life from the dead for the nations. Israel moved into a period of blindness and estrangement from God until a point of time called the fullness of the Gentiles (Rom.11:25).

At this point, God promises to work in goodness and severity with His people so that, under the discipline of the Tribulation, Israel will be brought to a place of decision and faith. This is always the intention of divine discipline for His own, in any era of history.

The Tribulation, then, will be a time of the conversion of Israel. Most boldly, the Scripture announces,

> And so all Israel shall be saved: as it is written, There shall come out of Zion the Deliverer, and shall turn away ungodliness from Jacob; For this is my covenant unto them, when I shall take away their sins (Rom. 11:26-27).

Spiritual Revival

The Tribulation will, therefore, be a time of great spiritual revival. It will mark the conversion of Israel and great activity by Israel for the conversion of the world.

The Book of The Revelation, therefore, announces an amazing multitude of 144,000 witnesses who represent the twelve tribes of Israel. These will have been converted during the days of the Tribulation and will have a profound effect upon the world. When one remembers that there is only a fraction of this number of Christian missionaries in the world today, one is impressed with the zealous response that will come out of Israel in the form of faith in Jesus Christ as its Messiah. "The gospel of the Kingdom" will be preached with great zeal by them to the world.

The Tribulation will also be a time of massive conversion of Gentile multitudes. The Revelation says,

> After this I beheld, and, lo, a great multitude, which no man could number, of all nations, and kindreds, and people, and tongues, stood before the throne, and before the Lamb, clothed with white robes, and palms in their hands (Rev. 7:9).

So remarkable is this sight that one of the elders around God's throne asked who these people are. The answer from the Word of God is: "These are they who came out of the great tribulation, and have washed their robes, and made them white in the blood of the Lamb" (Rev. 7:14).

Amazing spiritual results occur when the world comes to the end of itself, realizing that nothing on earth has any value. It then turns in great numbers to faith in Christ as Messiah, bringing in a time of evangelism that will be one of the largest and most effective in the history of the world. The anguish of the Tribulation produces a most salutary result. But a fearful time it will be!

God's Wrath Poured Forth

The Tribulation is the time of the outpouring of the wrath of God upon a wicked world. In the account of the horsemen of the Apocalypse, when the fourth horseman rides forth, the Scripture says,

> ... And power was given unto them over the fourth part of the earth, to kill with sword, and with hunger, and with death, and with the beasts of the earth (Rev. 6:8).

In the beginning days of the Revelation, therefore, approximately 25 percent of the world is killed in the opening wars and pestilences of those days.

Very quickly, the Scripture says,

> And thus I saw the horses in the vision, and them that sat on them, having breastplates of fire, and of jacinth, and brimstone: and the heads of the horses were as the heads of lions; and out of their mouths issued fire and smoke and brimstone. By these three was the third part of men killed, by the fire, and by the smoke, and by the brimstone, which issued out of their mouths (Rev. 9:17-18).

A third part of men killed! This already mounts up to one-half of the world's population, and beyond this point in the Revelation many other natural catastrophes take place. As the Tribulation unfolds, there are mighty earthquakes, occasions of scorching heat, the advent of the Antichrist, world occult religious organization, and finally, the Battle of Armageddon, which will be fatal to scores of millions of soldiers. This time of natural catastrophe combined with divine judgment will bring awesome carnage across the face of the earth.

The Day of the Lord

The Tribulation is the beginning of "the day of the Lord." As we have seen, the Christians were conscious — because they read about it in the Old Testament — that there was a time of fearful judgment coming upon the world called the day of the Lord. The churches, however, needed instruction as to how to discern the presence of the day of the Lord and the way to know that the day of grace was finished. Concerning this, the apostle Paul wrote to the Thessalonians, saying,

> Now we beseech you, brethren, by the coming of our Lord Jesus Christ, and by our gathering together unto him, That ye be not soon shaken in mind, or be troubled, neither by spirit, nor by word, nor by letter as from us, as that the day of the Christ is at hand (2 Thess. 2:1-2).

Here, the apostle Paul admonishes the believers of that faithful early church at Thessalonica not to think that the day of the Lord had in fact come upon the world. Paul says they should not be troubled by the idea of this prospect being present by (reason of) the coming of our Lord Jesus Christ and by (reason of) our gathering together unto Him. In other words, the day of the Lord was not present because Christ had not yet come and gathered the saints to himself.

The apostle Paul is, therefore, saying that the rapture of the Church, concerning which he had carefully instructed the Thessalonians, was the watershed point ending the day of grace and beginning the day of the Lord. In that the Rapture had not taken place, the day of the Lord was not yet present.

Here, the apostle Paul gives us a clear line of demarcation between the Church Age, the day of grace, and the day of the Lord, which is the day of divine judgment. That line of demarcation is the rapture of the Church.

During this day of Grace, God deals with the world with near-infinite forbearance. The Lord has said that unrepentant, sinful man is to be seen as follows:

> But after thy hardness and impenitent heart treasurest up unto thyself wrath against the day of wrath and revelation of the righteous judgment of God; Who will render to every man according to his deeds (Rom.2:5-6).

During this age of grace, therefore, God tells us that man is, as it were, putting iniquity in the bank. He is treasuring it up, but the judgment of man's iniquity is sure to come. It does not come by way of naked vengeance from God during this gracious era, but it will come during the period of time called the day of the Lord, which begins with the Tribulation.

What Can We Expect?

Why does not the judgment of God come strongly upon the world in our time? It is because of the presence of the Church, the bride of Christ, in the world. Christ is not intending to bring His bride to heaven bruised, battered, bleeding, and badly damaged by the dreadful persecutions of the Antichrist, which will come upon the world during the Tribulation. Rather, He has promised to take His Church home in timely fashion, so that she will be kept from the hour of Tribulation in the world.

Speaking to the Church in the last days of church history,

the Lord himself says,

> Because thou has kept the word of my patience,
> I also will keep thee from that hour of temptation,
> which shall come upon all of the world, to try them
> that dwell upon the earth (Rev. 3:10).

What then is coming upon the world? An hour of temptation, an hour of trial, an hour of tribulation.

What promise does Christ make to the Church concerning that time of Tribulation? The promise is that she will be kept from that hour. Here we have a remarkable clue as to the timing of the rapture of the Church relative to the Tribulation. The Rapture is positioned in Scripture as coming before the Tribulation, by reason of which the Church will be unscathed from the judgment of the Tribulation.

Some have expressed concern about the teaching of the Bible that the Church is the bride of Christ. This will be dispelled when we read the Scriptures, which say,

> Therefore, as the church is subject unto Christ,
> so let the wives be to their own husbands in every-
> thing. Husbands, love your wives, even as Christ
> also loved the church, and gave himself for it; That he
> might sanctify and cleanse it with the washing of
> water by the word, That he might present it to him-
> self a glorious church, not having spot, or wrinkle, or
> any such thing; but that it should be holy and without
> blemish. So ought men to love their wives as their
> own bodies. He that loveth his wife loveth himself.
> For no man ever yet hated his own flesh; but
> nourisheth and cherisheth it, even as the Lord the
> church: For we are members of his body, of his flesh,
> and of his bones. For this cause shall a man leave his
> father and mother, and shall be joined unto his wife,
> and they two shall be one flesh. This is a great
> mystery: but I speak concerning Christ and the church
> (Eph. 5:24-32).

We think Paul was speaking of human marriage . . . and he was. But, in the highest sense, he has Christ and His bride, the Church, in mind.

Does the Church deserve to escape the Tribulation? Of course not! But, the condemnation which every Christian knows he richly deserves has already been vicariously absolved via the condemnation of Jesus Christ on Calvary's cross. Because the iniquity of us all was laid upon Christ, we are, therefore, saved by righteousness which is imputed, accredited to us by virtue of the shed blood of the Lord Jesus. The result is that we have the announcement, "There is therefore now no condemnation to them which are in Christ Jesus . . ." (Rom. 8:1). No condemnation!

Kept from the hour is the faithful promise Christ gives to His church and that can be the object of joyous confidence on the part of us all.

This Day of Grace

In this day of grace, we who are Christians have been made custodians of the most precious possession imaginable, the gospel of the grace of God.

It will be different once the Tribulation begins!

The message which the Church has presently to preach to the world is the thrilling word that, "For by grace are ye saved through faith; and that not of yourselves: it is the gift of God: Not of works, lest any man should boast" (Eph. 2:8-9). Here we have this wonderful offer of salvation by the unmerited favor of God because of Christ. It is the core of the gospel.

What is the core of the gospel? It is grace. By what price does this precious gift become ours? The apostle Paul clearly says,

> For I delivered unto you first of all that which I also received, how that Christ died for our sins according to the scriptures; And that he was buried, and that he rose again the third day according to the scriptures (1 Cor. 15:3-4).

This marvelous message the apostle Paul declares to be "the gospel." It consists of the announcement of the death, the burial, and the resurrection of Jesus Christ. The declaration is that the sacrifice of Christ on Calvary's cross was fully sufficient, enough to save us to the uttermost who believe in Him.

Therefore, the apostle Paul is able to declare, "For all have sinned, and come short of the glory of God; Being justified freely by his grace through the redemption that is in Christ Jesus" (Rom. 3:23-24).

We are saved, therefore, not by our own righteousness but because we are justified freely by the grace of God. To be justified means to be declared righteous. It does not mean to be made righteous but, rather, the righteousness by which we are saved is that which we have by imputation. Therefore, the apostle Paul is able to expand on his message and declare that, Abraham believed God, and it was imputed unto him for righteousness.

In this passage, the word for "believed" is the word *amen*. Salvation, therefore, because the world is guilty and unable to work for God, comes "to him that worketh not, but believeth on him that justifieth the ungodly . . ." (Rom. 4:5).

The Church of our time, therefore, is custodian of the thrilling message that God has a gift for the world and it comes on an absolutely free basis. No work of man — before, during, or after salvation — is a part of that salvation, nor does it make his eternal life any more sure. This is the day of grace and salvation, and salvation is by grace alone. So, the gospel of the grace of God is the message that everlasting life is available to all by faith alone.

The Gospel of the Kingdom

During the Tribulation, however, the message that will be announced to the world is called "the gospel of the Kingdom." What is this message? It was the same message our Lord Jesus presented to the nation of Israel in His earthly ministry, particularly as is represented in the Gospel of Matthew.

The earthly ministry of Christ was the King speaking to his errant subjects and announcing, as Matthew describes it,

> From that time Jesus began to preach, and to say, Repent: for the kingdom of heaven is at hand (Matt. 4:17).

So, Matthew describes the ministry of Christ by saying,

> And Jesus went about all Galilee, teaching in their synagogues, and preaching the gospel of the kingdom, and healing all manner of sickness and all

manner of diseases among the people (Matt. 4:23).

The people of Israel, as we have seen, rejected both the King and the kingdom He offered — the kingdom of heaven. This rejection was not merely verbal, but the Scripture announces that, with utter cynicism, they nailed Christ to the cross.

Stupendous is this blindness, this cruel rejection of their King, this deocide. That's when everything changed. A sinful humanity was now utterly disqualified from salvation merely by repenting and receiving the kingdom. Without moral credentials or capacity, man, if he is to be saved at all, must be saved by utter grace. No deal, no arrangement, no nothing.

Man is guilty! All humanity is bankrupt! God, if He would save man, must open a bankruptcy court. There, He can declare guilty sinners, when they admit their bankruptcy, to be forgiven. He has been conducting that bankruptcy court for nearly 2,000 years. There, He declares sinners guilty (Rom. 3:19) and then, if they agree, they are cleansed in the blood of Christ. That agreement is called "faith." There is, there could be, no other way.

The parenthetical period (the Church Age) that followed the death, the murder, of Christ was not characterized by the announcement that "the kingdom of heaven is at hand" but, rather, that a guilty humanity by faith in Christ could be saved by grace. By this, they would inherit not merely the kingdom of heaven but, rather, be heirs and perhaps rulers of the universe. What incredibly fortunate people form the body of Christ!

There is coming a day, however, when the body of Christ will be complete, and the group to rule the universe will have been raptured out of the world. At that time, God will renew His program with the nation of Israel, and then will come again the announcement: The kingdom of heaven is at hand. So it is that believers in Jesus Christ during the Tribulation are saved by faith as has been the case in all ages. However, they are saved into participation in the kingdom of heaven. That is the Kingdom that will, during the Millennium, and then throughout eternity, produce heaven on earth.

We must remember, therefore, that believing Jews and believing Gentiles during the Tribulation will be heirs of the world (Rom. 4:13). Believing Christians, saved during the day of grace, will be heirs of the universe. The event of demarcation between those two eras in the divine dealings with mankind is the rapture of the Church.

The Day of the Lord

This is a point not well understood by Christians in our time and understood not at all by the world. This pitiful world still believes a sadly mistaken view of Christianity. It thinks that the Church makes the announcement, "If you come to church, you will go to heaven" or "If you clean up your life and go straight, you will be forgiven of God and you may make heaven some day." This is, of course, not at all the message of the Church.

The message of the Church is that, because of the death, burial, and resurrection of Christ, God has a free gift for man. "For the wages of sin is death; but the gift of God is eternal life through Jesus Christ our Lord" (Rom. 6:23).

All who believe in the finished work of Calvary's cross and accept salvation as a free gift from God are given everlasting life. Upon making this decision, they become heirs of God, joint heirs with Christ, and objects of His blessing for all of eternity.

But the message of the Tribulation as presented to us by Jesus Christ is not the same. Christ warns about the coming of the "abomination of desolation" as signaling that the Tribulation is fully upon the world. Continuing in that same address, He then says,

> And woe unto them who are with child, and to them that give suck in those days! But pray ye that your flight be not in the winter, neither on the sabbath day (Matt. 24:19-20).

So there will be a reconstitution of the Sabbath Day.

The rule is that a Sabbath Day's journey must not be violated on that day. In the very next verse, Christ reveals of what era He is speaking: "For then shall be great tribulation, such as was not since the beginning of the world to this time, no, nor ever shall be" (Matt. 24:21).

The religion of the Tribulation will also bring the rebuilding of the temple (2 Thess. 2:4), the establishing of temple sacrifice (Dan. 9:27), and other forms of Old Testament-like Jewish worship. So, the certified religion in the world during the Tribulation will be Judaism, or as some moderns might call it, "neo-Judaism."

It is clear that the Church must be taken out of the world before the days of the Tribulation. This is because it would be impossible to have the message of the gospel of the grace of God and, at the same time, the gospel of the Kingdom as concomitantly certified by the Lord. The Rapture is the event that pointedly punctuates the end of the era of the Church and the beginning of the era called the day of the Lord, which commences with the Tribulation.

The Middle East

The timing of the Rapture with reference to the Tribulation is clear — the Rapture will take place before the days of the Tribulation. The timing of the Rapture with reference to the Church Age is also clear — the Rapture will end the Church Age.

This being the case, thinking people everywhere wonder how soon the Rapture will take place when we observe the remarkable developments of this present time.

Across the nations of earth there now is transpiring a set of events that has set the world to thinking once again. Not since World War II has there been such a spirit of expectation in the world — the religious world and the secular society. We do well to take a brief look at some of the areas and occasions that have newly ignited an interest in the prophetic Word.

In the Middle East, and especially with reference to the state of Israel, we have observed a set of circumstances that appear to be remarkably similar to the events predicted in the prophetic Word. In our time, the Jews have been regathered from a period of dispersion among the nations of the world, and they are in their own land once again.

The Israeli nation, having been reconstituted in 1948, has been able to survive despite hopeless odds and the many wars leveled against her. In the more recent Gulf War, called "Desert Storm," Israel was the only non-belligerent nation attacked by those devilish Scud missiles. Still, doubtless by divine protection, the casualties were very light — one person killed by direct debris from the sky. That's an amazing statistic.

Now, Israel is being forced by the major powers — particularly the United States — to make peace with the Palestinians and Israel's Arab neighbors. This amounts to the program of "Land for Peace," which should be considered absurd by all thinking people.

But alas, that absurdity will become a reality! Israel will make a peace treaty with the prince that shall come (Dan. 9:24-27), the leader of Europe. This treaty will virtually signal the beginning of the Tribulation.

Europe — the Revived Roman Empire

We look also at Europe and find ourselves provoked by a new set of thoughts coming from the developments there. The Scripture indicates that Gentile world power will be encompassed in the hegemony of but four great empires. These are Babylon, Media-Persia, Greece, and Rome. The last of these, the empire of Rome, will be revived at the end of the age. The closest approximation to that is present day Europe. As we hear of "the United States of Europe," we sense an empire creating itself before our very eyes.

Europe — Rome revived — will bring to pass the rise of Antichrist. His emergence must take place after the rapture of the Church. It is at the beginning of the Tribulation that "the man of sin" will be revealed.

Russia continues its strange course as well. The leaders of the world announce "the breakup of the Soviet Empire," and "communism is dissolving before our very eyes." These things are true, but the troublesome aspect is that they are too good to be true. When observing this, we must remember the adage that "If something is too good to be true, it probably is." (Meaning, of course, that it is an illusion or a falsehood.)

Still, despite all these strange gyrations of the former Soviet Union, the cold reality is this: the central establishment of what was the Soviet Union has, despite all the rhetoric, eleven thousand nuclear warheads pointed at the United States. Just prior to the Soviet Union's dissolution, General Colin Powell reminded us that "the Soviet Union could destroy the United States in thirty minutes."

All other developments notwithstanding, we must remember that the Commonwealth of Independent States, as Russia and her fellow republics presently call themselves, forces us to face two considerations. The first is that it has a diamond-hard military establishment. The second is that it is running short of everything else, including oil.

We must bear in mind, therefore, that the Communist empire is not going to be allowed by God to die with a whimper, saying, "Sorry about that." Its doom will take place as it loses its army on the northern mountains of Israel. Whatever our hopes may be, the shortages of everything and the unfulfilled ambitions in the former Soviet Union will force it to attempt a lightning strike to the South.

This presses a serious question for the United States! Over the years, there has been but one entity, humanly speaking, that has prevented Communist world conquest. That entity is the United States of America, its nuclear capability and willingness to use it. What then has happened to the United States that makes the Prince of Rosh feel that he can move with impunity to the South? Many things, of course, are possible.

One of the great possibilities, however, is the rapture of the Church. This event would take from America its leadership class. The United States, if it lost fifty million of its people, would be hard-put to reconstitute itself quickly as a major power. Certainly this reconstituting, if it were even possible, would take a large amount of time. This potential scenario alone may explain why it is difficult to find America in the final prophetic picture as is presented in the Word of God.

Babylon Revisited

Think again of the Middle East as we consider the situation in our present world. During Operation "Desert Storm," thirty-two nations gathered against "Babylon" and its mad, unstable leader. This remarkable gathering was the assembling of the most powerful army that history has ever known.

We must not ignore the similarity of this gathering to the prediction of the prophet Isaiah against Babylon; "They come from a far country, from the end of heaven, even the Lord, and the weapons of his indignation, to destroy the whole land" (Isa. 13:5).

We must notice, then, that in the very next verse, Isaiah says, "Howl ye; for the day of the Lord is at hand; and it shall come as a destruction from the Almighty" (Isa. 13:6).

Now, as we have seen, the day of the Lord, that time of divine judgment upon the world, cannot come until first comes the Rapture. Isaiah, being an Old Testament prophet, did not foresee the rapture of the Church or even the Church itself. What might Isaiah's warning be were he to speak in our time? Might he not say, "The day of the Lord is at hand and therefore, the Rapture comes soon. Wail, for a time of judgment is coming upon the world from which the Church will be delivered."

The prophet Jeremiah indicates that there will be three stages in the destruction of Babylon; three military powers will cause its downfall. Those will be:

1) An international military alliance.

For, lo, I will raise and cause to come up against Babylon an assembly of great nations from the north country: and they shall set themselves in array against her; from thence she shall be taken: their arrows shall be as of a mighty and expert man; none shall return in vain (Jer. 50:9).

2) A single nation from the north.

For out of the north there cometh up a nation against her, which shall make her land desolate, and none shall dwell therein: they shall remove, they shall depart, both man and beast (Jer. 50:3).

3) The nation of Israel.

. . . Israel is the rod of his inheritance: the Lord of hosts is his name. Thou art my battle axe and weapons of war: for with thee will I break in pieces the nations, and with thee will I destroy kingdoms (Jer. 51:19-20).

Thinking students of the prophetic Word will agree as to the similarity of the action taken in Desert Storm to the first stage in the destruction of Babylon — the similarity to the prophetic description. There, then, awaits stages two and three. Stage two, the coming of Russia and her allies against Babylon, can also be seen as described in Ezekiel 38. This battle takes place after the beginning of the Tribulation.

Stage three, the destruction of Babylon by Israel, could well be the act that draws international consternation and even military action against what the nations will see as "presumptuous" Israel. This is indicated by Jeremiah in saying, "At the noise of the taking of Babylon the earth is moved, and the cry is heard among the nations" (Jer. 50:46). Reading this, we remember Zechariah's prophecy. He tells us that at a day to come, all nations will gather to war against Israel.

What could be the aggravation, the trigger mechanism that could bring this to pass? It could be that "arrogant" Israel has taken independent action against Babylon, even at a nuclear level. The indication is that the last two of these judgmental events take place during the days of the Tribulation. This would, therefore, suggest that the Rapture may happen between stages one and two. If this is indeed the case, we must not disallow the possibility that the Rapture could be a part of the near-term plan of God.

It is most instructive to think of the possibilities linked within the Old Testament announcement that "the day of the Lord is at hand." The timing of the fulfillment of that expression is in the midst of events that certainly resemble the events of our time.

Prophetic Timing

At this point, a helpful word may be said about the timing of prophetic events. The indication of the Scripture is that the events themselves are inevitable, but the timing is always subject to adjustment in the hand of God.

This is apparent from the account of the prophet Jonah. Jonah was sent to Ninevah with the announcement that Ninevah would be destroyed in forty days. Jonah arrived in Ninevah — via a circuitous route — and began preaching with that announcement central to his message. After forty days of preaching, he stepped outside of the city and waited in the anticipation of beholding before his eyes the destruction of Ninevah. To the chagrin of the prophet, this destruction did not happen. In fact, God gave Ninevah eighty-five more years of opportunity.

Why was this the case? It was because Ninevah repented. These pagan people turned to the Lord and, therefore, saw the forestalling of divine judgment that was scheduled for them.

That lesson should be learned by all. The events delineated in the prophetic Word are a part of this mysterious continuum called "time." The total picture is controlled by the

God who stands above time and is certainly able to do with it what He will. For this reason, we are to have a sense of surety about the events of prophetic history and the certainty that comes from faith that God will bring it all to pass.

Of the timing, however, we are advised against announcing that we know the day and the hour of His return. Still, the provocative developments we are seeing in our contemporary world surely should cause us to look up for a redemption that draws nigh. Christ is coming again for His own! Each of us must be ready.

The Believers Attitude

What then is the recommended attitude of the believer when he thinks about the future, especially the rapture of the Church? In thinking of this, we recall that there have been dramatic occasions where whole companies of people went to nearby fields to await the rapture of the Church. Dressed in white gowns, they looked up with ecstatic faces, believing that Jesus would return at any moment. One element in the attitude of these believers was commendable, that of bright anticipation. They really believed that Jesus was coming again and were moved to a form of action in response to that belief.

The weakness, however, was in biblical exegesis. Their lack of careful knowledge of Holy Scripture led them to be excessively specific about the time of the return of Christ. Believers do well to sing, "Jesus *may* come today," but they are excessively specific if they sing "Jesus *will* come today." He denies us the knowledge of the day and the hour of His return because He would have us to be expecting His coming at every day and in every hour.

Other believers have reacted in a different fashion, becoming fearful at the prospect of the return of Christ. Excessively settled in the things of time, they resent even the suggestion that all of that will be quickly gone some day. It is a mistake to attach oneself to the things of time in any manner that would make the instant initiation of eternity the object of our resentment. Nothing in this life should be held with so tight a clutch.

The proper attitude when one contemplates the return of Christ is suggested to us by our Lord himself. Speaking to His disciples and intimating the special nature of His return of His own, Christ said,

> Let not your heart be troubled: ye believe in God, believe also in me. In my Father's house are many mansions: if it were not so, I would have told you. I go to prepare a place for you. And if I go and prepare a place for you, I will come again, and receive you unto myself; that where I am, there ye may be also (John 14:1-3).

In these words to His disciples, the Lord Jesus makes to them the promise that He will come again and receive them to himself. In this passage, He also suggests an attitude on their part. In fact, there are a number of lessons that we do well to learn from these instructions by our Lord himself.

1) We are not to be troubled but confident in faith. The believer who knows that his eternity is secure and who walks by faith will be characterized by an untroubled heart. Fear of the future is dispelled when we believe in God and truly believe in Christ.

2) There is plenty of room in heaven. Christ promises us that His Father's house is characterized by many mansions. We may be confident of a splendid dwelling place on high that is infinitely better and more beautiful than the best we can know in this world. There is room also in heaven for neighbors and friends, and we do well to be inviting them to share heaven with us.

3) Christ is preparing a special place for His own. What is Jesus doing now in heaven? He is making the arrangements — perhaps the final arrangements — for our accommodations in glory. We may be sure that such accommodations, prepared by the loving hand of the Lord Jesus, will be splendid beyond our ability to describe them.

4) Christ is coming again for His own. Here we have the promise of the "special coming" of our Lord Jesus, the rapture of the Church. He is not now speaking of His coming in power and great glory, but rather, of His intimate, special relationship with those who believe in Him. For them, He is to make a special journey.

Reviewing this set of wonderful promises from the Lord Jesus, the believer will see grow within him the confidence of solid anticipation, looking forward to that day in which the promises of Christ will come to pass for him.

The proper attitude of the believer, therefore, is that he is neither fearful nor cynical. Bright anticipation is to be recommended, especially in our time.

Bright Anticipation

Yes, before the sun returns again to the morning landscape, Christ may come again for His own. Before we live another day, we may be translated from this world into the wonderful environs of heaven. Before too many hours, the commerce of earth may shudder and then stop, awe-stricken by the disappearance of the world's best people. Each one of these things is well within the realm of possibility and the certainty of their occurrence grows more sure every day. Bright anticipation, that is the proper attitude.

But someone will ask — perhaps with sincerity — the question, "Will not anticipation produce irresponsibility?"

"If a person is constantly anticipating the return of Jesus Christ, will he not become so heavenly minded that he is no earthly good?"

We may remind ourselves again that there was a group of Christians in the New Testament whose lives and testimonies became the answer to that question. The apostle Paul compliments his friends of Thessalonica and says that they were waiting for the return of Jesus Christ, the Son of God, to come from heaven (1 Thess.1:10). We have the word for it; their attitude was bright anticipation, watchful, waiting.

What was the result of this attitude? It was not laziness nor disinterest, not at all. Rather, the church at Thessalonica became one of the classic churches of the New Testament as a result of their anticipating the return of Christ. The apostle Paul says that they did a number of things that made them one of the great churches of the early age of Christianity.

1) They received the Word in much affliction, with joy in the Holy Spirit (verse 6). Constantly conscious of the reality of heaven, these people had little confidence in the word of man. Correspondingly, they had ultimate confidence in the Word of God.

We may well remind ourselves that the rapture of the Church will bring an abrupt end to the foolish, mindless, human discourse of this world. Grandiose schemes and vast human enterprises will be of little or no consequence when Jesus comes again. Our generation is greatly mistaken by living on philosophy and vain deceit rather than the Word of God. Our foolish generation is ruled by human philosophers who are already in the grave. This would never be if proper attention had been given to the Word of God.

2) They became followers of Christ. The path of life is a deep mystery to many as they wonder about the purpose of their life. For the dear Christians at Thessalonica, this was no problem. They should live for Christ, of course. Soon, they believed, He would come again and, therefore, every step taken in pursuit of His perfect will would be certified and validated by that coming.

A reminder here is also appropriate. The rapture of the Church will not merely deliver a generation of living Christians who are caught up to be with Him. It will also vindicate the purpose for which every Christian has lived a godly life in all of the ages of the Church. His coming will be a testimony to this and all previous generations that the life committed to Christ was not that of a fool. The wisdom of consecration will certainly be forever certified when Jesus comes again.

3) These Christians became an example of the believers. The onlooking world, looking at the lives of "anticipatory believers" in that day, was much impressed. These individuals exemplified the Lord Jesus as against being mere creatures of time.

One who anticipates the return of Christ is careful not to go anywhere, to do anything, to commit himself to any principle of which he will not be proud when Christ comes again. So it is that the doctrine of the return of Christ is a purifying hope. And every man that hath this hope in him purifieth himself even as he is pure (1 John 3:3).

4) These believers became broadcasters of the Word of the Lord (1 Thess. 1:8). Being totally confident in the return of Jesus Christ, the believers saw themselves as having a great message, a transforming hope to bring to the world. The result was a mighty and most effective program of evangelism so that, "In every place your faith toward God is spread abroad, so that we need not to speak anything."

Much could be said of this. In the Church of our time, the need for a strong, explosive program of evangelism and world missions is great. Still, a major proportion of the world, probably 75 percent, awaits the opportunity to hear the gospel of Jesus Christ. Preoccupied with other things and overly engaged in time-serving efforts, the Church of our day could well use a new motivation for global conquest.

Broadcasting the gospel everywhere became the activity of the Thessalonians. Why? Because they believed that Christ was coming again. This doctrine produced such motivation as the world had seldom seen. No one must miss the opportunity of hearing that Jesus is coming back and that, therefore, we should trust Him. This was the motivating hope of the Thessalonians and could well be ours today.

A Glorified Body

The bright anticipation of the Christian could be greatly enhanced by remembering one glorious fact that is promised in connection with the rapture of the Church. What is that glorious fact: we shall receive a glorified body. With great conviction, the apostle Paul declares,

> But our citizenship is in heaven. And we eagerly await a Savior from there, the Lord Jesus Christ, who, by the power that enables him to bring everything under his control . . . (Phil. 3:20-21;NIV).

Echoing this same wonderful promise, the Scripture says,

> Beloved, now are we the sons of God, and it doth not yet appear what we shall be: but we know that, when he shall appear, we shall be like him; for we shall see him as he is (1 John 3:2).

Yes indeed, a glorified body will be ours when Christ comes back for His own. This means, of course, that we will instantly move beyond pain, sorrow, human suffering, and death itself. We will receive bodies like that of the Lord Jesus and be glorified forever in His presence.

This means that the unfortunate characteristics of life in this sinful world will be forever past. Our bodies of flesh, even though we are Christians, are forever subject to the process of deterioration. Paul declares that the outward man must perish while in this life the inward man is renewed day by day.

When Christ comes, however, this will all be changed. Never again will the shocks and sicknesses of this world beset the believer. Forever transformed into his glorified body, he will be beyond that. That change will take place the instant that Christ comes again for His own.

For all of these reasons, therefore, may we suggest that each believer be confident and filled with anticipation about the return of Christ. For many reasons, the prospect of the deliverance of the Church into the arms of the Lord Jesus grows with every day that passes. Upon hearing this, the earnest believer will surely say, Amen, even so, come, Lord Jesus!

Questions and Answers

There are hundreds of prophetic questions that live in the minds of people. Many of them are asked openly at prophetic conferences, on radio programs, and certainly in private conversations. We do well to deal with some of the frequently asked questions, believing that the answers will be helpful to us all.

What qualifies a person to be caught up in the rapture of the Church?

The Word of God teaches that Christ will return again for the delivering of His Church. Everyone who is among those called "brethren" (1 Thess. 5:10) is a member of the body of Christ and will be the object of the deliverance that will come at the Rapture. The single qualification, therefore, is that an individual be a Christian. A Christian is one who has believed the gospel of Jesus Christ and knows God's Son as his personal Saviour.

What prophetic events must be fulfilled before the Rapture?

There are no prophetic events that must precede the Rapture. The predicted events of prophecy have to do with the period of time following the Rapture leading up to the glorious return of Jesus Christ. Therefore, the Rapture could take place at any given moment. It is well for the believer to regularly tell himself, "Perhaps today!"

How shall I prepare for the Rapture?

Surely the greatest experience in life will be to be brought into the presence of God as a good soldier, a faithful servant. The essential preparation for the Rapture is that I be a Christian. Then, the fact that I could be taken to heaven at any given moment should motivate me to exemplary Christian service. Earnest prayer, faithful witnessing, godly living — all of these will be a part of the approval that can come in heaven. We all must so live so as to hear Jesus say in that day, "Well done, good and faithful servant."

When the Rapture comes, what will happen to the children of Christians?

All children who have not yet reached the age of account-ability are counted as "believers" under the doctrine of preve-nient grace. We, therefore, conclude that the children of unbe-lievers will also be included with the children of believers and taken home to be with the Lord. As one person said, "All the children of the world will be taken to heaven and all the unborn children of the world as well."

What impression will the Rapture make on the world?

The answer, of course, depends upon the preoccupations and involvements in which the world finds itself at the time of the Rapture. Still, we must conclude that the disappearance of the Christians of the world and the children of the world will leave a stunning impression upon the minds of people. The Antichrist will be hard-put to come up with an explanation. In lieu of this, the dismay at the teaching of Scripture now being so well proved by the Rapture may well cause millions to come to faith in Christ during the Tribulation. They, as Tribulation saints, will face a time of fearful persecution.

Can we take anyone with us at the Rapture?

Certainly not by holding on to them, as much as we might desire this. But, we can take all of our loved ones and friends with us to heaven if we will have led them to Christ so that they themselves have become Christians before the time of the taking away of the Church. When the Rapture comes, it will be too late to do any additional things in this world for Christ. The record of each person's life will stand as indelible forever after that instant of translation.

How can heaven receive and process so many millions of individuals all arriving at the same time?

This is no problem to God. The arrival of the Church, the body of Christ, at heaven will be a time of great reunion and rejoicing. A home in heaven will have long since been prepared for every individual by Christ himself (John 14:3). A place at the feast of welcome, of betrothal, called "the marriage supper of the Lamb," will have been set for each one. No one will arrive at heaven as a stranger; rather, as a brother beloved.

Isn't it cowardly to wish for the Rapture to deliver us from the problems of life?

Anyone who does not particularly wish to be beheaded during the days of the Tribulation can certainly be expected to anticipate with a welcoming sentiment the rapture of the Church and the deliverance from the wrath to come. To want to go into the Tribulation is not courage; it is mere foolish bravado. The doctrine of the Rapture is true, unrelated to human attitudes. Especially remember that we are to love His appearing (2 Tim. 4:8).

Didn't the doctrine of the Rapture come from a strange source?

The doctrine of the Rapture comes from the Word of God. It is the apostle Paul, under the inspiration of the Holy Spirit, who presents this marvelous truth. It is best to avoid silly stories, from whatever source, related by people who would draw our attention away from any doctrine of the Word of God.

What is the difference between the Rapture and the second coming of Christ?

The Rapture is a very special mission by the Lord to deliver the Church from the awful scenes of the Tribulation. The Rapture, therefore, comes before the Tribulation and takes Christians out of this world before that seven-year period of the wrath of God. Notice that, in the Rapture, Christ does not come all of the way to this world. Rather, Christians are caught up to meet Him in the air (1 Thess. 4:17).

At the second coming of Christ, His glorious return, He comes with His saints. In fact, He returns with an army from heaven for the conquest of the world (Rev. 19:11-16). Remember, since this is an army of His saints (Jude 14), you and I will be a part of that glorious conquest that centers on the return of Christ in power.

Why is the Rapture not mentioned in the Old Testament?

The prophets of the Old Testament were not given the

revelation of the Church, the body of Christ. Neither were they told of the rapture of the Church. This is particularly a New Testament revelation. The Scripture speaks of the message of salvation by grace, given to the Church to preach to the world, and testifies of the concern of the prophets. It says,

> Of which salvation the prophets have inquired and searched diligently, who prophesied of the grace that should come unto you: Searching what, or what manner of time the Spirit of Christ which was in them did signify, when he testified beforehand the sufferings of Christ, and the glory that should follow. Unto whom it was revealed, that not unto themselves, but unto us they did minister the things, which are now reported unto you by them that have preached the gospel unto you with the Holy Ghost sent down from heaven; which things the angels desire to look into (1 Pet.1:10-12).

So, the Church and its message was a mystery in the Old Testament. Paul says,

> For this cause I Paul, the prisoner of Jesus Christ for you Gentiles, If you have heard of the dispensation of the grace of God which is given me to you-ward, How that by revelation he made known unto me the mystery; (as I wrote afore in few words, Whereby, when ye read, ye may understand my knowledge in the mystery of Christ) Which in other ages was not made known unto the sons of men, as it is now revealed unto his holy apostles and prophets by the Spirit; That the Gentiles should be fellowheirs, and of the same body, and partakers of his promise in Christ by the gospel (Eph. 3:1-6).

Does Israel then have a different calling and destiny from that of the Church?

The Scripture teaches that Israel is the heir of the world (Rom. 4:13). But it teaches that the Church is the heir of the universe. "All things" are the inheritance of the Christian, of the Church (1 Cor.3:21-23).

If the Kingdom is now, why the Rapture? Why can't the Church just grow and take over everything?

There are various kinds of "kingdom now" teachings in the world. The fact, however, is that the Kingdom was rejected by Israel and will not be instituted in the world until Christ comes in power and great glory. The Kingdom in its external form is not promised to the world in our time. In this day and age, God represents himself in this world via the unseen body of Christ and through the seen, observable lives of individual believers. The program of God becomes "visible" in Christians who testify for the Lord Jesus and live holy lives before the watching world. The Kingdom, by the way, will not "grow in the world," but it will come suddenly, imposed upon the world by its King, the Lord Jesus Christ.

Where does the Rapture fit into the "big picture" of history?

The Rapture ends the day of grace and begins the day of the Lord, which begins with the Tribulation. It will end a day of grace, the time of divine forbearance, and begin a time called the day of the Lord, in which God is at liberty to work with His promised program of judgment upon the world.

I recommend a book called *The Two Futures*, which will give you a presentation of "the big picture." To get it, write and ask for it by title to: Christian Destiny, Inc., P.O. Box C, Hillsboro, KS 67063, or call (316) 947-5560.

The Glory to Come

Let each of us be finally reminded that the story of the future is not simply that of one day after another ad infinitum. No indeed! There is a glorious future for the Church, and there is a dismal future for the world. The sojourn of the Church in this world will come to an instantaneous end, at which time every believer will be taken from this dark planet to the glory which is to come.

At the moment of that transition, each of us will receive a new body, a glorified body that is not unlike the body of Christ himself. We will at this point be given the capacity to feel, to appreciate, to enjoy all of the unspeakably wonderful things that will be ours in eternity. The Scripture says, "In thy presence is fulness of joy; at thy right hand are pleasures for evermore" (Ps. 16:11).

So great will be the delights of heaven that they are impossible to describe under the constraints, the limitations of human language. It may, therefore, be well to exercise a sanctified imagination, to ask the question, "What will it be like when Jesus comes?" The answer, of course, is that it will be like nothing we can imagine in all of life. There is no human experience that resembles in any but the palest fashion the ecstasy that will be ours when we step across the great divide into the fadeless light of heaven.

What is heaven like?

The answer must be that heaven is not exactly like anything that we know in this world. We do well to take the greatest joys of earth and multiply them by a thousand times. Only then do we have even the beginning of the joys that will be ours in heaven.

The Christian is invited to use his "sanctified imagination" to think of golden streets, ivory palaces, a city where there is no night, and endless "pleasure forevermore." In heaven also, we will have the opportunity to meet the saints who have gone before and, of course, loved ones who have in earlier days moved from the Church militant to the Church triumphant. How wonderful to contemplate that golden moment when the Church will be translated from this world to the world to come. What a moment that will be!

The real point is that we be prepared for that moment. The preparation is that we must be Christians. A Christian is one who believes the gospel of Jesus Christ, who has accepted the Son of the living God as personal Saviour. Because of the shed blood of Jesus Christ, the sufficient sacrifice for sin, each person in all of the world is invited to receive the free gift, the gift of God, which is everlasting life. The single requirement is faith alone. By believing in Jesus Christ — who He was and what He did for man on the cross — by that act of faith I receive the gift of God, which is life eternal.

Meanwhile, in these days, let us gather together at the cross, recognizing Jesus Christ as the Saviour whose sacrifice made eternal life possible. While laboring for Him here, let us also anticipate the sound of the trumpet when we will be caught up to be with Him.

Conclusion

It's Not Too Late

by *William T. James*

We are the world! A few years ago, a celebrity-studded chorus added yet another stanza to the developing one-world anthem. Later, John Lennon's infectious song, "Imagine," was played in the spirit of world unity for the cause of world peace at a 1991 session of the General Assembly of the United Nations.

Globalism as an irresistible force thrusting into earth's future is quickly gaining momentum. There can be no turning back; the planetary thinkers-elite have determined, like Lennon, like Lenin, that all the world will be as one.

There are two books, written from two different perspectives, one titled *Educating for the New World Order*, the other titled *Education for a New World Order*, in which the authors analyze factors involved in the process implied by the titles. What appropriate titles they are for America in this day and how true!

America's public school systems are effusive with great swelling texts pronouncing man his own savior. Our children are being systematically indoctrinated by critical thinking techniques that turn Christian precepts of morality upside-down. Through values clarification that preaches there are no moral absolutes in this enlightened age, they apparently would have our children — and us — accept that one plus one now equals anything we want it to.

Such teaching injects, through the syringe of New Age false promises, the heady, ego-centric serum of humanism. They proclaim unabashedly that collective man is indeed an island of self sufficiency — with no need of God. It is indoctrination built upon revisionist propaganda, perverse half-truths, and outright lies from the same Lucifer who told the first man and woman they needed no deity to govern themselves or their world.

The U.S. Supreme Court's decisions to keep God out of public schools has America swallowing the satanic lie that we can best govern ourselves apart from God. The correlation between those tragic actions and the degeneration and decay of our society at every level is undeniable.

The Global Campaign

The astonishing Humpty-Dumpty fall of the Soviet Union and immediate forming of a Commonwealth of Independent States has snatched attention away from the equally astonishing flood of circumstances and events that is sweeping the United States into the much heralded New World Order. Fact is, for decades America has been in the process of being slowly poisoned by the incessant ugly American portrayal. Sadly, most of the character assassination, painting this nation as the affluent Satan most detrimental to the family of man, has come from the American press and the American entertainment industry.

The liberal message is always one that berates as callous, vicious, and evil American free enterprise. Coupled with the invective against big business in America is the demand that all nations — especially the rich capitalist Western ones — demonstrate compassion for the individual and collective have-nots. One world philosophy espouses that the cause of planetary equity must forge ahead into the next century and that the way it can happen is to educate the haves to think globally.

The campaign is on, gushing in a torrent that is swamping common sense in a frothy mixture of occultism, mythology, and fantasy that Mother Earth is the giver and sustainer of life. They are pleading that we must, as "her children," take dramatic and immediate actions to save "her."

Globalist media mogul Ted Turner's TBS network on February 23, 1992, began the deluge with the program series, "One Child, One Voice." Actor Jason Robards' voice mouthed the exhortation that together, collective man must create a "deafening roar" in the call to "save the world" for the children. A little girl, then, gently scolded us, saying that her father fought in a war so the earth would be a better place, but she said that now, in effect, we are instead brutalizing her and generations of children to come if we don't come together as the people of one planet to save earth.

Actor Robards then announced that a "summit of global leaders" was to take place at Rio De Janerio, Brazil, in June, 1992, to plan strategy for saving the planet. That summit turned into a New Age campmeeting complete with Hindu chanting, yoga, and meditation, and attended by delegates whose main purpose was to promote their New Age philosophy.

The true, living God, the Creator of all things, who gives all life and sustenance, is totally left out of their grandiose planning. Therein lies the evil in their desire to clean up the earth's environment. By worshiping and serving the creation more than the Creator, they are professing themselves to be wise, but they have in so doing become fools (Rom. 1:22,25).

The Chosen Model

If the European Community is the engine that will provide locomotion while the world steams toward the twenty-first century, the dynamics of economics is most assuredly the fuel that will fire that engine. Each day we are witness to the transfer of economic influence from the U.S. to the developing E.C. while it transforms before our eyes into a new Roman order — the neo-Roman Empire.

Within economy resides power; within economy of such awesome potential lurks power of massive dimension. Make no mistake, Europe united will soon become a political leviathan whose strength is in its unprecedented economic power. It already demands obeisance from such still-voracious monsters as the Russian bear! A bear, which God's prophecy foretells, will at some momentous point in time cease begging handouts and instead will turn southward to devour the rich spoils of the Middle East and Israel.

The European Community is obviously the chosen model around which must rally all other countries as the New World Order is built. And so a united Europe rises while the United States declines in power, prestige, and influence. Nationalism — like, communism — recedes into history.

Russia's Next Move

Christmas Day 1991 brought events involving matters that constitute the very nucleus of biblical end-time prophecy.

Mikhail Gorbachev, after six and one-half years as president of the Soviet Union, resigned, effectively dissolving the USSR. The red flag with gold hammer and sickle was lowered from its domed spire in Moscow. The little suitcase, as the Kremlin masters term it, (the case containing keys and codes needed to unleash their nuclear arsenal in an attack upon other nations) was peacefully transferred from Gorbachev to Russian President Boris Yeltsin.

Russia, not the Union of Soviet Socialist Republics, is now in control of the ultimate power to take peace from the earth. Russia (Rosh), precisely the geopolitical entity the prophet Ezekiel foretold would instigate war in the powder keg we now call the Middle East, is in place and in turmoil. Needing desperately to give its hungry, hurting populations the essentials of life, and its angry, confused military direction and loot that will satisfy them, the new Commonwealth's leaders must make dramatic choices in the very near future.

The so-called independent states of Kayakstan, Uzbekistan, Turkmenistan, Kirgizia, Armenia, Moldovia, and Azerbaijan are heavily Muslim populations, making them pre-eminently supportive of their Islamic brothers to the South and just as intense in their hatred for Israel. Anti-Semitism has for decades been, and is now more than ever, seething within the other "states" that comprise the Commonwealth that was formerly the USSR.

The chief prince of Rosh, whom Ezekiel under inspiration of the Holy Spirit termed Gog, realizes the potential for consolidating power. How long before the rider on the red horse focuses the lusts and hatreds of his hordes on the spoils ripe for the taking in the vast oil and mineral rich Middle East?

Peace and Safety?

That same Christmas Day in 1991, Pope John Paul II stood above the throngs of adoring people in St. Peter's Square at the Vatican in Rome and pronounced blessings on and future hopes for the on-going peace process between Israel and its Arab neighbors. These two Christmas Day events — the USSR's demise and the Pope's address — have much significance as the world rushes toward the end of one Millennium and the start of another.

They bring the Word of God into sharp focus in two separate yet very interconnected portions of Holy Scripture.

For when they shall say, Peace and safety; then sudden destruction cometh upon them, as travail upon a woman with child; and they shall not escape (1 Thess. 5:3).

Thus saith the Lord God; It shall also come to pass, that at the same time shall things come into thy mind, and thou shalt think an evil thought: And thou shalt say, I will go up to the land of unwalled villages; I will go to those who are at rest, that dwell safely .... To take a spoil, and to take a prey ... (Ezek.38:10-12).

Clouds signaling Apocalypse are already gathered. Brilliant rays of unquenchable light, however, laser through blackening skies as during no other period of man's sin-obscured time on the planet.

The Last Laugh

On December 25, 1991, one could almost literally hear God's voice — tinged with omniscient irony and humor — as He displayed His absolute control over all things. That Christmas Day, the Soviet Union, the governmental, ideological embodiment of hatred for God, which for 74 years did all within its power to deny its victimized peoples access to Him, died ignominiously with a stroke of a pen.

As if symbolically punctuating the total failures and collapse of the Soviet Communist system, Mikhail Gorbachev's own fountain pen failed as he tried to sign his resignation document. He had to borrow a pen from a nearby Western journalist.

To God's honor and glory, it happened on the very day Christians celebrate the birth of His precious Son. Yes, God's voice could almost literally be heard chiding the former Communist masters — and all who reject and/or oppose Him.

> Because I have called, and ye have refused; I have stretched out my hand, and no man regarded; But ye have set at nought all my counsel, and would none of my reproof: I also will laugh at your calamity; I will mock when your fear cometh; When your fear cometh as desolation, and your destruction cometh as a whirlwind; when distress and anguish come upon you.
>
> For that they hated knowledge, and did not choose the fear of the Lord: They would none of my counsel: they despised all my reproof. Therefore shall they eat of the fruit of their own way, and be filled with their own devices. For the turning away of the simple shall slay them . . ." (Prov. 1:24-27,29-32).

God is not mocked; He is in control! His wisdom is foolishness to those who perish. He laughs at the small creation called men who oppose His majestic, eternal purpose and who reject His beloved Son Jesus Christ. What a price such folly exacts from them!

The Spirit and the Bride Say Come

But now the marvelous, wondrous light breaks through! Although judgment and wrath are near, God's great love and mercy is still offered!

In the next verse in Proverbs, God tells all mankind: "But whoso hearkeneth unto me shall dwell safely, and shall be quiet from fear of evil" (Prov. 1:33).

The resurrected Lord Jesus says to all men, women, boys, and girls:

> I, Jesus, have sent mine angel to testify unto you these things.... And the Spirit and the bride [the true

Christian Church] say, Come. And let him that heareth say, Come. And let him that is athirst come. And whosoever will, let him take the water of life freely (Rev. 22:16-17).

While Apocalypse looms ominously above the horizon, while this doomed world system storms toward Armageddon, there yet remains time. God's Spirit calls His children (those saved through belief in the shed blood of Jesus) to do His work while they watch and pray for Christ's return for them in the air.

Jesus said:

And when these things begin to come to pass, then look up, and lift up your heads; for your redemption draweth nigh (Luke 21:28).

God's Spirit calls, especially, to those who have not accepted Jesus, although they have heard the truth of the gospel message and have been convicted of their lost condition. God calls you to believe, repent, and be saved from the deadly curse of sin.

Christ's return is imminent. Physical life is frighteningly fragile. All we have is this fleeting moment in time. Today, right now, is the moment of decision. We have no guarantees of second or third chances.

. . . behold, now is the accepted time; behold, now is the day of salvation (2 Cor. 6:2).

Accept Jesus Christ today. He is the way, the *only* way to eternal life in heaven with God. He says to us, "Behold, I come suddenly. . . ." Even so, come, Lord Jesus!

William T. James, "Terry" as he is addressed by those who know him, prefers to be thought of as an intensely interested observer of historical and contemporary human affairs, always attempting to analyze that conduct and those issues and events in the light of God's Holy Word, the Bible.

As public relations director for several companies he has written and edited all forms of business communications, both in print and electronic media. Prior to that he worked as creative director for advertising agencies and did extensive political and corporate speech writing, as well as formulated position papers on various issues for the clients he served. In addition to writing, he worked closely with clients and broadcast media in putting together and conducting press conferences and other forums.

Mr. James received his education at Arkansas Polytechnic Institute, Russellville, Arkansas; the Memphis Academy of Arts, Memphis, Tennessee; and Little Rock University (now University of Arkansas at Little Rock). In addition, he has done graduate level course work in journalism during his career.

He and his wife, Margaret, have two sons, Terry Jr., currently a pre-med student, and Nathan, a ninth grade student. He has taught Bible classes at various age levels throughout his years as a Christian, and at present conducts weekly Bible study preparation sessions for Sunday school teachers at his local church.

His overriding desire in this book, as well as in his life's conduct, is that Christ be lifted up so that all people might be drawn to the Saviour, that the lost might be redeemed, and that the child of God might be exhorted to watch for the soon return while working diligently for the Lord.

David Breese is an internationally-known author, lecturer, radio broadcaster, and Christian minister. He ministers in church and area-wide evangelistic crusades, leadership conferences, student gatherings, and related preaching missions.

He is president of Christian Destiny, Inc. of Hillsboro, Kansas, a national organization committed to the advancement of Christianity through evangelistic crusades, literature distribution, university gatherings, and the use of radio and television.

Dr. Breese is active in a ministry to college and university students, speaking to them from a background of theology and philosophy. He graduated from Judson College and Northern Seminary and has taught philosophy, apologetics, and Church history. He is frequently involved in lectures, debates, and rap sessions on university campuses.

Breese travels more than 100,000 miles a year and has spoken to crowds across North America, Europe, Asia, the Caribbean, and Latin America. His lectures and debates at universities in the United States and overseas center on the confrontation of Christianity and modern thought.

Breese is also the author of a number of books, including *Discover Your Destiny, His Infernal Majesty, Know the Marks of Cults, Living For Eternity* and the latest, *Seven Men Who Rule from the Grave*. His books, booklets and magazine articles have enjoyed wide readership across the world. He also publishes "Destiny Newsletter," a widely-circulated periodical presenting the Christian view of current events.

For many who comprise the cable television audience across America, "God's News Behind the News" and the name Ray Brubaker are synonymous. As director, Mr. Brubaker's on-air reports and fascinating interviews, as well as those conducted by his colleagues on "God's News," bring biblically prophetic insights into the issues and events that shape our times.

Mr. Brubaker was introduced into the broadcast arena during one tense moment of the Moody Bible Institute in Chicago's program which had no announcer at the mike at air time. A student at that time, Mr. Brubaker was employed as a "studio assistant," setting up studios, turning pages for musicians, assisting with the sound effects and related duties.

Aware of the split-second timing essential in broadcasting and with no announcer in sight, Ray grabbed the script, signaled for the mike, and introduced the broadcast on the air.

That was the beginning of an announcing career that in six months found Mr. Brubaker with his own newscast, and soon becoming the director of the news department.

"God's News Behind the News" was one of several news features originated back in 1946.

This television version of "God's News Behind the News" is now carried on four Satellite Networks as well as on select stations across America.

With news clips and film footage, along with the powerful application from the Word of God, Ray continues in his unflinching, dedicated drive to let the world know that "Jesus is coming soon" and they must "be ready."

Dr. Joseph Chambers, senior pastor of Paw Creek Church of God at Charlotte, North Carolina, has achieved renown as a champion in promoting godly principles in society and government.

While preaching the uncompromising Gospel message of Jesus Christ from the pulpit and through his broadcast and writing ministries, he has at the same time been a rising force on the evangelical-political scene for more than 25 years.

He is president of Paw Creek Christian Academy which he founded in 1974. The school includes an enrollment of 500, infancy through twelfth grade.

Since 1969 he has been involved in Echoes of Calvary, a traditional radio ministry, and since 1972 has hosted "Open Bible Dialogue," a 60-minute open forum discussing current issues — a program which covers half of North Carolina.

His published works include two books, *The Challenge of the Ministry*, edited by Dr. Robert E. Fisher; *Miracles, My Father's Delight*, copyright May 1986, Pathway Press, and many articles in a number of publications, e.g., *Church of God Evangel*, official publication of the Church of God denomination, Cleveland, Tennessee; *The Carolina Watchman*, a newspaper covering both Carolinas in which Dr. Chamber's weekly column appears; and *The Pentecostal Minister*, an award-winning journal for pentecostal ministers.

Dr. Chambers, through his education and demonstration of analytical skills in dealing with social and political issues, his obvious gift in the area of eschatology — and most of all, his calling to ministry by God — make him well qualified to address Bible prophecy as it relates to the days in which we live.

Dr. Tim LaHaye is an author, minister, TV and radio commentator, and family life speaker. He and his wife, Beverly, have four children and eight grandchildren. He earned his Doctorate of Ministries Degree at Western Baptist Seminary, Portland, Oregon.

For 25 years he pastored one of the nation's outstanding churches in San Diego, California, where he founded two accredited Christian high schools, a Christian school system of ten Christian schools, and founded Christian Heritage College. He has counseled over 6,000 people, many of these dealing with family and marriage problems.

As founder and president of Family Life Ministries he has conducted over seven hundred Family Life Seminars throughout the U.S. and Canada to help strengthen families by teaching biblical principles for family living. Thousands of couples testify that their marriages were enriched, and many claim they are still together because they attended one of these seminars.

In 1985 he and his wife, Beverly, who is president of the largest women's organization in America (Concerned Women for America), moved their offices to Washington, DC, within blocks of the nation's capitol. There he produces the daily TV and radio versions of the "Capital Report," a Christian conservative commentary on news events that have an impact on the family, traditional moral values, and religious liberty. In addition, he produces a bi-monthly "Prophecy Report" that highlights current events which seem to be fulfilling Bible prophecy. Prophecy books by Dr. LaHaye are the following: *Revelation: Illustrated & Made Plain; How to Study Bible Prophecy for Yourself; The Beginning of the End; The Coming Peace in the Middle East;* and *Life in the Afterlife.*

He also presently serves as an associate minister at Montrose Baptist Church, located in Rockville, MD.

David A. Lewis is a clergyman, author, lecturer, researcher, publisher, and is active in national and international circles in promoting the welfare of the Church, of Israel, and the Jewish people. His ordination has been with the Assemblies of God for over 35 years.

Dr. Lewis speaks at churches, conferences, minister's seminars, colleges, camp meetings, district events, etc. He has taught short courses in eschatology and apocalyptic literature in both secular and theological colleges, also short-term seminars and spiritual life emphasis in Bible colleges.

He has traveled to the Middle East over fifty times. He has visited and done research in Israel, Egypt, Turkey, Syria, Lebanon, Jordan, and Cyprus. He has also ministered in Hong Kong, Kowloon, Barbados, Virgin Islands, Iceland, Mexico, Canada, and has traveled to mainland China and many European countries.

David Lewis has conferred on numerous occasions with heads of state including Prime Ministers Begin, Peres, and Shamir of Israel, as well as members of Israel's Parliament, Mayor Teddy Kolleck of Jerusalem, Moderate Palestinian Arab leaders, various U.S. senators, congressmen, and has met with former President Reagan.

He was invited and appeared as a witness on the Middle East before the Senate Foreign Relations Committee in Washington, DC.

He has strong contacts with religious leaders in a broad spectrum of churches, with many Jewish religious and political leaders, and in diverse disciplines of the scientific communities.

Books by Lewis include *Prophecy 2000, Smashing the Gates of Hell, Magog Cancelled 1982, Dark Angels of Light, Coming Antichrist,* and *Holy Spirit World Liberation.*

Dr. Robert Lindsted, whose Ph.D. is in Mechanical Engineering, taught for nine years in the Department of Mechanical Engineering at Wichita State University. As an engineering consultant he worked with over one hundred companies on various products and problems in the area of heat transfer and process modeling.

For the last seven years he has committed his time to a daily radio program entitled, "Bible Truth." In great demand as a speaker and author in areas including Bible prophecy and science, he is a frequent guest speaker on such forums as "The Southwest Radio Church" radio program in Oklahoma City, Oklahoma, and "The Family Bible Hour" radio program in Canada.

Dr. Lindsted is the author of *The Next Move*, as well as a number of other booklets dealing mostly with the subject of current events and Bible prophecy.

Even before Operation Desert Storm began he produced a video entitled "Sadam Hussein, The Persian Gulf, and the End Times." This video showed how the prophecies of Jeremiah 50 and 51 promised the eventual destruction of Iraq because of its invasion into Kuwait.

Dr. Lindsted travels extensively to places like Russia where he and his fellow servants of God continue to distribute thousands of Bibles to the long-oppressed Russian people who hunger for God's Holy Word.

He boldly proclaims the validity of God's promises made many centuries ago by holding the prophetic word up to the scenario of events unfolding at a quickening pace in the 1990s.

Texe Marrs is perhaps the foremost authority in researching, analyzing, and reporting matters involving the New Age movement in the United States and the world. His reference book on that subject, *New Age Cults and Religions* is the classic guide to New Age groups while his newest book, *Millennium: Peace, Promises, and the Day They Take Our Money Away*, is a bestseller that explains the coming money crash, and the drive by conspiratorial forces for a New World Order.

Mr. Marrs is president of Living Truth Ministries in Austin, Texas, and a frequent guest on radio and TV talks shows throughout the United States and Canada in response to the public's search for greater insight into Bible prophecy, the New Age movement, and world affairs.

The well-known author of the #1 landmark national Christian bestseller, *Dark Secrets of the New Age*, Texe Marrs has also written thirty other books for such major publishers as Simon & Schuster, John Wiley, Prentice Hall/Arco, Stein & Day, and Dow Jones-Irwin. His books have sold over 700,000 copies.

Mr. Marrs was assistant professor of aerospace studies, teaching American Defense Policy, strategic weapons systems, and related subjects at the University of Texas at Austin from 1977 to 1982. He has also taught international affairs, political science, and psychology for two other universities. A graduate Summa Cum Laude from Park College, Kansas City, Missouri, he earned his Master's degree at North Carolina State University.

As a career United States Air Force officer (now retired), he commanded communications-electronics and engineering units. He holds a number of military decorations, including the Vietnam Service Medal.

Texe Marrs' dynamic monthly newsletter, *Flashpoint*, is distributed around the world.